ASSYRIOLOGICAL STUDIES · No. 23

THE ORIENTAL INSTITUTE OF THE UNIVERSITY OF CHICAGO

KANIŠŠUWAR

A TRIBUTE TO HANS G. GÜTERBOCK

ON HIS

SEVENTY-FIFTH BIRTHDAY

May 27, 1983

Edited by

HARRY A. HOFFNER, JR.

and

GARY M. BECKMAN

THE ORIENTAL INSTITUTE OF THE UNIVERSITY OF CHICAGO

ASSYRIOLOGICAL STUDIES · No. 23

CHICAGO · ILLINOIS

Library of Congress Catalog Card Number: 86-60384

ISBN: 0-918986-44-3
ISSN: 0066-9903

The Oriental Institute, Chicago

Published 1986. Printed in the United States of America

TABLE OF CONTENTS

EDITORS' FOREWORD

It is universally recognized today in the world of ancient Near Eastern studies that few scholars have contributed as much to the discipline of Hittite and Ancient Anatolian Studies as Hans Gustav Güterbock, who celebrates today his 75th birthday, and that his name will always stand high in the list of those who have studied and published in this area from the very beginnings. His bibliography compiled in his two festschrifts speaks for itself of both the quantity of his scholarly output and the variety of subjects he has addressed. The uniformly high quality of these publications cannot be seen from a bibliography, but everyone who has read any of Güterbock's writings knows the uncompromising standard of excellence which he maintains.

Hans Güterbock is not only a peerless scholar but a truly generous and selfless teacher and colleague. Many are those who have been the beneficiaries of his criticism and advice. It is generally known that Hans Güterbock's "students" in the broader sense of that word—young colleagues who have associated themselves with him for longer periods of time in order to learn from him—make up a large segment of today's active Hittitologists. Therefore it was appropriate that the editors of his first festschrift in 1973 applied to him the famous quotation from the prayer of Ḫattušili III and Puduḫepa about the debt owed to one who raises children for their parents. The editors of the first festschrift applied this to Güterbock's "raising the child of Hittitology" brought into being by the decipherer Hrozný. But we can also apply it to his ceaseless efforts to "raise" other teachers' "children."

Although this written tribute comes from all of Hans Güterbock's colleagues, it comes in a special, personal way from his associates on the staff of the Hittite Dictionary Project, to which he has devoted so much of his time in recent years. That this dictionary has been well begun is due in large measure to his participation. The Chicago Hittite Dictionary occupies a central place among his many publications. We who have shared the work with him consider ourselves fortunate.

All of your colleagues greet you, Hans Güterbock, and wish you Happy Birthday and many happy returns of the day!

THE EDITORS

Chicago, May 27th, 1983

BETROTHAL OF GIRLS DURING CHILDHOOD IN ANCIENT ASSYRIA AND ANATOLIA

Kemal Balkan

Ankara

On behalf of his uncles, residing in Assur, Sūinēa's son Pūšu-kīn came to Anatolia in his younger years as a merchant.[1] He had been in correspondence with the woman Lamassī. It is not very likely that she was the wife of Pūšu-kīn, but perhaps a close relative of his, who resided in Aššur.[2] She sent textiles and other invaluable items, which were rare or not found in Anatolia, to Pūšu-kīn to be sold for some money and to take care of a certain *ṣuḫārtum* (a girl), whose growth she gave news of in the supplementary passages of her letters written to him. In BIN 4.9: 20ff. Lamassī discusses the young girl in the following words: *ṣú-ḫa-*[*ar*]*-tum* (21) *ir-tí-bi*$_4$ *ku-ta-bi*$_4$*-it-ma* (22) *al-kam-ma a-na sú-un* (23) ^{d}*A-šùr šu-ku-ší* "The girl has grown up (and) so do (us) the honour of coming here (to the city of Aššur) and place her in the lap of the god Aššur." In the letter BIN 6.7: 6ff. the same Lamassī gives Pūšu-kīn the following advice: *ku-ta-bi-it-ma* (7) *ku-ur-ṣí-kà pá-ri-ir* "Do (us) the honour (of coming to the city of Aššur) and break your obligations (over there)." We may assume that in this brief statement Lamassī is referring to Pūšu-kīn's coming to the city of Aššur for the purpose of placing the girl in the lap of the god Aššur. In another letter CCT 3.20: 17ff. to Pūšu-kīn, Lamassī stresses the fact that the young girl has grown up enough (to marry): *ki-ma ṣú-ḫa-ar-t*[*um*] (18) *i-ir-ta-bi-ú-ni* "as the girl has grown up. . . ." In the same letter Lamassī tells Pūšu-kīn in lines 38ff. the following: *ṣú-ḫa-ar-*

1. Eisser-Lewy, MVAeG 35/3 p. 31f.; H. and J. Lewy, HUCA 17 (1942–43) pp. 82f. note 237; Landsberger, Türk Tarih, Arkeologya . . . Dergisi 4 (1940) 15 note 1; J. Lewy, HUCA 27 (1956) 79 and note 333; Garelli, Les Assyriens, index; Veenhof, Aspects, index; Larsen, The Old Assyrian City-State . . . , index.

2. Garelli, RA 59 (1965) 158 "Toutes ces allusions, . . . , invitent à croire que Lamassī était la femme de Pūšu-kīn"; Larsen, Old Assyrian Caravan Procedures 55, 60 "perhaps . . . wife (of Pūšu-kīn)"; according to some other scholars she was the wife of Pūšu-kīn: Veenhof, Aspects 20, 11ff., 90, 116ff.; Matouš, BiOr 32 (1975) 334; Larsen, The Old Assyrian City-State . . . , index; M. Darga, Eski Anadolu'da Kadın (Turkish), 11ff. "kesinlikle" (definitely).

tum da-ni-iš (39) *ir-tí-bi té-eb-a-ma a-tal-kam a-na sú*(!)*-ni A-šùr* (40) *šu-ku-ší ù šé-ep ì-lí-ka ṣa-ba-at* "and the girl has (indeed) fully grown up. Get up and come here (to the city of Aššur), place her (the girl) in the lap of the god Aššur, and seize the foot of your own god."

In the letter MAH 16209[3]: 3ff. Lamassī approaches the problem of the young girl in a different manner. The letter to Pūšu-kīn begins directly by saying: *ta-ša-mì-ma ta-ni-iš*(!)*-tum* (4) *il*$_5$(!)*-té-mì-in* (5) *a-ḫu-um a-na a-ḫi-im* (6) *a-na ḫa-lá-tim i-za-az* (7) *ku-ta-bi-it-ma* (8) *ù al-kam-ma ku-ur-ṣí-kà* (9) *pá-ri-ir ṣú-ḫa-ar-tám* (10) *a-na sú-un A-šùr* (11) *šu-ku-un* "You also hear that humanity has become bad. One is ready to swallow the other.[4] (So) do (us)

3. Preserved at the Musée d'art et d'histoire de Genève. See Garelli, RA 59: 156–160.

4. *ḫalātum-ʾalātum* "to swallow," Garelli, ibid. 160; CAD A/1 s.v.; AHw s.v. The following new evidence for OA *ḫ* may be added from the unpublished Kültepe tablets:

(a) *ḫ* is rendered with (ʾ), as was seen in *arpum,* "(tablet) enclosed in a case" (CAD A/2 292; cf. AHw 69); Kültepe b/k 499: 8ff. "I owe ⅓ mina of gold to the Colony (of Kaniš). (10) . . . *ik-ri-bu* (11) ⌜*ma*⌝*-lá ṭup-pí-i* (12) ⌜*ar*⌝*-ma-am ú-kà-lu* "the offering according to my tablet enclosed in a case which (the Colony) holds. . . ."

(b) *ḫ* in *mašāḫum,* CAD M/1 360f. s.v. *mašāʾum,* "to take away by force, . . . , to rob a person"; AHw 624f. s.v. *mašā'um* "gewaltsam wegnehmen, rauben." Besides the evidence in the above sources the following may be mentioned: Kültepe a/k 548 b (tabl.): 8ff. . . . *a-ta a-ma-kam* (9) *mì-li-kà ú-lá ta-áš-ta-pár* (10) *ki-ma Ì-lí-il*$_5$*-ma-ad* (11) [*i*]*m-šu-ḫi-ni ú* 5 MA.NA (12) KÙ.BABBAR *ḫa-al-qú-ni* "You have not sent (me) there your thoughts (saying that) 'Ili-ilmad has robbed me, from me 5 minas of silver have been lost' . . ."; Kültepe c/k 45: 9ff. *um-ma a-ta-ma* (10) *ni-ma-lam ù-ša-ar-ší-kà* (11) *a-pu-ùḫ ni-me-lim ša-ar-šu-im* (12) {*ša-ar-šu-im*} *a-ta-ma i-na* (13) É^{tí}*-kà ta-am-ta-áš-ḫu-ni* (14) ⅔ MA.NA KÙ.BABBA[R] (14) *ta-áš-ku-nam-ma* . . . (28) *mì-ma a-nim i-na Za-al-pá a-na* (29) *bi*$_4$*-tí-kà ta-am-šu-ḫa-ni ú-lá a-we-lu-um* (30) *ḫa-al-pu-um* . . . , "You said thus: 'I will let you make some profit.' Instead of making profit, you yourself in your home robbed me; you have caused losses (to me) of ⅔ mina of silver. All these you have taken away for your (own) home, in the house at Zalpa, (but) I am not an accursed man." Kültepe c/k 1229: 31ff. *u*$_4$*-me-e ša-na-at* (32) *ir-ša-ni-ma ra-mì-ni* (33) *lá ú-ma-ša-aḫ* "ask (imp. pl.) from me the days of a year, (but) you should not rob me"; Contenau, TTC 27: 13 *ú-ma-ša-aḫ-kà* (cf. CAD M/1 361a). *mešiḫtum,* "robbing"; *mašḫātum* (pl.). Kültepe c/k 45: 38ff. *ki-ma i-a-tí me-ší-iḫ-tám* (39) *ú-*KU*-ur-šu-ma ù a-na* (40) *me-ší-ḫi-tim a-wi-lam ú-kà-an* "as my representatives . . . the robbing to him and against the robbing I assign the (right) man." Kültepe c/k 1604: 4ff. *um-ma A-šùr-ma-lik-ma* (5) *ḫa-ra-ni a-mì-ša-am* (6) *ki-ma a-wa-tim* (7) *ma-áš-ḫa-tim* (8) *áš-ta-na-me-ú* (9) *e-ra-ba-am* (10) [*lá*] *a-mu-a-am* "Aššur-mālik said thus: 'My way was over there (to you), as I regularly heard of the unfair things (that) I was not able to enter over there.'"

(c) *šuḫʾudum* "to warn, to threaten by force"; *šuʾūdum* (***âdum,* CAD A/1 136a; *âdu* AHw 14a; Kültepe a/k 1368 b (tabl.): 18ff. . . . 5 MA.NA SÍG.ḪI.A (19) *ku-nu-uk-ma a-na A-ki-a* (20) *še-bi*$_4$*-lam-ma* ITU.2.KAM *sí-ki* (21) *ú-kà-il*$_5$*-ma e-mu-qú-tám* (22) *e-ba-ru-tí-a ú-ša-ḫi-du-šu-ma* (23) *ú-šé-ra-ni* "Seal (there) 5 minas of wool and send to Akia over there and (for) two months he has been holding my hem, (but) my colleagues have threatened him by force and (then) he set me free."

the honour and come here and break your obligations (over there). (And) place the girl in the lap of the god Aššur."

In reminding Pūšu-kīn of the behaviour of humanity, Lamassī apparently intended to warn him of the unpleasant consequences that might be expected from not fulfilling a promise. Such an act ordinarily might be expected to cause serious concern to a respectable merchant.

To date no other documents dealing with the subject in question have been discovered in the archive of Pūšu-kīn at Kültepe. Perhaps the above letters refer to a solution of the problem concerning the young girl (cf. ATHE 31; p. 4).

Before dealing with the results to be drawn from the letters just mentioned, let us examine the legal protocol of Kültepe i/k 120, discovered at level 2 during the Turkish excavation and published for the first time here. The

---

(d) *usḫiʾum* is probably identical with *ú-ús-e-en* (dual), Īrišum Inscription, Belleten 14 (1950) 224: 13. In the latter it is said that in each of the double *ḫubūrum,* each *usʾum* weighing one talent has been attached to each beer-vessel (2 *ú-ús-e-en ša* 1 GÍN.TA (14) *i-*[*n*]*a qar-bi-šu-nu a-di*). Thus *usʾum* is a Sum. lw. meaning "duck" (AHw 1438b s.v. *ūsu(m)* II). For animal attachments to earthenware see T. Özgüç, Ausgrabungen in Kültepe 1948 (TTKYayın V/10), No. 313 a, b–314; idem, Kültepe-Kaniş (TTKYayın V/19), Fig. 85, pls. 33 2, 39 1, 40 1a–1b, 41 2, cf. pls. 31 1, 3, 47 1–2.

usḫiʾum appears in Kültepe c/k 1517 (see OLZ 1965: 160, text B): 1f. 1 RI-*bu-um* 1 *ús-ḫi-um* (2) 1 *ta-áp-šu-ḫu-um* (the rest in OLZ ibid.). Here *usḫiʾum* is probably a duck-shaped figure. All the objects in the text are made of bronze (ZABAR, cf. B line 17). In Kültepe h/k 87 (OLZ 1965: 160, text C; [. . .] in line 2 is to be deleted): line 3 reads 2 *ús-ḫi-ú ša bi-ṣí-ni* "two duck-shaped figures for lamp wicks"; here, too, *isḫiʾums* are made of bronze (line 22). A clay bowl with a duck-shaped clay figure attached to the bottom, was excavated from the Kārum Kaniš in Kültepe: T. Özgüç, Ausgrabungen in Kültepe 1948, pl. 48 No. 224. The bowl shows a black sooted spot in the bottom: T. Özgüç, "Bei der grosseren Tasse mit Schwan [duck?] . . . , ist nur der Schwan und der Mündungsrand mit kurzen Linien verziert (. . .). Der Schwan mit kurzem Hals und spitzem Schwanz ist auf die Mitte der Russpuren tragende Tasse geklebt."

usḫiʾū ša biṣinni in Kültepe h/k 87: 3 which corresponds to the cup, described by T. Özgüç, might be assumed as a Cappadocian type of lamp of which the wick has perished. Cappadocian lamps consisted apparently of the following parts: *bīt biṣinni* "the lamp" (CAD B 348b, 3; AHw 143, 2), duck-shaped figure (*usḫiʾum ša biṣinnim* CAD B 348b 3; AHw 143 2), and the wick itself *(biṣinnum)*. According to CAD B 348 and AHw 143, the plant *buṣinnum* is *Verbascum thapsus,* the leaves of which were used as a lamp wick. [Ed.—Compare CHD 3: 45 sub *lappina*-**(SAR)**.]

In a newly excavated Kültepe contract *biṣinnum* is used, as in OB documents (AHw 163), to mean "the lamp" itself. In this contract (Kültepe d/k 38 a, b), the purchaser of the house attaches great importance to the fact that the seller should reimburse (his) *biṣinnum* "lamp," in case he is legally obliged to return the house to his vindicator: Kültepe d/k 38 b (tabl.): 11ff. IGI *Ta-li-a* (12) IGI *Ḫu-zi-ú-ma-an* (13) *be-zi-nam ú-*[*ša*]*-ba* "Before: Talia; before: Ḫuziuman. He (also) will sa[tis]fy (him, that is Peruwa) regarding the lamp." Cf. OIP 27: 19 A: 18 IGI *Ka-ma-li-*[*a*] *be-el* bi_4*-ṣí-*[*nim*?] (or *be-el* bi_4*-tim*?).

plaintiff in the new text is Aḫu(w)-waqar, the defendant is Zuba, both of whom are Assyrians.[5] The document runs as follows[6]:

(Obv.) (1) *A-ḫu-wa-qar ù Zu-ba-ma* (2) *iṣ-bu-tù-ni-a-tí-ma* (3) *um-ma A-ḫu-wa-qar-ma* (4) *a-na Zu-ba-ma a-ḫa-tí* (5) *ir-tí-bi$_4$ ba-a-am* (6) *a-ḫa-tí i-na Kà-ni-iš* (7) *a-ḫu-úz um-ma Zu-ba-ma* (8) [*l*]*u tù-ší-ib* (9) [*u*]*m-ma A-ḫu-wa-qar-ma* (10) [*i*]*-na Kà-ni-iš* (Lower edge) (11) [*dí-i*]*n kà-ri-im dí-šu* (Rev.) (12) *šé-ep-kà ru-qá-at* (13) *a-dí ma-tí a-ḫa-tí* (14) *lu tù-ší-ib* (15) *um-ma Zu-ba-ma a-lik* (16) *a-ḫa-at-kà a-šar* (17) *li-bi-kà a-na mu-tim* (18) *dí-in* IGI *En-nam-A-šur* (19) DUMU *Bu-da-tim* (20) IGI [d]AB*-ba-ni* DUMU *A-ba-ba* (21) *a-na a-wa-tim a-ni-a-tim* (22) {*A-ḫu-wa-qar*} *kà-ru-um* (23) *Té-ga-ra-ma im-ḫu-ur-ni-a-tí-ma* {*ú* (on erasure)} (Lower edge) (24) *kà-ru-um* (Left edge) (25) *i-dí-in-ni-*⌜*a*⌝-[*tí-ma*] (26) *tup-pá-am* ⌜*ša*⌝ *ší-*[*bu-t*]*í-*[*ni*] (27) *i-ba-áb* DINGIR *ni-dí-i*[*n*] (end of the tablet)

(1) "Aḫu-waqar and Zuba (2) seized us (as witnesses) and (3) Aḫu-waqar spoke as follows (4) to Zuba, 'My sister (5) has (now) grown up, come here (6) (and) at the town of Kaniš (7) marry[7] (6) my sister.' (7) Zuba answered thus: (8) 'Let her stay.' (9) Aḫu-waqar spoke as follows: (10) 'At the town of Kaniš (11) give it[8] (i.e., the decision about her). (12) Your foot is far away (i.e., you live in a distant place).[9] (13–14) How long should my sister stay?' (15) Zuba replied

5. PN *Zuba* is used apparently both by Assyrians and Anatolians. Different *Zuba* appear as sons of the following Assyrians: *Aššur-idi* (Kültepe f/k 35: 13); *Aššur-rēʾum* (unpubl. B 9: 9); *Aššur-ṭāb* (ICK 2.125: 37); *E-lá-li* (Kültepe 125: 2); *Iddi(n)-abum* (BIN 4.189: 15); *Ištar-palil* (BIN 4.174 (= MVAeG 33 No. 61): 3–4; TCL 4.86 (= MVAeG 35/3 No. 305): 1, 13–14; BIN 6.174 (= MVAeG 33 No. 6): 3; ICK 2.132: 35; 305: x+17; Kültepe a/k 906: 12; Kültepe c/k 487: 13–14; Kültepe c/k 512: 9); *Puzur-Ištar* (TCL 4.30: 16).

Together with *Elama* a certain *Zuba* is found as *ḫamuštum* (ICK 1 56: 5; Kültepe a/k 1206: 4–5). *Zuba* also appears as *mušāridum* (CAD M/2 260 a; cf. AHw 681b s.v. *mušarriṭ/tum*).

In some documents persons named *Zuba* are the sons of the following natives: *Wa-ar-ki-tí-iš* (Kültepe f/k 166:14; f/k 168: 17); *Gazana* (Kültepe f/k 73 (tabl.): 20–21, (its case) f/k 76: 3–4); *Šadaḫšu* (Kültepe f/k 158: 3); *Zuba ša* [(f)]*Ilališka* (Kültepe c/k 183: 15).

Zuba, I 552 (cited Studies Landsberger [AS 16] 177): 17 (witness; together with other Anatolians); OIP 27: 49 A: 4, B: 7; passim. Cf. [m]*Zuba* in the Hittite texts, Laroche, NH No. 1572.

6. According to lines 4, 7, 15, line 1 *Zu-ba*{*-ma*}. Some irregularities may also be observed in lines 22–23.

7. Imp. I of *aḫāzum;* see CAD A/1 175b, 176b.

8. Hecker, Grammatik §49 a; Kültepe d/k 48 b (FsGüterbock 35): (21) *I-li-dí-na-šu* "my god give it (the child) to him"; unpubl. Ankara c 33: 6.

9. AHw 971a *rêqu(m)* "fern sein, sich entfernen"; CAD M/1 417 (s.v. *mātu* 1) *rūqtum* (fem. sg.) "far-off," *ruqūtu;* ARM 4.70: 17 *ina eqlim ru-qí-im;* Late Babylonian, AHw 971b "Weg für die Füsse"; cf. Landsberger, Türk Tarih, Arkeologya . . . Dergisi 4: 15 note 1; J. Lewy, HUCA 27: 79 note 333; idem, OrNS 29 (1960) 25ff. The following unpublished text should be also considered, Kültepe c/k 1046: 8ff. *eq-lam ru-qàm* (9) *a-lá-ak lá té-té-qàm-ma* (10) *lá ta-na-ma-ar* "I go to a distant field, (but) you do not want trespassing and not seeing (me) regularly."

thus: 'Go! (18) Give (16) your sister to a husband[10] who pleases (17) your heart!' (18) Before Ennam-Aššur, (19) son of Budatum; (20) before ^{d}AB-bāni, son of Ababa. (21) After these words (22) {Aḫu-waqar} the Colony (23) of Tegarama accepted us and {and (on erasure)} (24) the Colony ordered u[s] (as witnesses) and (27) we gav[e] (i.e., we have recorded) (26) the tablet of [our] tes[timo]n[y] (27) at the Gate of the God."

While the legal protocols were usually concluded by Assyrians,[11] and to a lesser degree also by Anatolians,[12] a decision of the Colony, particularly of the head of the Colonies, the Kārum Kaniš, was obtained only by Assyrians (see MVAeG 33 No. 273ff.). Though *Zuba* could be an Anatolian name (cf. Garelli, Les Assyriens 130ff.), he was considered an Assyrian. In this legal protocol, the girl's brother urged the defendant Zuba to marry his sister, because she had now grown up. This is a clear indication that the young girl had been promised to her fiancé while she was a child. Probably her fiancé also was a very young person.

In the legal protocol just examined a simple declaration by the man sufficed to dissolve the betrothal. It must be noted that no written betrothal contracts have been found among the Cappadocian tablets. However, in at least one particular case, we have evidence that the legal proceedings were recorded in a legal protocol.

The dissolution of the betrothal by means of a formal declaration by the man apparently deprived him of the right to reclaim the betrothal gifts which might have been given by his to the girl's family. However, there is no mention of any betrothal gifts in the Cappadocian tablets concerning the engagement. One may assume that in the *irtibi* ("she has grown up")–clauses in the

10. *ana mutim nadānum* "to give (a girl) to a husband," CAD M/2 314f. (s.v. *mutum*); CAD Ṣ 230a, 236 (s.v. *ṣuḫārtu, ṣuḫru*). Kültepe c/k 137 may be added to the above given examples: (Obv.) 1ff. *i-nu-mì ṣú-ḫa-ar-tám* (2) *a-na mu-tim* (3) *a-dí-nu* 10 GÍN (4) KÙ.BABBAR *Šu-Ku-bu-um* (5) *ub-lam* (Rev.) (6) 2 GÍN (7) *E-lá-ma* (8) *ub-lam* (end of the tablet) "As I gave the girl to the husband, Šu-Kubum brought 10 sheqels of silver to me; Elama brought 2 sheqels (of silver) to me." Cf. BIN 6.20: 22ff. . . . *mì-šu ša* . . . (23) . . . (24) *ú a-na mu-tim ta-li-ki-ni,* CAD M/2 314 translates the passage as "why is it that you go (to live) with a husband?", but the same passage is translated in CAD A/2 302b (s.v. *alāku*) as "what is it that (I hear) that you went to (stay with) a man?"

11. Eisser-Lewy, MVAeG 33 pp. 244ff.; passim.

12. Only one party of the legal protocol is a native: MVAeG 33 No. 252: 1 (*Ša-ar-ni-ga-at*), 4, 10 (*-ga*); ICK 1.61: 2, 7, 16 (*-ga*); *Du-ùḫ-ni-iš*: MVAeG 33 No. 261: 1, 8, 12; $^{(f)}$*Zu-uš-ga(-na)* (DAM *Ù-zu-a*) MVAeG 35/3 No. 292 (= CCT 5.17a): 2, 8, 21 (*-na*), dupl. TCL 21.266: 1 (*-na*), 9 (*-ga*), 23 (*-na*); *Ma-la/i-(a)-wa-áš-ḫa/i*: MVAeG 35/3 No. 303 A: 1 (*Ma-li-wa-aḫ-ší*), 12 (*-áš-ḫa*), B: 5 (*Ma-li-a-wa-áš-ḫi*). Both of the partners in the legal protocol are natives: *Ša-ak-tù-nu-wa* against *Ni-ki-li-e-wi-i-it, Ni-ki-li-e-it* MVAeG 35/3 No. 297: x+3, x+7, x+14, x+19 (*Š.*), and x+20, x+28 (*N.*).

Cappadocian texts a betrothal might be indicated between girls and men. That is, an arrangement could have been made while the girl was still a child; cf. ARM 1.64—the letter of Šamši-Adad I to Iasmaḫ-Adad, his son: 7 ff. SAL.TUR.MEŠ *ša Ia-aḫ-du-Li-im* (8) *ša a-di-na-kum* (9) SAL.TUR.MEŠ *ši-na ir-ta-bé-e:* "the young girls of Iaḫdu-Lim whom I gave to you, these young girls have (text: has) (now) grown up."

It should be noted that in the aforementioned letters the *irtibi*-clause is followed by the sentence "place her (the girl) in the lap of the god Aššur." But, in the legal protocol already seen, the *irtibi*-clause[13] is followed by the clause "take my sister as your wife," or, "marry my sister." It is inadmissible to maintain that putting a girl in the lap of the god Aššur refers "très vraisemblablement à sa consécration religieuse" (Garelli, RA 59 [1965] 157) because of the following reasons: It would be a sacrilege to the god Aššur who has been waiting for such a long time that Lamassī has sent at least four letters to Pūšu-kīn. It would also be considered an act of disrespect both to the temple of the god Aššur and Aḫaḫa, *kubabtum (ugbabtum)* priestess (NIN.DINGIR, MVAeG 33 No. 11: 16, 22; ATHE 24 A: 11–12, 34–35, B: 14–15, 26) who was Pūšu-kīn's own daughter. There is, therefore, a parallelism between "putting a girl in the lap of the god Aššur" and "to marry a girl."

Our own assumption is that it was an euphemistic usage only occurring in Old Assyrian which probably means "under the protection of the god Aššur[14] to take a girl as a wife."

It remains to be seen whether Pūšu-kīn's wife (ATHE 31: 8, 11) was the mother of his sons and the daughter, and whether she, whose death is mentioned in TCL 4.30: 3–4 is identical with *ṣuḫārtum,* who was placed in the lap of the god Aššur.

In two letters VAT 9230[15] and BIN 6.104 the marriages of two adult couples are mentioned. In VAT 9230 Šū-Ḫubur, a banker in Aššur, asks his colleague Pūšu-kīn in Kaniš to send to him in Aššur the young merchant Ennum-Aššur, that is his (Šū-Ḫubur's) son(-in-law). The idea seems to be

13. Cf. TCL 19.35: 19 *i-il$_5$-tum i-ir-tí-bi* "the goddess is already angry," CAD I/J 89b; but AHw 191b (s.v. *eli*ʾ*ltum*) "Opferverplichtung wurde gross." BIN 4.88: 18 *a-wi-lúm ar-tí-bi* "(as) a man I have grown up."

14. CAD Ṣ 230a translates BIN 4.9: 20 and CCT 3.20: 38 as "place her in the lap of (i.e. dedicate her to?) Aššur," but CAD K 18 (s.v. 10 *kutabbutu*) offers the translation of BIN 4.9: 20 as "put her (the girl) into the 'lap of Aššur' "; AHw 1059b (s.v. *sūnu*) "c) Schutz auf dem Schoss. a) v Gott . . . ,)".

15. Communicated by J. Lewy, AnOr 18/3 (1950) 374 note 49.

that Ennum-Aššur would marry Šū-Ḫubur's daughter at a home in Aššur and bring her (to his house).[16]

The second letter, BIN 6.104, addressed by Puzur-Aššur, writes to Nuḫšātum that her father asked him to marry[17] her and goes on to say: "As soon as you (Nuḫšātum) hear my letter, consult your father and . . . come here. . . ." At the end Puzur-Aššur tells Nuḫšātum what he intends to do if she does not come to Kaniš to be his wife: ". . . at the town of Waḫšušana (in Anatolia) I shall marry a girl of Waḫšušana." We may observe that in this letter the girl must have reached puberty. Here the prospective husband is apparently ready to take her as his wife, but acknowledges the girl's right to make the final decision whether to marry him or not. As a result, we may conclude that a refusal by the girl could dissolve the engagement. Although there is no mention of betrothal gifts in the Cappadocian texts, by not accepting the man as her husband, she probably loses her right to the supposed gifts.

In Old Assyrian, as in other dialects of Akkadian, *aḫāzum* connotes "to take a woman, to cohabit in marriage, to marry."[18] It is used only in connection with the husband. The woman is the subject, not the object of the act (see note 10).

We have already noted that in VAT 9230, the marriage took place in a home in Aššur. It seems that according to Old Assyrian rules, a man and a woman were considered to have been joined in marriage in the home of the man. VAT 9230 is in favour of Koschaker's view (ArOr 18/3 [1950] 216 note 11) that in Old Babylonian *aḫāzum* reaches its destination by bringing the woman to the home of the man.

MVAeG 33 No. 1 (= TCL 4.67) cannot be considered a betrothal,[19] since *aḫāzum* ("to marry a girl") already has taken place (lines 6–7).[20]

Neufeld makes a distinction between two different forms of betrothal in Hittite Laws,[21] §§28–29.[22] For the girl §28 uses the term *taranza* meaning

16. 20ff. *a-na-kam i-na* É^{tim} (21) *ṣú-ḫa-ar-tám e-ḫa-az* (22) *ṣú-ḫa-ar-tám li-it-ru*.

17. 3ff. *a-bu-ki a-šu-mì-ki* [*a-na*] (4) *ṣé-ri-a a-na a-ḫ*[*a-zi-ki*] (5) *iš-pu-ra-am*.

18. CAD A/1 175b; to be corrected CAD Ṣ 229–230a, TCL 4.67: 6 "has been betrothed to the girl"; AHw 19a; cf. also Driver-Miles, The Assyrian Laws 169ff. "(sexually) to marry"; Koschaker, ArOr 18/3 (1950) 214, note 11 (p. 238).

19. Eisser-Lewy, MVAeG 33 No. 1 "Verlobung?"; for CAD Ṣ 229–230a see note 18 above.

20. For the Old Babylonian usage cf. Driver-Miles, The Babylonian Laws, Vol. I 250, 262; for Middle Assyrian usage see Driver-Miles, The Assyrian Laws 185, §43: 29.

21. The Hittite Laws (1951) 143ff.

22. Friedrich, Die hethitischen Gesetze (1959), 24–25, 94–95.

"promised,"[23] §29 uses *ḫamenkanza* meaning "bound."[24] Probably, against Koschaker, ArOr 18/3: 216 n. 11, the age of the girl and the man obliged the Hittites to use two different forms of engagement. Since *taranza* discloses the fact that the girl was promised by her parents to the family of the man as an eligible wife for their son, we may assume that the girl (TUR.SAL) in §28 was not old enough to marry and was perhaps still a child. We may also assume that the man (LÚ) was very young (cf. Goetze, Kl² 112).

On the one hand, it reminds us that in Old Assyrian (perhaps in Old Anatolian) *irtibi*-documents the girl and the man were not allowed to marry because they were not grown up. On the other hand, it brings to mind the so-called Cradle-Tally, or Cradle-Engagement (Turkish: Beşik Kertmesi, Beşik Nişanı[25]), which still exists in some parts of Turkey and perhaps in some other oriental countries.

The girl, for whom the Hittite Law §29 uses the term *ḫamenkanza,* "bound," cannot be taken to be the wife of the man (cf. Goetze, Kl² 112). This form of betrothal requires a *kušata* (*tirḫātu*) "bride price," which covers the betrothal of adults.

We should pay attention to the fact that the gifts of the man('s family) bestowed on the young girl in §28 have no particular Hittite name, but are simply mentioned as *ku-it ku-it* [*pí-eš-ta*] (freely restored): "whatever (the first man) [has given] (to her) . . ." Eloping with another man is apparently allowed in §28, if the girl has reached the age of being able to make up her own mind, and if the eloper compensates the first man for his gifts.

It is a special pleasure for the present author to present this paper to his teacher Professor Hans Gustav Güterbock on his birthday. He taught Hittitology many years ago in Ankara. Those who have sought information about the ancient cultures of Turkey, have always found Güterbock by their sides. We feel very indebted to Professor Güterbock for his many excellent contributions to Ancient Anatolian studies.

23. Goetze, Kl² 112, note 8; Friedrich, HG 24f. 135b; Koschaker, ArOr 18/3: 216ff. ("versprochen"); Neufeld, The Hittite Laws 28 ("promised"), 143 ("declared"); for the views of other scholars see Neufeld, ibid. 143.

24. Güterbock, apud Koschaker, ArOr 18/3 note 49 (p. 260); Friedrich, HG 24f., 120 ("gebunden"); Neufeld, The Hittite Laws 9 ("affianced"), 143 ("bound"). Goetze, Kl² 112 (". . . verheiratet . . . jedoch nicht . . . den Beginn der ehelichen Gemeinschaft. Ehen sind . . . im Kindesalter geschlossen"). For the views of other scholars see Neufeld, The Hittite Laws 143.

25. E. Ercan, Beşik Kertme, Folklora Doğru 30: 28–30; A. Petekçi, Bozkır Ilçesinde Beşik Kertme, Türk Folklor Araştırmaları 271: 6223; S. V. Örnek, Türk Halk Bilimi 187f.; idem, Geleneksel Kültürümüzde Çocuk, 206, 195ff.; M. Tezcan, Beşik Kertmesi, Kongre Bildirileri 11: 498ff. (all Turkish).

Fig. 1.-Obverse

Fig. 2.-Lower edge

Fig. 3.-Reverse

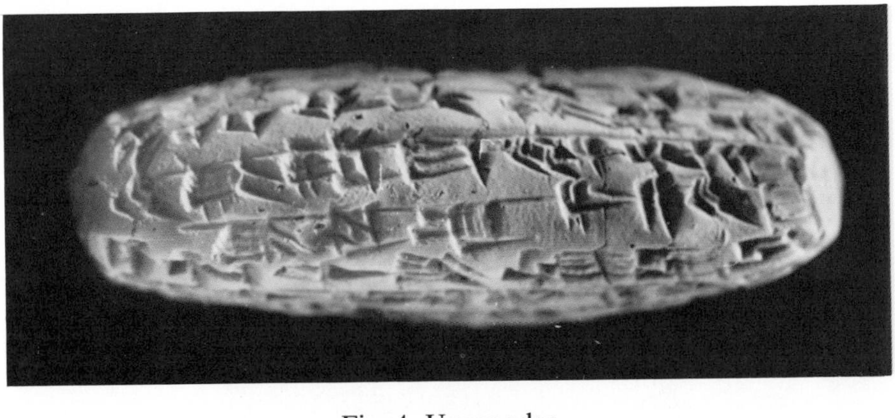

Fig. 4.-Upper edge

Fig. 5.-Left edge

Fig. 6.-Right edge

INHERITANCE AND ROYAL SUCCESSION AMONG THE HITTITES*

GARY BECKMAN

Yale University

> Let only a prince of the first rank, a son, become king! If there is no first-rank prince, then whoever is a son of the second rank—let this one become king! If there is no prince, no (male) heir, then whoever is a first-rank daughter—let them take a husband for her, and let him become king![1]

While this, our only general statement of the principles of royal succession in Ḫatti, is straightforward, it is contained in the late Old Kingdom Proclamation of Telepinu (CTH 19), and it is presented there as a reform. Consequently there has been ample room for scholarly debate concerning the character of the rules of succession to the Hittite throne in force before Telepinu's edict. Two of the most influential interpretations of the relevant Old Hittite material have been that suggesting an elective kingship, a position which I have discussed and dismissed elsewhere,[2] and that supporting a matrilineal succession.[3]

*In the preparation of this study I have made use of the lexical files of the Hittite Dictionary Project of the Oriental Institute, access to which was generously granted by the co-editors of the Project, Professor Harry A. Hoffner, Jr., and the *Jubilar*. I am honored to contribute this piece to a volume in celebration of Professor Güterbock, who has taught me much—through his writings, through conversations concerning my research, and through his example.

1. KBo 3.1 ii 36–39 (with restorations from KBo 7.15 + KBo 12.4 ii 11ff.):

    36. LUGAL-*uš-ša-an ḫa-an-te-ez-zi-ya-aš-pát* DUMU.LUGAL DUMU-*RU ki-ik-k*[(*i-iš-*)]*ta-ru ták-ku* DUMU.LU[GAL]
    37. *ḫa-an-te-ez-zi-iš* NU.GÁL *nu ku*[!]*-iš ta-a-an pé-e-da-aš* DUMU-*RU nu* LUGAL-*uš a-pa-a-aš*
    38. *ki-ša-ru ma-a-an* DUMU.LUGAL-*ma* DUMU.NITA NU.GÁL *nu ku-iš* DUMU.SAL *ḫa-an-te-ez-zi-iš*
    39. *nu-uš-ši-iš-ša-an* [LÚ]*an-ti-ya-an-ta-an ap-pa-a-an-du nu* LUGAL-*uš a-pa-a-aš ki-š*[(*a-ru*)]

2. JAOS 102 (1982) 435–42.
3. This position is set forth most fully by K. K. Riemschneider in H. Klengel, ed., *Beiträge zur sozialen Struktur des Alten Vorderasien* (1971) 79–102 (hereafter BSS), based largely on

In addition to analysis of the events narrated by the historical sources of the Old Kingdom, evidence adduced for this latter view includes the independent position within Hittite society of the woman bearing the title Tawananna,[4] the enigmatic self-reference of Ḫattušili I in his annals (CTH 4) as "the brother's son of Tawananna" (*ŠA* ᶠ*Ta-wa-an-na-an-na* DUMU ŠEŠ-*ŠU*),[5] and the important role played by goddesses in the Hittite pantheon. I will offer my own interpretation of most of these questions in the course of this paper, but I must remark here that the position of female deities within a religious system is hardly a direct reflection of the power or influence enjoyed by human females within that society.[6]

Matrilineality within a social group in which political power is hereditary and exercised by males entails the succession to a man's property and/or office by the son of his sister.[7] I do not believe that such a system obtained in Ḫatti in any period. Indeed, the very vocabulary employed in connection with royalty in Hittite texts indicates a patrilineal succession. Note first of all the New Hittite royal genealogies which stress direct descent in the male line. For example, Ḫattušili III identifies himself at the beginning of his "Apology" (CTH 81) as:

studies of the Soviet scholar Dovgjalo (cited p. 80, n. 5) inaccessible to me. Many writers have imputed some degree of matriarchy and/or matrilineality to Old Hittite society—see, for example, A. Goetze, *Hethiter, Churriter und Assyrer* (1936) 63, Kl 92ff.; G. Pugliese Carratelli, AttiAccTosc 23 (1958/59) 116; J. G. Macqueen, AnSt 9 (1959) 171–88; F. Cornelius, XIXᵉ CRRAI 325; R. Lebrun, Hethitica 3 (1979) 112; and V. Haas, KN 315–18, WZKM 69 (1977) 150–56, *Hethitische Berggötter und hurritische Steindämonen* (1982) 12, 43f., 63ff. As M. Liverani, OA 16 (1977) 118f. with n. 48, points out, discussion of this problem has been carried out largely within the context of modern racialist mythology. For a particularly striking formulation, see F. Hančar, AfO 13 (1939/41) 289.

4. This point is stressed particularly by Macqueen, AnSt 9 (1959) 184ff. On this office for females, see S. R. Bin-Nun, *The Tawananna in the Hittite Kingdom,* THeth 5 (1975) esp. pp. 11–29, but note my comments, JAOS 98 (1978) 513–14.

5. Preserved fully only in KBo 10.2 i 3. The duplicate KBo 10.3:2 has [DUMU ŠE]Š-*ŠU,* while the Akkadian KBo 10.1 obv. 1 preserves only *ša* ᶠ*Ta-w*[*a-* . . .].

6. A "forerunner" to the alleged Hittite matriarchy is not to be found in the occasional rule of native princesses (*rubâtum*)—among a great majority of princes—in the Anatolian towns of Ankuwa, Kaneš, Luḫušaddiya, and Waḫšušana during the Old Assyrian period. No historian would see matriarchy or a matrilineal rule of succession in sixteenth-century England, based on the reign of Elizabeth I. See M. T. Larsen, *The Old Assyrian City-State and its Colonies,* Mesopotamia 4 (1976) 121, n. 44, who suggests that the attested princesses were the widowed surviving members of original ruling pairs. Cf. also Bin-Nun, THeth 5:11–14.

7. On matrilineality see J. Gould and W. L. Kalb, eds., *Dictionary of the Social Sciences* (1964) 416–17.

> Ḫattušili, the Great King, King of the Land of Ḫatti; son of Muršili, the Great King, King of the Land of Ḫatti; grandson of Šuppiluliuma, the Great King, King of the Land of Ḫatti; descendant[8] of Ḫattušili, King of Kuššar.[9]

Such genealogies could, of course, be adduced in great numbers.[10]

Secondly, in the description of the actual assumption of royal office, the most frequently employed terminology—after such obvious and unhelpful locutions as "be or become king"—is:

$$\left\{\begin{matrix}\begin{Bmatrix}\textit{INA}\\ \textit{ANA}\end{Bmatrix} \begin{Bmatrix}{}^{\text{GIŠ}}\text{GU.ZA}\\ {}^{\text{GIŠ}}\text{ŠÚ.A}\end{Bmatrix} \begin{Bmatrix}\textit{ABĪYA/ŠU}\\ \text{LUGAL-}\textit{UTTI}\end{Bmatrix}\\ \text{LUGAL-}\textit{uiẓni}\end{matrix}\right\} \begin{Bmatrix}\textit{eš-/WAŠĀBU}\\ \textit{ELÛ}\end{Bmatrix}$$

"to sit on[11]/go up to the throne of the father/of kingship." That is, "throne of the father" and "throne of kingship" are interchangeable terms. There is no apparent development through time in the use of this vocabulary.[12]

I proceed to a closer examination of the Hittite sources:

If within a particular society tenure of a political office is hereditary, its transmission from generation to generation ought to follow for the most part the rules in force for other types of property. Of course, the office of king is special in at least two respects—it is non-divisible, unlike most other forms of property, and its "ownership" is of great interest to many members of the society beyond those individuals who actually transfer it. Therefore some special rules may govern its inheritance, but the general principles applicable within a society—e.g., patrilineality or matrilineality, strict primogeniture or parental choice—will be in force here also.[13]

Despite the small amount of material available for the study of Hittite inheritance practice, we may be certain that it was patrilineal. While no para-

8. On ŠÀ.BAL.BAL see StBoT 24 (tr. Nachfahre on p. 3, Nachkomme on pp. 31, 111):34. [Ed.—Note that in Ḫatt iv 86–7 the ŠÀ.BAL.BAL must be of *both* Ḫattušili and Puduḫepa.]

9. KUB 1.1 + 19.62 i 1–4 and dupls. (Ḫatt)—see StBoT 24:4f.

10. Similarly, scribes often employ patronymics in colophons—see E. Laroche, ArOr 19 (1949) 10ff.—as do other individuals on occasion, e.g., KUB 26.58 obv. 6 (cf. rev. 4a): ^{m}GAL-^{d}IM-*aš-ma* DUMU ^{m}*Kán-t*[*u-uz-zi-li*].

11. (*ḫaššuiẓnani*) *ašatar,* "seating (in kingship)," seems to have been the general Hittite expression for the installation of the monarch. Note the oracles carried out concerning LUGAL-*iz-na-ni a-ša-a-tar* (KUB 23.13), and the EZEN *a-ša-an-na-aš* (KUB 18.36:19f.). See A. Ünal, THeth 6:15, for a complete list of relevant oracles. For *ašātar/ašanna* in the meaning "to seat" cf. Hoffner, JAOS 103 (1983) 192.

12. See Appendix.

13. See J. Goody in id., ed., *Succession to High Office* (1966) 1ff., and cf. Liverani, OA 16 (1977) 118.

graph of the Hittite Laws focuses on inheritance, there are several sections dealing with the closely related problem of marriage. §27 reads:

> If a man takes a wife and carries her [to his house], he takes her dowry along. If the woman [should die] t[here], then he, the man, will bur[n] her (personal) goods, (but) her dowry he shall take for himself. If she should die in (her) paternal household [. . .?] (and) she has a male child, the man shall no[t take] her dowry.[14]

Whatever the significance of the incineration of the personal effects, it is clear from this law that normal marriage was virilocal, with the dowry of a deceased wife devolving upon her husband or upon her children,[15] if she had remained in her paternal household. This is in keeping with patrilineality, as is §46 of the Laws, which stipulates that a man who has received the lesser portion of a piece of landed property as an inheritance (*iwaru*[16]) should not be responsible for the services due to the state, but that these should be rendered "from his paternal household" (*IŠTU* É *ABĪŠU*—KBo 6.2 ii 40 and dupls.).[17] Note here also the levirate marriage set forth in §193:

> If a man has a woman (as his wife), and (that) man dies, his brother will take his wife. Then his father will take her. When secondly his father also dies, the son of his brother will take the wife whom he had. It is not an offense.[18]

A final law concerned with marriage is §36:

14. KBo 6.5 ii and dupls.:

4. *ták-ku* LÚ-*aš* DAM-*ŠU da-a-i na-a*[*n pár-na-aš-ša*]
5. *pé-e-ḫu-te-ez-zi i-wa-ru-uš-ši-*[(*it-az*)]
6. *an-da pé-e-da-a-i ták-ku* SAL-*za* [(*a*-)*pí-ya a-ki*]
7. *na-aš* LÚ-*aš a-aš-šu-še-et* BIL-*n*[*u-zi*? (*i-wa-ru-še-ta-az*)]
8. LÚ-*aš da-a-i ták-ku* [*a*]*d-da-aš* É-[(*ri a-ki*)]
9. DUMU.NITA-*ši i-wa-ru-ši-it* LÚ-*aš Ú-U*[*L da-a-i*]

On the interpretation of this paragraph, see Hoffner, AlHeth 33.

15. Probably not only a male heir as in the text quoted—the older dupl. KBo 6.3 ii 3 has DUMU.MEŠ-*Š*[*U*] in place of DUMU.NITA here.

16. As Goetze, Kl 105 and 113 recognized, an *iwaru* could be bestowed by a father upon either a son or a daughter. In fact, the *iwaru* seems to have constituted the share of the family estate due to a child leaving the paternal household before his father has died (so Hoffner, *Hittite Laws* [1964] 301f.). In the case of a woman this would be her dowry.

17. Cf. F. Imparati, JESHO 25 (1982) 233.

18. KBo 6.26 iii:

40. *ták-ku* LÚ-*iš* SAL-*an ḫar-zi ta* LÚ-*iš a-ki* DAM-*SÚ*
41. ŠEŠ-*ŠU da-a-i ta-an A-BU-ŠU da-a-i*
42. *ma-a-an ta-a-an A-BU-ŠU-ya a-ki* SAL-*na-an-na ku-in ḫar-ta*
43. ⟨DUMU⟩ ŠEŠ-*ŠU da-a-i Ú-UL ḫa-ra-tar*

> If a slave pays the "bride-price"[19] for a free young man and takes him as an *antiyant*-husband (for his daughter), no one shall alienate him (i.e., the young man) (from the household of the slave).[20]

As several scholars have already noted,[21] reflected here is a practice similar to the Mesopotamian *erēbu*-marriage[22] by which the father of the bride pays, rather than receives, the "bride-price," and the bride-groom therefore becomes a member of the wife's family in inversion of the usual custom. Thus when Queen Ašmunikal endows a mausoleum estate with what she intends as a permanent population of workers, she forbids to this group any alienation of its younger members through "brideship or *antiyant*-ship."[23]

antiyant-marriage is otherwise known in Ḫatti from one of the versions of the Illuyanka myth[24] and from the Old Hittite Inandık tablet.[25] In this latter legal document, an important person by the name of Tuttulla, whose own son has been dedicated to the priesthood of a deity and thus removed from normal societal relationships, gives his daughter in marriage to the man Zidi. At the same time Tuttulla adopts Zidi as his son. Any future legal challenge by the physical son of Tuttulla and his descendants to the ownership of Tuttulla's property by Zidi and his offspring is forbidden.

19. On *kušata* see most recently J. J. S. Weitenberg, IF 80 (1975) 67f.

20. KBo 6.3 ii:

> 27. *ták-ku* ÌR-*iš A-NA* DUMU.NITA *EL-LIM ku-ú-ša-ta píd-d[a-iz-]zi*
> 28. *na-an* ^{LÚ}*an-ti-ya-an-ta-an e-ep-zi na-an-kán pa-ra-a [Ú-]UL ku-iš-ki tar-na-i*

21. See K. Balkan, Dergi 6 (1948) 147–52; Güterbock, Cor.Ling. 64, MAW 152; Hoffner, Or 35 (1966) 393f.

22. See most recently C. H. Gordon, FsLacheman 155–60. Despite Kammenhuber's objections—HW^2 108f.—^{LÚ}*antiyant-* must be understood as a participle of *anda(n) iya-*, i.e., "the one entering." Even if Kammenhuber is correct in her view that *anda(n)* is not attested with certainty as a preverb with *iya-*, the Hittite term is probably a calque on Akkadian *errebu* and thus may not reflect correct Hittite usage. For an example of an *erēbu*-marriage at Kaneš, see K. Veenhof, CRRAI 25 (1978) = BBVO 1 (1982) 151.

23. KUB 13.8 i:

> 13. *A-NA* LÚ.MEŠ É.NA$_4$-*ya-kán AŠ-ŠUM* É.GI$_4$.A-*TIM an-da-an pé-eš-kán-du*
> 14. *pa-ra-a-ma-kán* DUMU.NITA DUMU.SAL *AŠ-ŠUM* É.GI$_4$.A-*TIM* ^{LÚ}*an-da-i-ya-an-da-an-ni-ya le-e*
> 15. *ku-iš-ki pa-a-i*
>
> Let them give (their daughters) for the purpose of brideship internally, to the men of the mausoleum (estate)! Let no one give out(side of the estate) a male or female youth for brideship or *antiyant*-ship!

24. See Hoffner in H. Goedicke and J. J. M. Roberts, eds., *Unity and Diversity* (1975) 137f., and, in general, BiOr 37 (1980) 200.

25. K. Balkan, *Inandık* (1973). The text is transliterated and translated into German on pp. 41–44.

Inheritance of property in the male line is clear, but what of a situation in which there were several children? The royal documents conferring land upon an individual speak only of its devolution upon posterity in general,[26] but the Šaḫurunuwa text (CTH 225)[27] of the Empire period records the *ante mortem* gift by this high courtier of many scattered properties to the sons of his daughter (obv. 8ff.). Also mentioned in passing is a previous donation to his own sons of much land (obv. 4–7). This tablet reveals the possibility of choice by a man in the disposition of his property among his heirs, and it possibly also indicates that a daughter could not inherit land in her own right.[28]

Turning to the inheritance of the office of King of Ḫatti, a subject most easily studied through injunctions to vassals in treaties, we see again that most texts speak only generally of the posterity of the overlord. Thus Muršili II informs Duppi-Tešub of Amurru:

> I have hereby caused you to swear an oath in regard to the King of Ḫatti, to the Land of Ḫatti, and to my sons, (and) my grandsons . . . You, Duppi-Tešub, must protect the King of Ḫatti, the Land of Ḫatti, my sons, (and) my grandsons in the future![29]

Other treaties, however, indicate that the incumbent King of Ḫatti might exercise a choice. Šuppiluliuma I enjoins one vassal:

> Now you, Ḫuqqana, recognize only My Majesty in regard to lordship! My son of whom I, My Majesty, say: "Let everyone recognize this one," and whom I thereby distinguish among (his brothers)—you, Ḫuqqana, recognize him![30]

26. E.g., KBo 5.7 (= LS 1) rev. 48: *UR-RA-AM ŠE-E-RA-AM ŠA* ^f^*Ku-wa-at-ta-al-la A-NA* DUMU.MEŠ-*ŠU* DUMU.DUMU.MEŠ-*ŠU MA-AM-MA-A-AN LA-A I-RA-AG-GUM*, "In the future no one shall contest (the property) with the sons or grandsons (or, 'children or grandchildren'?) of Kuwattalla." On these clauses in the royal land donations, see Riemschneider, MIO 6 (1958) 332ff.

27. KUB 26.43 + KBo 22.56 and dupl., edited by Imparati, RHA XXXII (1974).

28. See Imparati, op. cit. 16. That a woman could *hold* property, however, is clear from KBo 5.7, cited above in n. 26, a royal grant in favor of the "maid" (SAL.SUḪUR.LAL) Kuwattalla. Cf. also Law §171, where a (widowed?) mother seemingly disinherits her son—see H. C. Melchert, JCS 31 (1979) 62–64, and R. Haase, RIDA 17 (1970) 63f.

29. KBo 5.9 i:

> 21. *nu-ut-ta ka-a-aš-ma A-NA* LUGAL KUR ^URU^*Ḫa-at-ti* KUR ^URU^*Ḫa-a*[*t*-]*ti*
> 22. *Ù A-NA* DUMU.MEŠ-*YA* DUMU.DUMU.MEŠ-*YA še-er li-in-ga-nu-nu-un*
> 27. . . . *zi-ik-ma* ^m^*Dup-pí-*^d^U-*aš*^!^(Text: -AN) LUGAL KUR ^URU^*Ḫa-at-ti*
> 28. KUR ^URU^*Ḫa-at-ti* DUMU.MEŠ-*YA* DUMU.DUMU.MEŠ-*YA zi-la-du-wa pa-aḫ-ši*

See J. Friedrich, SV 1:12f.

30. KBo 5.3 i:

> 8. *nu̦-za zi-ik* ^m^*Ḫu-uq-qa-na-a-aš* ^d^UTU-*ŠI-pát A̦Š-ŠU̦M BE-LU-TIM ša-a-a̦k*

and the same ruler informs another subordinate king:

> Whichever son of his My Majesty speaks of to Šunaššura for kingship, Šunaššura will guard that one.[31]

Therefore inheritance of the office of king, as well as of other property, was in the male line and was subject to the will of the previous holder as to its disposition within the group of eligibles.[32] The texts just quoted date from the Empire period, well after the promulgation of the Telepinu Proclamation.[33]

9. DUMU-*YA-ya ku-in* ^{d}UTU-*ŠI te-mi ku-u-un-wa-za ḫu-u-ma-an-za ša-a-ak-du*
10. *na-an-kán iš-tar-na te-ek-ku-uš-ša-mi nu-za zi-iq-qa* ^{m}*Ḫu-uq-qa-na-a-aš*
11. *a-pu-u-un ša-a-a*[*k*]

See Friedrich, SV 2:106f.

31. KBo 1.5 i:

57. . . . *a-i-ú-me-e*
58. ^{d}UTU-*ši* DUMU.NITA-*šu a-na* LUGAL-*ru-tim ša a-na* ^{m}*Šu-na-aš-šu-ra*
59. *i-qa-ab-bi* ^{m}*Šu-na-aš-šu-ra šu-ú-tam a-na* LUGAL-*ru-tim i-na-aṣ-ar-šu*

See E. Weidner, PD 94f.

32. See already Otten, MIO 5 (1957) 27, n. 5, and below, n. 59.

33. Not surprisingly, rules of succession in the appanage kingdoms of Ḫatti were similar to practices involving the Great Kingship. The treaty between Tutḫaliya IV and Ulmi-Tešub of Tarḫuntašša (CTH 106) well demonstrates that the kingship was hereditary, and that the male line had precedence. KBo 4.10 obv.:

9. *ma-a-an* DUMU-*KA* DUMU.DU[MU-*KA kat*?-*t*]*a wa-aš-ta-i ku-iš-ki na-an* LUGAL KUR ^{URU}*Ḫat-ti pu-nu-uš-du nu-uš-ši-kán ma-a-an wa-aš-túl a-aš-zi*
10. *nu* GIM-*an A-NA* LUGAL [KU]R ^{URU}*Ḫat-ti* ZI-*an-za na-an QA-TAM-MA i-ya-ad-du ma-a-na-aš ḫar-kán-na-aš-ma na-aš ḫar-ak-du* É-*TUM-ma-aš-ši-kán*
11. KUR-*TUM-ya le-e* [*d*]*a-an-zi na-at da-me-e-el* NUMUN-*aš le-e pí-ya-an-zi ŠA* ^{m}*Ul-mi-*^{d}U-*ub-pát* NUMUN-*aš da-ad-du*
12. *da-ad-du-ma-at ŠA* DUMU.NITA *ŠA* DUMU.SAL-*ma le-e da-an-zi ma-a-an* NUMUN DUMU.NITA-*ma Ú-UL e-eš-zi* EGIR-*an-at-kán tar-na-at-ta-ri*
13. *nu* NUMUN *ŠA* DUMU.SAL *ŠA* ^{m}*Ul-mi-*^{d}U-*ub-pát* EGIR-*an ša-an-ḫa-an-du ma-a-na-aš a-ra-aḫ-zi-na-ya* KUR-*e na-an a-pí-iz-zi-ya*
14. EGIR-*pa ú-wa-d*[*a-*]*an-du nu I-NA* KUR $^{URU\,d}$U-*ta-aš-ša AŠ-ŠUM* EN-*UT-TI a-pu-u-un ti-it-ta-nu-wa-an-du*

(The Great King assures his junior colleague: Your descendants shall possess the kingship, but) if any son or grandson of yours should commit an offense, then let the King of Ḫatti question him. And if an offense is proven against him (lit. "remains for him"), then let the King of Ḫatti treat him as he pleases: If he is deserving of death, let him perish! But his household and country will not be taken and given to (someone) of another family. Let only (someone) of the descent of Ulmi-Tešub take (them)! Let (someone) of the male line take them—(those) of the

How does this Hittite theory of succession compare to the practice actually attested in historical documents? Aside from the Proclamation of Telepinu, our most important source for the Old Kingdom period is the Bilingual Edict of Ḫattušili I (CTH 6), drawn up when the king was quite ill and possibly on his death bed.[34] The ruler addresses the assembly:

> I spoke to you of the young Labarna (saying:) "Let him sit securely (upon the throne).' " I, the King, had named him as my son; I continually instructed him and constantly looked after him. But he showed himself a youth not fit to be seen . . . No one will ever again raise the son of his sister! . . . But enough! He is no (longer) my son! . . . Muršili[35] is now my son! H[im you must acknowledge!] Him you must enthrone![36]

The text continues with advice and commands for both the new heir[37] and the assembly, frequently buttressing these instructions with admonitory tales drawn from recent history. Most importantly for the present topic we learn in ii 63ff. that a son Ḫuzziya had led an unsuccessful revolt against Ḫattušili in a provincial town, and that afterward a daughter of Ḫattušili had been brought to rebellion by plotters who incited her:

> female line shall not take (them). But if there is no male line of descent, (and) it is extinguished [Ed.—Cf. Otten, StBoT 24.29 tr. "einziehen."]—then let (someone of) the female line of Ulmi-Tešub alone be sought out! Even if he is in a foreign country, let him be brought back from there! And let him be installed for lordship in the land of Tarḫuntašša!

See Imparati, RHA XXXII (1974) 98, n. 153 and H. Winkels, Diss. Hamburg (n.d.) 64f. As opposed to E. Neu, StBoT 5:168, and Götze, KlF 1 (1927–30) 229f., I understand the second occurrence of the pronoun *-at* in line 12 as referring to NUMUN (always a neuter noun—see Otten, ZA 61 [1971] 236 with n. 7) and not to *per* and/or *utne*. It is clear that *tarnattari,* in the indicative, forms part of the description of the situation, rather than of its consequences, which are all expressed in the imperative or the prohibitive.

34. Note the colophon (KUB 1.16 iv):

> 73. *tup-pí Ta-ba-ar-na* LUGAL.GAL *i-nu-ma*
> 74. LUGAL.GAL *Ta-ba-ar-na i-na* URU*Ku-uš-šar*KI *im-ra-aṣ-ṣú-ma* TUR-*am* m*Mu-u*[*r-ši-li*]
> 75. *a-na* LUGAL-*ru-tim ú-wa-a-ru*

For *wârum* D as "einsetzen, abordnen," see W. von Soden, AHw 1472b, citing BoSt 8:36 *ana šarrūti . . . limeršu.*

35. Muršili was probably the physical grandson of Ḫattušili—see KBo 1.6 obv. 13: m*Mu-ur-šị-li* LUGAL.GAL DUMU.DUMU-*šụ ša* m*Ḫa-at-tu-ši-li* LUGAL.GAL.

36. KUB 1.16 i–ii 1ff., 9, 14, 37f.—see F. Sommer and A. Falkenstein, HAB 2–7 for transliteration, but in i 4 read *ú-ʾ-ú-ri-šu* with E. Forrer, BoTU p. 10, and AHw 1472a. This was called to my attention by Professor Hoffner.

37. This aspect of the text renders unlikely the suggestion of Liverani, OA 16 (1977) 115 with n. 35, that the "true author" of the Bilingual Edict was Muršili himself.

[For] your father's [throne there is no heir. A se]rvant will sit (upon it)![38]

It is obvious that the naming of the young men as "son," i.e., their adoption, is equivalent to their proclamation as heir to the throne, and that Labarna's dismissal as son cannot be divorced from his removal as heir. The successive adoptions of these two were necessitated by the prior revolt of Ḫuzziya, which apparently left the old king without an eligible physical son. There can be no doubt as to either the patrilineal character of this succession, or as to the freedom of the ruler to choose among the eligibles, shown by the Bilingual Edict to include in practice most male members of the younger generation of the royal family.[39]

As for Ḫattušili's reference to himself in his Annals as "the brother's son of Tawananna," I can only suggest that this phrase expresses Ḫattušili's own biological relationship to the previous generation,[40] for it is likely that he was not the physical son of his predecessor,[41] but was probably himself adopted by King Labarna.[42] Even if we grant that this singular filiation might invoke legitimation according to matrilineal principles, it remains the sole possible piece of evidence for the existence of such a system in Ḫatti. No other king in all of Hittite history was followed in rule by his nephew, and the murders and usurpations by brothers-in-law attested by the Telepinu Proclamation may be better explained as examples of the exercise of *antiyant*-claims to the throne than as preemptive revolts on behalf of the claims of children of the next generation.[43]

It is important to note that many of the (male) victims chronicled in the Telepinu Proclamation perished along with their children (*QADU* DUMU^{MEŠ}-

38. KUB 1.16 ii 70f.: *at-ta-aš-tạ-aš-wa* [^{GIŠ}ŠÚ.A-*ši* DUMU.NITA NU.GÁL Ì]R-*iš-wa-aš-ša-an e-ša-ri.*

39. Uncertainty persists only as to whether a king could pass over an otherwise eligible physical son of the first rank and adopt a more distant relative as son and heir to the throne.

40. Cf. Hoffner, OrNS 49 (1980) 297. T. R. Bryce, AnSt 31 (1981) 13, hypothesizes that Ḫattušili suppressed mention of his father because he had been among the rebels against the "grandfather" mentioned in KUB 1.16 iii 41ff. (HAB 12ff.).

41. Note KUB 1.16 iii 41f.: *ḫu-uḫ-ḫa-aš-mi-iš* [*La-ba-a*]*r-na-an* DUMU-*ša-an* ^{URU}*Ša-na-ḫu-it-ti iš-ku-na-aḫ-ḫi-iš*, "my grandfather *i.*-ed [Laba]rna his son in Šanaḫuitta." If, as I believe, the Labarna treated here is the same person as the predecessor of Ḫattušili, then he cannot have been his father, for the younger man would certainly have referred to the older as "my father."

42. Bryce, AnSt 31 (1981) 12, believes that Labarna, too, may have been adopted, but since his view hinges upon interpretation of the passage quoted in n. 41, and therefore upon the meaning of the obscure verb *iškunaḫḫ-* (on which see J. Puhvel, IF 83 [1978] 141–43) we cannot be certain.

43. This latter opinion, of course, is that of proponents of the matrilineal analysis—see Riemschneider, BSS 84ff., 94. Cf. also Bin-Nun, THeth 5:213–17.

ŠU).[44] Since these grisly actions were only necessary—or at least were only mentioned in the context of the Proclamation—because they represented the extinction of a line and a claim to the throne, they serve as additional evidence for patrilineal succession.[45] It may well be that in those instances when a reigning king (Muršili I, Zidanta I) himself was murdered, the crime was committed before he had made known his choice of successor. We must remember that while the Proclamation informs us of the identity of the murderers, this information may not have been widely available at the time of succession.

It is also useful to bear in mind that Telepinu was himself the son-in-law of his penultimate predecessor, Ammuna, and brother-in-law of the ruler whom he deposed, Ḫuzziya (see §22). Since this Ḫuzziya had come to power as the result of a bloodbath which eradicated the lines of Tittiya and Ḫantili, and since he had in addition threatened the lives of Telepinu and his wife Ištapariya, the sections of the Proclamation providing for the punishment of a murderous monarch by the assembly (§§27, 29ff.) were certainly directed against him. Thus the goals of the Proclamation may be seen not only as the elimination of bloodshed within the royal family and the concomitant rise in the fortunes of Ḫatti, but also the justification of the very career, accession, and policies of Telepinu.[46] The centerpiece of the entire text, of course, is the rule of succession with which we began.

However, it seems that the will of Telepinu was thwarted soon after his own death, for his immediate successor was apparently not his son-in-law Alluwamna, as he had undoubtedly intended,[47] but rather the poorly attested Taḫurwaili, in all probability a brother of Ḫuzziya.[48] Early in the following "Middle Hittite" period there was also a struggle for the throne—apparently between two rival lines—again in clear contravention of the Telepinu Proc-

44. Kaššeni (§18), Tittiya (§21), Ḫantili (§22).

45. See Riemschneider, BSS 92. On p. 84, with n. 27, he quite rightly dismisses the idea of Dovgjalo that DUMU might indicate both "son" and "nephew" (i.e., "matrilineal successor") in Hittite texts.

46. Cf. Hoffner in *Unity and Diversity* (1975), pp. 51–56, esp. bottom of p. 51 ("The defense of both usurpers had to rest upon grounds other than descent.") and OrNS 49 (1977, pub. 1980) 307f., followed by Liverani, OA 16 (1977) 118ff., esp. n. 45, where he remarks that the purpose of the Proclamation was more to justify the present than to regulate the future.

47. Cf. Goetze, JCS 11 (1957) 57, and Gurney, CAH 3 II/1, 669. Note that Alluwamna is given the title DUMU.LUGAL in KUB 11.3:6. Does this perhaps indicate that he, like Arnuwanda later, was adopted by his father-in-law?

48. On this recently re-discovered Hittite king, see O. Carruba in K. Bittel et al., eds., *Anatolian Studies presented to Hans Gustav Güterbock on the Occasion of his 65th Birthday* (1974) 73–93, esp. 91. Cf. also Otten, Hist. Quellen 115, and Liverani, OA 16 (1977) 113f.

lamation. These troubles were seemingly resolved by an agreement reached by the two parties, as recorded in the fragmentary "Protocoles de succession dynastique" (CTH 271).[49]

Later in the "Middle Hittite" period a vexing problem is posed by Arnuwanda and Ašmunikal, whom the sources refer to both as brother and sister and as a married couple, in seeming violation of Hittite concepts of incest.[50] We may resolve this difficulty by understanding Arnuwanda as the son-in-law and adopted son of his predecessor Tutḫaliya.[51] This would thus be a situation similar to that of Tuttulla and Zidi adduced earlier. Note that Tutḫaliya further strengthened the claim of Arnuwanda to the throne by instituting the only known coregency in Hittite history.[52]

Under the Empire, succession was most often from father to first-rank son,[53] but on two occasions to the brother of the deceased ruler (Muršili II, Šuppiluliama II). Whereas it is said of Šuppiluliama II that his brother had not left even a pregnant woman behind,[54] we have no such statement of the lack of issue of Arnuwanda II, succeeded by his brother Muršili II.[55] There were two celebrated usurpers in the Empire period: The army seems to have been instrumental in the installation of Šuppiluliuma I in place of Tutḫaliya the Younger,[56] who may well have been his brother,[57] and Ḫattušili III re-

49. On these and related documents, see Carruba, SMEA 18 (1977) 175–95, and Košak, Tel Aviv 7 (1980) 163–68. See also Košak, AnSt 30 (1980) 37f. I cannot, however, accept Košak's view of the role of the *panku-* in this period—see my study cited in n. 2.

50. See Gurney, CAH 3 II/1, 671f., and Otten, Hist. Quellen 105f.

51. This interpretation is presented by Beal, JCS 35 (1983) 115–119. I am grateful to Mr. Beal for allowing me to read a preliminary version of his study. Cf. also C. Kühne, CRRAI 25 (1978) = BBVO 1 (1982) 254, n. 139, and 261, n. 215.

52. See Ph. H. J. Houwink ten Cate, Records 58, n. 2.

53. See below, n. 59. Other than for Muwatalli—see Ḫatt i 9–11 (StBoT 24, 4f.)—we cannot be reasonably sure that any succeeding son was actually the eldest of the first rank.

54. In KUB 26.33 ii an unnamed official reports of Arnuwanda III:

> 7. *nu-uš-ši* NUMUN NU.GÁL *e-eš-ta ar-m*[*a-aḫ-ḫu-wa-an-ta-an*]
> 8. SAL-*an pu-nu-uš-šu-un nu ar-ma-aḫ-*[*ḫu-wa-an-za*]
> 9. SAL-*aš Ú-UL e-eš-ta*

Cf. Carruba, SMEA 18 (1977) 151–53.

55. See the description given by Muršili II in his annals of his becoming king—Götze, AM 15–21.

56. Muršili II relates in his "First Plague Prayer" (CTH 378.I), KUB 14.14++ and dupl. obv. 13–19:

> Because Tut[ḫaliya] the Younger was Lord of the lands of Ḫatti, the princes, the nobles, the commanders of the thousands, the officers (LÚ.MEŠ DUGUD), [the subalterns(?) (LÚ.MEŠ SIG_5)], and all [the infantry] (and) chariotry of Ḫattuša swore an oath to him. My father also swo[re] an oath to him. [But when m]y

volted successfully against his nephew Muršili III/Urḫi-Tešub.[58] Whatever the ultimate glories of the reigns of these two usurpers, their initial claims to kingship must have rested on some basis within the acknowledged system of succession.[59]

It seems that the choice of successor within the male line remained somewhat free down to the end of Hittite history. That is, the old king chose the best candidate among his first-rank sons,[60] born to his sole legitimate queen.[61] In the absence or disqualification of such *šaḫuiḫu(i)ššuwali*-sons,[62]

> [father] mistreated Tutḫaliya, al[l the princes, the noble]s, the commander(s) of the thousands (and) the officers of Ḫattuša [went] over to my father. And the oath (deities) [seized Tutḫaliya. Then they kil]led [Tutḫaliya,] (and) furthermore, such of his brothers as [stood with him?] they killed.

For transliteration, see Lebrun, *Hymnes* (1980) 194, and cf. Götze, KlF 1 (1927–30) 166. For the military connotation of LÚ DUGUD and LÚ SIG_5, see E. von Schuler, OrNS 25 (1956) 209–13.

57. See Götze, KlF 1 (1927–30) 181–82, and Laroche, NH no. 1389.5. With the newly discovered seal impression from Maşat (S. Alp, Belleten XLIV/173 [1980] 57) proving that Tutḫaliya (II) was the father of Šuppiluliuma, we see that the function of the epithet DUMU-*RU* in the case of Tutḫaliya "the Younger" was precisely to distinguish father from son in the historical records.

58. See Ḫatt, esp. iii 63–iv 37 (StBoT 24:20–25).

59. Riemschneider's suggestion—BSS 96, n. 89—that the provisions of the Telepinu Proclamation had been forgotten over time is made unlikely by the fact that all known copies of this text may be dated by their script to the Empire period.

60. As Sturtevant, Chrest. (1935) 189 and 198 and Liverani, OA 16 (1977) 118, n. 44 have shown, *ḫantezziyaš* DUMU.LUGAL and DUMU.LUGAL *ḫantezziš* in the Telepinu Proclamation—see n. 1 here—must refer to a rank, even though *ḫantezzi(ya)š* DUMU in other contexts may mean "firstborn." Of the two variant expressions, the first probably involves an ellipsis, i.e., *ḫantezziyaš* (*pedaš*) DUMU.LUGAL—cf. *tān pedaš* DUMU-*RU* in the same context and DUMU-*aš* SAG.DU-*aš* (nom.) in KUB 26.33 ii 15—while the second features an attributive. Cf. also Götze, ArOr 2 (1930) 158, n. 2. It seems reasonable that a rank might be occupied by more than one person; if so, even the Telepinu Proclamation leaves the king some degree of choice as to his successor, and the plans of Šuppiluliuma I to pick a successor mentioned earlier would not necessarily involve a violation of this edict.

61. So Sturtevant, Chrest. 189 "of the first (wife)," sometimes referred to as *šakuwaššaraš* SAL.LUGAL, "legitimate queen," e.g., KUB 21.42 iv 16. Note that in the greeting formulae of the letter of Ḫattušili III to Kadašman-Enlil II of Babylon (KBo 1.10—CTH 172), the Hittite ruler mentions only one wife (DAM) of his own (obv. 3), while attributing several to the addressee (obv. 5). Likewise, Šattiwazza of Mitanni, when given a Hittite princess in marriage, is told by his overlord/father-in-law Šuppiluliuma I that while he may make no other woman equal in rank to his new queen, he might enjoy SAL.MEŠ *EŠ-RI-*TU_4 (KBo 1.1 obv. 59ff.—see Weidner, PD 18f.). [Ed.—Cf. also the class/rank of DAM.MEŠ *paḫḫuwaršeš* KUB 29.1 iii 42 and Güterbock apud Kellerman Diss. 65–6 (all the wives of the king but the queen).]

62. See Götze, NBr 24f.

the purple might fall on a son-in-law espoused to a first-rank daughter,[63] or on a son of the second rank, offspring of a secondary wife (*ESERTU* or *NAPṬARTU*).[64] Such was the position of Muršili III/Urḫi-Tešub,[65] who in the eyes of some, however, was not well-enough-born to sit upon the throne.[66] Unfortunately the sources yield no information as to how or when a ruler made known his choice of successor.[67] In normal cases this would probably not have occurred until the king had ruled for at least a few years. When on two occasions under the Empire a monarch died early in his reign, he was succeeded by a brother, rather than by a minor son, illustrating the priority of competence over a strict rule of succession.[68] That is, the claims of an entire generation of eligibles were not always in practice vacated by the accession of one of their number.

This system had as an advantage the securing of the most able of several young males for the demanding position of king, but it carried within itself the seeds of intradynastic struggle and bloodshed, as exhibited in both the Telepinu Proclamation and the "Apology" of Ḫattušili III. It is the large number of persons with some—perhaps remote—claim to consideration for the highest office to whom Tutḫaliya IV refers in his Instructions to the Eunuchs (CTH 255.2):

63. See the passage of the Telepinu Proclamation quoted in n. 1, and note that Ištapariya, wife of Telepinu, is called the "first-rank sister" (*ḫa-an-te-ez-zi-ya-an* NIN) of Ḫuzziya (KBo 3.1 ii 10). Cf. Pugliese Carratelli, AttiAccTosc 23 (1958/59) 105, n. 1.

64. Despite the work of Götze—see esp. ArOr 2 (1930) 153–63, and Kl 87 and 94f.—many details of the organization of the Hittite royal family and harem remain obscure.

65. Ḫatt iii 41 (StBoT 24:20) refers to Urḫi-Tešub as DUMU *EŠERTI*.

66. In his treaty with Šaušgamuwa of Amurru (CTH 105), Tutḫaliya IV recounts the objectionable behavior of a previous ruler of that kingdom, Mašturi (KUB 23.1++ ii 20–29):

> When Muwatalli "became a god," then Urḫi-Tešub, son of Muwatalli, became king. [My father, however,] wrested the kingship away from Urḫi-Tešub. [Maš]turi committed treachery—(Although) it was Muwatalli who had taken him up and had made him his son-in-law, afterwards he (Mašturi) did not protect his son, Urḫi-Tešub, but went over to my father, (thinking:) "Will I protect even a 'bastard' (^{LÚ}*paḫḫurši-*)?"

For transliteration see StBoT 16:10, and see pp. 37f., on ^{LÚ}*paḫḫurši-*.

67. The Hittites were not alone in the ancient Near East in allowing their king to choose, within limits, his own successor. Note the comments of Liverani, CRRAI 19 (1971, publ. 1974) 336, on Late Bronze Age Syria, and R. N. Frye, Acta Antiqua 25 (1977) 81, on ancient Persia. On this latter culture cf. also G. Widengren, *Commémoration Cyrus—Congrès de Shiraz 1971* (1974) 84ff.

68. These are the sole instances of succession by a brother attested in Hittite history, and although I cannot give a detailed rebuttal here, I believe that there is no evidence to support the thesis of Bin-Nun, set forth in RHA XXXI (1973) 5–25, and THeth 5, passim, that brother-succession was the rule in ancient Anatolia.

My Majesty has many brothers and many [co]usins (lit. [sons of] his "fathers"). The Land of Ḫatti is full of the seed of kingship. The seed of Šuppiluliuma, the seed of Muršili, the seed of Muwatalli, (and) the seed of Ḫattušili, is numerous. You must not recognize any other man in regard to lordship! In regard to lordship, down to the second and third generations, protect the seed of Tutḫaliya![69]

APPENDIX

The Terminology of Succession and Rule[70]

I have included the approximate date of the tablets on which each Old and Middle Hittite attestation is inscribed. For the system of dating and abbreviations employed, see CHD III/1 xiv–xv. When more than one occurrence of a single expression are attested for a particular ruler, in most cases only the oldest example is cited. I have also omitted duplicate texts. Citations in brackets are those involving substantial restorations.

OLD KINGDOM

Labarna		
active[71]		
	LUGAL.GAL *eš-*	KBo 3.67 i 2 (OH/NS)
passive[71]		
	PN *iškunaḫḫ-*	KUB 1.16 iii 41f. (OH/NS)
Ḫattušili I		
active		
	ḫaššuwai-	[KBo 10.2 i 3] (OH/NS); KBo 3.1 i 12 (OH/NS)
	LUGAL-*utta epēšu*[72]	KBo 10.1 obv. 1 (OH/NS)

69. KUB 26.1 i 9–16—for transliteration see von Schuler, Dienstanw. 9, and cf. Laroche, RA 47 (1953) 76f. On the restoration [DUMU] ⌜*A*⌝-*BI*^{MEŠ}-*ŠU* cf. Goetze, JCS 13:66 (space is adequate). A similar passage is found in KUB 23.1++ ii 8ff. (StBoT 16:8–11). On the difficult successions in the last era of Hittite history, see Otten, Jahresbericht des Instituts für Vorgeschichte der Universität Frankfurt a.M. (1976) 30f.

70. On the related question of Hittite royal titulary, see H. Gonnet, Hethitica 3 (1979) 3–107.

71. Seen from the point of view of the king. In instances where the action is thus "passive," the actor may be either a powerful human being or a deity.

72. For this expression, see CAD E 219f.

Muršili I		
active		
	LUGAL *eš-*	KBo 3.57 ii 5 (OH/NS)
	ḫaššuwai-	KBo 3.1 i 23 (OH/NS); KBo 3.57 ii 4 (OH/NS)
	^{GIŠ}ŠÚ.A *ABĪŠU da-*	KBo 3.27 obv. 14 (OH/NS)
passive		
	PN *ašeš-*	KUB 1.16 ii 38 (OH/NS)
Zidanta I		
active		
	ḫaššuwai-	KBo 3.1 i 65? (OH/NS) [KBo 3.67 ii 11] (OH/NS)
Ammuna		
active		
	ḫaššuwai-	KUB 11.1 ii 4 (OH/NS)
	INA ^{GIŠ}GU.ZA *ABĪYA eš-*	[KUB 26.71 i 8] (OH/NS)
	utne maniyaḫḫ-	[KUB 26.71 i 8] (OH/NS)
Ḫuzziya I		
active		
	ḫaššuwai-	KBo 3.1 ii 9 (OH/NS)
Telepinu		
active		
	INA ^{GIŠ}GU.ZA *ABĪYA eš-*	KBo 3.1 ii 16 (OH/NS)
miscellaneous (pretenders, general statements, uncertain)		
active		
	LUGAL-*uš kiš-*	KBo 3.22 obv. 22, rev. 49 (OS); KUB 21.48 obv. 7(?)
	INA ^{GIŠ}ŠÚ.A *eš-*	[KUB 1.16 ii 71] (OH/NS)
	INA ^{GIŠ}GU.ZA.GAL *eš-*	KUB 11.3:2(?)
	wašābu[73]	KUB 1.16 i 3 (OH/NS) (of the Young Labarna)
passive		
	LUGAL-*un iya-*	[KBo 3.38 rev. 6] (?) (OH/NS)
	PN *ašeš-*	KUB 1.16 iii 44 (OH/NS) (of Papaḫdilmaḫ)
	PN ^{GIŠ}ŠÚ.A-*mi ašeš-*	KBo 3.28 ii 24 (OH/NS)
	PN *te-/qabû*	KUB 1.16 i–ii 3 (OH/NS) (of the Young Labarna)

73. For the use of *wašābu* with *kussû,* "throne," see AHw 515 and 1481. In the present context *ina kussî* has been ellipsed.

"MIDDLE HITTITE" PERIOD

Tutḫaliya I
active

ana ^{GIŠ}GU.ZA LUGAL-*utti elû*	KBo 1.6 obv. 15 (NH)

Tutḫaliya II *tuḫkanti*
active

ANA ^{GIŠ}GU.ZA *ABĪŠU eš-*	KBo 10.34 iv 12 (MH/NS)
LUGAL-*uizni eš-*	KBo 10.34 i 1 (MH/NS)

miscellaneous
passive

LUGAL-*uizni lamnai-*	KUB 36.109:6 (MH/MS)
LUGAL-*uizni tittanu-*	KUB 36.114:22 (MH/MS)
LUGAL-*uizni iškiya-*	KUB 36.119:5 (MH/MS?)
ANA LUGAL-*TIM iškiya-*	KBo 16.24 (+) 25 i 66 (MH/MS)

EMPIRE PERIOD

Šuppiluliuma I
active

LUGAL.GAL *kiš-*	KBo 22.10 iii 10f.[74]
ANA ^{GIŠ}ŠÚ.A LUGAL-*UTTI eš-*	KBo 6.28 obv. 16f.
ana ^{GIŠ}GU.ZA LUGAL-*utti wašābu*	[KBo 1.6 obv. 33]
LUGAL-*uizni eš-*	KUB 23.124 i 36

Arnuwanda II
active

ANA ^{GIŠ}GU.ZA *ABĪŠU eš-*	KBo 3.4 i 5

74. Košak, Tel Aviv 7 (1980) 164f., suggests that this passage was spoken by Muršili II in reference to Šuppiluliuma I.

Muršili II		
active		
	ḫaššuwai-	KUB 19.8 i 19
	ANA DINGIR^{MEŠ} ^{LÚ}SANGA *kiš-*	KUB 14.12 obv. 4
	ANA ^{GIŠ}GU.ZA *ABĪYA eš-*	KBo 3.4 i 3
	ANA ^{GIŠ}ŠÚ.A LUGAL-*UTTI eš-*	KUB 26.43 obv. 13
	ana ^{GIŠ}GU.ZA *abīya wašābu*	[KUB 3.14 obv. 12]
	ana ^{GIŠ}GU.ZA LUGAL-*utti wašābu*	KBo 1.8 obv. 8
Muwatalli		
active		
	LUGAL-*izziya-*	KUB 23.1 i 29
	ANA ^{GIŠ}GU.ZA *ABĪŠU eš-*	KBo 6.29 i 23
	LUGAL-*iznanni eš-*	KBo 4.12 obv. 14
	ana ^{GIŠ}GU.ZA LUGAL-*utti ṣabātu*[75]	KBo 1.8 obv. 11
passive		
	ANA DN ^{LÚ}SANGA *iya-*	KUB 6.45 iii 29f.
	LUGAL-*iznanni dai-*	KUB 6.45 iii 31
Muršili III = Urḫi-Tešub		
active		
	LUGAL.GAL *eš-*	[Ḫatt (StBoT 24) iii 44]
	LUGAL-*izziya-*	KUB 23.1++ ii 21
	ANA ^{GIŠ}GU.ZA *ABĪŠU eš-*	[KUB 21.17 ii 17]
passive		
	LUGAL-*iznanni tittanu-*	KBo 4.12 obv. 21
	AŠŠUM LUGAL-*UTTI tittanu-*	KUB 21.37 rev. 18f.
	AŠŠUM LUGAL-*UTTI dai-*	KBo 6.29 i 38
	EN-*anni dai-*	[Ḫatt (StBoT 24) iii 43]

75. Muwatalli uses this expression to describe his own legitimate accession. Ṣabātu is not solely employed to describe accession in a critical or hostile manner—cf. A. Archi. SMEA 14 (1971) 200, n. 64.

Ḫattušili III		
active		
	LUGAL.GAL *kiš-*	Ḫatt (StBoT 24) iii 43
	LUGAL-*izziya-*	KBo 4.12 obv. 31
	LUGAL-*anni eš-*	KUB 26.43 rev. 9–11
	ana ^{GIŠ}GU.ZA *abīya wašābu*	KBo 1.8 obv. 16
	ina ašri ša abi abīka wašābu	NBC 3934 obv. 15 (JCS 1, 241)
	šarrūta ṣabātu	KBo 1.14 rev. 5, 7
	ANA PN LUGAL-*iznatar arḫa da-*	KUB 23.1 ii 22
passive		
	LUGAL-*UTTA mema-*	Ḫatt (StBoT 24) iv 7f.
	LUGAL-*iznanni tittanu-*	Ḫatt (StBoT 24) iv 65f.
Arnuwanda III		
active		
	LUGAL-*uš eš-*	KUB 26.32 i 9
Šuppiluliama II		
active		
	LUGAL-*uš kiš-*	[KUB 26.33 ii 23]
passive		
	EN-*an iya-*	KUB 26.33 ii 13
miscellaneous		
active		
	LUGAL *eš-*	KUB 31.66 + IBoT III 122 ii 5
	LUGAL-*uš kiš-*	KBo 6.28 rev. 19
	PN *lū inneppuš* LUGAL-*utti*	[KBo 1.7:40]
	LUGAL *išpart-*	KUB 31.66 + IBoT III 122 ii 7
	ANA ^{GIŠ}ŠÚ.A LUGAL-*UTTI eš-*	KUB 10.45 rev. rt. 25–27
	ANA LUGAL-*UTTI eš-*	KUB 9.10 rt. 17f.
	LUGAL-*iznanni eš-*	KBo 18.179 rt. 8
	^{GIŠ}GU.ZA *ABĪŠU ep-*	KUB 8.1 ii 8 (oracle trans.)
	INA ^{GIŠ}GU.ZA *ABĪŠU para nai-*	KUB 8.1 ii 10 (oracle trans.)

passive

ana šarrūti qabû	KBo 1.5 i 46f.
te-	KBo 5.3 i 9
IŠTU Ì DÙG.GA LUGAL-*UTTI* *iškiya-* . . . *ŠUM* LUGAL-*UTTI* *dai-* . . . TÚG LUGAL-*UTTI* *waššiya-* . . . TÚG*lupannin šiya-*	KUB 24.5+ obv. 19ff.

NEW BOGHAZKÖY JOINS AND DUPLICATES

HOWARD BERMAN

The Oriental Institute
Chicago, Illinois

As part of my work for the Chicago Hittite Dictionary Project I transliterated all of the Hittite texts in KUB 51, KBo 27, and FHL.[1] While doing so I found a number of new joins and duplicates, which I present here arranged in order of CTH number.

CTH 292: Les lois, deuxième série: "si une vigne"
FHL 90: 1′–4′ is a fragment of law 113 and is a duplicate of KBo 6.10 obv. i 27′–30′ (a_1), KBo 6.11 obv. i 24′–27′ (b), and KUB 29.24: 3′–8′ (p).

CTH 334.2: ^{d}MAH, déesse perdue et retrouvée (*mugawar*)
A. KUB 33.45 + 53 + FHG 2.
B. KUB 33.51 = A 5′–19′.
C. KUB 51.30 rev. = A 8′–16′ and B 4′–12′.
D. 637/f + 658/f (StBoT 2: 51): 7–10 = C obv. 13′–15′.
E. KBo 26.131 obv. 1′–5′ = C obv. 12′–15′ and D 7–13.

CTH 370: Fragments mythologiques
A. KUB 36.49.
B. KBo 27.15 = A obv. i?
C. FHL 146 = A obv. i?

These duplicates are uncertain because of the small size of B and C. They are based on *ka-ra-ap-ta* A i passim = B 3′ and C 3′, 4′, and *ḫa-az-zi-i-šar* A i 3′ = [. . . *ḫa-az-z*]*i-i-šar* B 4′. Laroche, FHL, p. 75, suggested that A and C belong to the same tablet.

1. Helmut Freydank, *Hethitische Rituale und Festbeschreibungen, Keilschrifturkunden aus Boghazköy,* vol. 51, Berlin (1981); Heinrich Otten and Christel Rüster, *Tafelfunde der Siebziger Jahre und Texte in Hurritischer Sprache, Keilschrifttexte aus Boghazköi,* vol. 27, Berlin (1982); and J.-M. Durand and E. Laroche, *Fragments hittites du Louvre, Mémorial Atatürk: études d'archéologie et de philologie anatoliennes,* Éditions Recherche sur les civilisations, Synthèse 10, Paris (1982), 73–107.

CTH 394: Rituel d'*Ašhella,* contre une épidémie dans l'armée

A. KUB 9.32 + Bo 4445 (ZA 64: 244f.).
B. KUB 9.31 rev. iii 14–iv 40.
C. HT 1 rev. iii–iv 43.
D. KUB 41.18 obv. ii 2′-rev. iii 20 = A obv. 1–26, B rev. iii 14–46, and C rev. iii 1–40.
E. KUB 41.17 rev. iii = A obv. 31–42 and B rev. iii 51–63; rev. iv 1′–24′ = A rev. 5–32, B rev. iv 7–40, and C rev. iv 13–43.
F. KBo 13.212 = A obv. 33–39, B rev. iii 55–63, and E rev. iii 5′–13′.
G. FHL 95 = A obv. 37–40, B rev. iii 61–63, E rev. iii 10′–14′, and F 7′–10′.

F may be an indirect join to C.

CTH 401.1: Rituel de [. . .]*banippi,* l'oiseleur

A. KUB 30.36.
B. FHL 115: 2′–4′ = A obv. ii 1–2.

CTH 419: Rituel de substitution royale

A. KUB 24.5 + KUB 9.13 + FHL 125.
B(+)C. KUB 36.92(+)93 = A obv. 6′–20′ and obv. 32′–rev. 7.
D. KUB 36.94 = A rev. 4–21 and C rev. 9′–13′.
E. KBo 15.14 = A obv. 32′–rev. 3 and C rev. 1′–7′.

FHL 125 joins KUB 24.5 rev. 1–4.

CTH 434.6: Fragments de rituels pour les divinités ^{d}MAḪ-^{d}GUL-*šeš*[2]

A. KUB 43.55.
B. Bo 2872 (AfO 23: 38 n. 21).
C. FHL 135 = A obv. iii 14–19.

CTH 435.3: Fragments de rituels au Soleil

A. KUB 41.4.
B. KUB 51.83 obv.? 2′–5′ = A obv. ii 19′–22′.

CTH 491.1: Rituels de purification

A. KUB 43.58.
B. KUB 15.42 obv. i = A obv. i 1–35; obv. ii = A obv. ii 13–47.
C. FHL 158 rev. = B rev. iii 17′–24′.

CTH 500: Fragments de rituels du Kizzuwatna

KBo 22.135(+?)KBo 27.136.

2. So classified by Laroche, RHA XXX (1972) 108. This is actually a Sammeltafel. A obv. ii 1–iii 9 is a ritual for ^{d}MAḪ-^{d}GUL-*šeš,* obv. iii 10–rev. iv 16′ is a ritual for ^{d}DÌM.NUN.ME, and rev. v is part of the colophon.

This indirect join is uncertain. Both fragments come from the Great Temple (K/19). If the join is correct, KBo 27.136 obv. ii 1 follows immediately after KBo 22.135 obv. i 9′ and KBo 22.135 rev. 1′ follows KBo 27.136 rev. 13′ with the loss of an intervening one or two lines. KBo 27.136 rev. 1′–13′ is parallel to KBo 22.135 rev. 3′–15′.

CTH 530: Fragments divers d'administration religieuse
KBo 13.234 + KUB 51.69.
The sides of KUB 51.69 are to be inverted. KUB 51.69 obv.! joins KBo 13.234 obv. i 5–19 and KUB 51.69 rev.! joins KBo 13.234 rev. 2′–19′.

CTH 580: Oracles mixtes: KIN et MUŠEN
KUB 5.17 + KUB 18.55 + FHL 187.
FHL 187 is a direct join to KUB 5.17 rev. iii 18′–25′.

CTH 628: Fête *(ḫ)išuwaš*
II. Tablettes sans numéro
a) A. KBo 15.48.
B. KBo 23.28 + KUB 32.65 + 61 obv. i 1′–34′ = A obv. i 1′–33′; obv. ii 1′–20′ = A obv. ii 29′–50′.
C. KBo 15.47 + KUB 25.42 obv. ii 1′–16′ = B obv. ii 10′–28′; obv. ii 1′–10′ = A obv. ii 38′–50′; obv. ii 18′–29′ = A obv. iii 1–17.
D. KUB 32.64 = C obv. iii 24′–rev. iv 6.
E. KUB 25.43: 7′–13′ = C rev. v 1–14.
F. KBo 23.20 obv.? 1′–13′ = C obv. ii 11′–29′; obv.? 1′–4′ = B obv. ii 22′–28′; obv.? 5′–13′ = A obv. iii 1–17.
G. KBo 27.156: 1′–11′ = A obv. iii 36–46.
H. KBo 27.196 rev. iii = A obv. iii 16–35; rev. iii 1′–2′ = C obv. ii 28′–29′ and F obv.? 12′–13′; rev. iv = A obv. ii 2′–14′.
I. KBo 27.194 left col. = A obv. ii 10′–26′; left col. 1′–6′ = H rev. iv 8–13; left col. 3′–6′ = B (KUB 32.61) 1′–6′; right col. = A obv. iii 30–38; right col. 1′–6′ = H rev. iii 15′–20′; right col. 6′–10′ = G 1′–3′.
The sides of A or H are to be inverted, but it is not clear which one. Fragments G and H may belong to the same tablet.
d) Offrandes aux rivières
2. A. KBo 15.68.
B. KBo 15.59 rev.? iv 1′–8′ = A rev. iv 8–15.
C. KUB 51.4 obv.? = A obv. iii 6′–rev. iv 8; rev.? = B obv.? iii 6′–17′.

Autres fragments
A. KUB 45.53.
B. KUB 51.16: 5′–17′ = A obv. iii 1′–rev. iv 9.

CTH 654.1: Fragments nommant les gens de Kurustama
A. KBo 10.9.
B. FHL 32: 2′–14′ = A rev.? 1′–12′.

CTH 663.4: Offrandes: noms des divinités en tête de ligne
A. HT 19 + FHL 177.
B. IBoT 2.65: 6′–11′ = A 1′–9′.
C. IBoT 3.23 obv. iii? 3′–13′ = A 1′–9′, then diverges.

CTH 670: Fragments divers de fêtes
1. A. KUB 41.30.
B. KUB 51.37 obv. 8′–18′ = A obv. iii 1′–12′.

2. KUB 20.19 + KUB 51.87.
KUB 51.87 right col. 6′–16′ joins KUB 20.19 rev. iv 1′–11′.

CTH 692: Fragments de la fête *witass(iy)as*
A. KUB 51.60.
B. KBo 24.28 obv. i 22′–29′ = A obv. 1′–8′.
A rev. 1–3 may be restored following the parallel KUB 17.24 rev. iii 20′–24′.

CTH 701: Libation au trône de Hebat
4. A. KBo 27.161 + KBo 27.139.
B. KBo 27.121: 1′–10′ = A rev.? iv 3′–12′, then appears to diverge.
C. KBo 27.137 = A rev.? iv 7′–12′.
KBo 27.139 obv.? joins KBo 27.161 rev.? iv 1′–13′ and KBo 27.139 rev.? joins KBo 27.161 obv.? i 7′–16′. The sides of either KBo 27.139 or KBo 27.161 should be inverted, but it is not clear which one. The references to A rev.? iv assume that the sides of KBo 27.161 are correct. A rev.? iv 2′–7′ may be restored following the parallels KBo 23.15 obv. i 31′–36′ + KBo 23.5 obv. i 4′–10′ and KUB 32.49b obv. ii 11′–15′.

5. A. KBo 23.45.
B. KBo 27.166: 1′–11′ = A rev. iv 6–17.

CTH 704.1: Listes de divinités hourrites dans des rituels et fêtes
A. KUB 34.102(+?)KUB 32.97.[3]
B. KUB 32.84 rev.? iv 7′–23′ = A iv.
C. KUB 10.51 right col. 10′–16′ = A iii 1′–6′.
D. KBo 27.195 right col. = B rev.? iv 10′–19′ and A (KUB 34.102 rev. 4′–13′(+?)KUB 32.97 obv.? 1′–2′).

3. If the join is correct, the sides of KUB 32.97 are to be inverted.

CTH 705: Fragments de listes divines analogues

1. A. KBo 24.59.
   B. FHL 132 = A rev.? iv 4′–8′.
2. KBo 27.200 joins KBo 27.167: 5′–11′.

CTH 744.1: Fragments de fêtes contenant des chants et récitations en hatti

A. KUB 1.14.
B. KUB 28.96: 4′–21′ = A obv. ii 1′–17′.
C. KUB 28.95 obv.? ii = A obv. ii 13′–22′ and B 16′–21′.
D. KBo 27.55 right col. = A obv. ii 5′–14′ and B 8′–17′.

CTH 771: Tablette de Lallupiya (louvismes)

KUB 25.37 + KUB 35.131 + 132 + KUB 51.9.

KUB 51.9 joins KUB 25.37 + KUB 35.131 obv. i 35′–44′ and rev. iv 5–17.

CTH 790: Fragments de rituels et conjurations hourro-hittites

1. A. KBo 24.63 + KBo 23.43.
   B. KUB 45.26 + KBo 27.159 obv. ii 1–9 = A obv. ii 4′–14′.[4]
   C. KUB 44.54 + IBoT 2.46 + KUB 41.5: obv. ii 7–16 = A obv. ii 4′–14′;[4] obv. ii 7–19 = B obv. ii 1–11.
   D. KUB 48.70 rev. 8′–12′ = A rev. iii 8′–14′.
   E. KBo 27.128 = A obv. ii 5′–15′,[4] B obv. ii 3–10, and C (IBoT 2.46) 3′–11′.

Cf. Otten and Rüster, ZA 68, 276f. and ZA 71, 132f.

2. A. KBo 19.144 + KBo 27.154.
   B. KUB 47.51 rev. iv 4′–25′ = A rev. iv 1′–22′.

KBo 27.154 obv. 1′–3′ and rev. 3′–6′ join KBo 19.144 obv. i 24′–26′ and rev. iv 1′–4′. CTH 790.1 and CTH 790.2 belong to the same composition, as may be seen by a comparison of the colophons. See Laroche, RHA XXX 126.

3. A. KBo 25.190.
   B. KBo 27.160: 5′–21′ = A obv. 7′–24′.

CTH 823: Ordalie par le feu (?)

A. ABoT 47.
B. FHL 53: parallel or duplicate to A obv. 11–15.

[This article was submitted before the appearance of Otten's review of KUB 51 in ZA 72 (1982) 160–61.]

4. The Hurrian in A ii 7′–10′ diverges.

BILDLICHE DARSTELLUNGEN ḪATTUŠILI'S III. IN ÄGYPTEN

KURT BITTEL

Heidenheim, West Germany

Die nahen Beziehungen zwischen Ḫatti und Ägypten, wie sie sich unter Ḫattušili III. und Ramses II. schliesslich herausbildeten und im Vertrag zwischen den beiden Ländern, endlich auch durch die Heirat einer hethitischen Prinzessin mit dem ägyptischen König ihren Ausdruck fanden, sind hinreichend bekannt. Zudem hat Elmar Edel in der letzten Zeit zu diesem Thema wichtige neuere Quellen erschlossen, welche die Vorgänge zum Teil genauer als bisher erkennen lassen.

Seit langem bekannt ist auch die sog. Hochzeitsstele auf der südlichen Seite des Vorplatzes vor dem Felstempel Ramses' II. in Abu Simbel in Nubien. Im Gegensatz zu den anderen Inschriften, in denen wenigstens noch zum Teil diese dynastische Hochzeit verewigt ist, nämlich in Karnak, Elephantine und ᶜAmārah-West[1], ist allein in Abu Simbel zuoberst eine bildliche Darstellung erhalten, auf der Ḫattušili und seine Tochter von rechts her (vom Beschauer aus gesehen) vor dem zwischen zwei Göttern sitzenden Pharao erscheinen. Die Tochter, die mehr nach ägyptischer Art gekleidet ist, berührt uns hier nicht. Ḫattušili dagegen trägt einen weiten, bis zu den Knöcheln reichenden Mantel oder Umhang, der stark nach hethitischer Manier zugeschnitten ist, auch in seiner Tragweise über den rechten Oberarm mit dem Saum vom Armgelenk senkrecht nach abwärts. Das entspricht weitgehend dem Mantel hethitischer Grosskönige, wie er von Muwatalli im Felsrelief bei Sirkeli in Kilikien und von Tutḫalija IV. zweimal in Yazılıkaya getragen wird[2]. Es ist also kaum daran zu zweifeln, dass man sich ägyptischerseits an

1. Karnak: Charles Kuentz, La 'stèle de mariage' de Ramses II, in: Annales du service des Antiquités d'Egypte XXV 1925, 183ff.; Elephantine: Kuentz a.O. 182f.; Gesamttext a.O. 185ff., Übersetzung 224ff. ᶜAmārah-West: H. W. Fairman, JEA 24, 1938, 155 (zur Lage ebenda 25, 1939, 140 mit Pl. XIII).

2. Sirkeli: Ignace J. Gelb, Hittite Hieroglyphic Monuments (OIP XLV 1939) Pl. LXIX Nr. 48. Ekrem Akurgal, Die Kunst der Hethiter (München 1961) Abb. 98 und Taf. XX. Kurt Bittel, Die Hethiter, die Kunst Anatoliens vom Ende des 3. bis zum Anfang des 1. Jahrtausends vor Christus (München 1976) 174/75 Abb. 195 und 197. Yazılıkaya: Boğazköy-Ḫattuša IX (Berlin 1975) Titelbild, Taf. VII, Taf. 48, 3, Taf. 49.

das beim hethitischen Hof Übliche gehalten hat. Freilich ist in Anatolien selbst kein entsprechendes Bild Ḫattušili's bekannt. Aber der ältere Muwatalli und der jüngere Tutḫalija legen es hinreichend nahe, dass auch unter dem Bruder bez. Vater Ḫattušili die gleiche Hoftracht benützt worden sein wird.

Man hat auch schon lange hervorgehoben, dass der hethitische König in Abu Simbel eine hohe Mütze trägt, die sich von der oberägyptischen Krone durch ihre mehr kegelförmige Gestalt deutlich abhebt und einem Typus hethitischer Kopfbedeckungen angehört. Im Bereiche der hethitischen Kunst lässt sich allerdings kein absolut gleiches Beispiel nachweisen, denn dort sind die Spitzmützen gewöhnlich steiler[3], ihre Vorderkante nicht leicht gewellt wie in Abu Simbel. Aber das ist eine kleine Abweichung[4], die nicht ins Gewicht fällt und an der generellen Übereinstimmung nichts ändert.

Bei Richard Lepsius ist der untere Mützenrand von der Stirn über dem Auge nur bis zum Ohr hin gezeichnet, so dass eine Trennlinie zwischen Mütze und Nackenhaar fehlt[5]. In Wirklichkeit ist sie aber am Original vorhanden, so dass auch dieser Teil der Kopfbedeckung wie auch das Nackenhaar selbst dem hethitischen Vorbild vollkommen entspricht. Das hat Walter Wreszinski und seitdem alle, die sich darüber geäussert haben, richtig gesehen. Doch glaube ich, dass sich Wreszinski irrt, wenn er meint, dass Ḫattušili ein Halsband trage[6]. Was er dafür hielt, ist viel eher der obere Saum des Mantels. So schien es mir wenigstens bei einem Besuch in Abu Simbel im März 1983. Bei dieser Gelegenheit glaubte ich auch, Längsstege im Inneren der Mütze des Königs zu erkennen, wie sie bei hethitischen Darstellungen dieser Art von Kopfbedeckung häufig, ja fast die Regel sind. Aber das erforderte eine genaue Untersuchung, denn es könnte sich auch um natürliche Linien oder leichte Auswitterungen im Stein handeln.

Das Bildnis Ḫattušili's in Abu Simbel ist nicht die einzige Darstellung des hethitischen Königs in Ägypten, was bisher, wie mir scheint, nicht gebührend hervorgehoben worden ist, und was jedenfalls Hans Gustav Güterbock, der selbst sozusagen am hethitischen Hofe zu Hause ist, gerne zur Kenntnis nehmen wird.

3. Steindenkmäler als Vergleichsbeispiele: Yazılıkaya: a.O. Taf. 56–58, 62–63. Akurgal a.O. Abb. 101 oben. Fraktin: Bittel a.O. 176 Abb. 198. Akurgal a.O. Abb. 99 oben. Gâvurkale: Bittel a.O. 178/79 Abb. 199 und 200. Akurgal a.O. Abb. 102. Karabel: Bittel a.O. 184 Abb. 206.

4. Die Kopfbedeckung des sog. Schwertgottes in Yazılıkaya zeigt, dass auch im hethitischen Bereich leichte Abweichungen von der Normalform vorkommen: Boğazköy-Ḫattuša IX Taf. 50, 1 und 51 (abgesehen von der Mütze mancher Berggötter).

5. Richard Lepsius, Denkmäler aus Ägypten und Äthiopien III 196 a.

6. Walter Wreszinski, Atlas zur altägyptischen Kulturgeschichte Taf. 46, Text zu Beibild 7.

Im grossen Tempelbezirk von Tanis (Sân el-Hagar) im nordöstlichen Delta befindet sich hinter dem linken Bein einer einst kolossalen, aber heute nur noch in ihren unteren Teilen erhaltenen, sehr verwitterten Sandsteinstatue Ramses' II. die hethitische Prinzessin Mat-neferu-re in Relief, das aber mit wenigen Ausnahmen sehr verdorben ist (Fig. 1 und 2). Jedoch ist die zugehörige Beischrift mit der Titulatur gut erhalten (Fig. 3). Darin heisst es "Tochter des grossen Fürsten von Cheta" (dh. Ḫatti). Das Ideogramm für diesen Fürsten ist nicht in der stereotypen Art wiedergegeben[7], sondern unter deutlicher Angleichung an die hethitische Tracht. Das nur 14,2 cm hohe Männchen (Fig. 4), mit dem Ḫattušili gemeint ist, steht mit dem Oberkörper leicht nach vorne gebeugt, hält die weit abstehenden Arme gesenkt, ist mit einem Gewand bekleidet, das bis zu den Waden reicht und an den Hüften etwas eingeschnürt zu sein scheint, und trägt eine hohe, spitze Mütze, die der bei den Hethitern gangbaren noch mehr entspricht als die Ḫattušili's in Abu Simbel[8]. Man wird bei einer vergleichsweise so kleinen Wiedergabe einer Darstellung als Schriftzeichen nicht zu sehr auf Einzelheiten sehen dürfen. Sicher ist aber, dass auch hier die Angleichung an Hethitisches, wie es namentlich in der Spitzmütze zum Ausdruck kommt, unverkennbar ist.

Nach Emmanuel de Rougé entspricht das Zeichen für den Grossfürsten von Cheta, [Ḫattušili], im Texte des bekannten Vertrages, der in Karnak an einer auf der südlichen Aussenseite des grossen Säulensaals anschliessenden Mauer steht und in dem dieses Zeichen mehr als dreissigmal vorkommt, dem

7. Etwa wie Alan H. Gardiner, Egyptian Grammar (Oxford 1927) 436 (Sign-List) oder 438 A 30.

8. Die vorliegenden Zeichnungen weichen darin sehr voneinander ab: A. Mariette, Fragments et Documents relatifs aux fouilles de Sân (Recueil de Travaux IX 1887, 13) gibt Ḫattušili mit rundem Kopf und ganz ohne Mütze; Emmanuel de Rougé, Inscriptions hiéroglyphiques I (Paris 1877) Pl. LXXIV unten zeigt ihn mit stark eingeschnürter Hüfte, aber richtig mit spitzer Mütze; Ders., Oeuvres divers 5, 134f. (leçon du 16 juin 1869, herausg. 1914 von G. Maspero) sagt: "La coiffure du personnage qui représente le roi de Khéta est ici la même que dans le texte du traité et sur la stèle d'Istamboul". W. M. Flinders Petrie, Tanis I (London 1885) Pl. V Nr. 36 B stellt die Mütze als oben nahezu flach dar. P. Montet gibt in Kêmi V 1935–37 zum Text 9/10 eine Photographie auf Pl. VII, die aber nicht brauchbar ist, weil das Entscheidende im Schatten liegt; Ders., Le drâme d'Avaris (Paris 1940) 128 Fig. 41; Ders., Tanis, Douze Années de fouilles dans une capitale oublié du Delta Égyptien (Paris 1942) 77 Fig. 15; Ders., Les énigmes de Tanis (Paris 1952) 71 Fig. 11 veröffentlichte einfache Zeichnungen, die aber in der Wiedergabe Ḫattušili's nicht genau sind. Dasselbe trifft für K. A. Kitchen, Ramesside Inscriptions, Historical and Biographical II (Oxford 1979) 440, 9 B zu.

Als meine Frau und ich zusammen mit Herrn Werner Kaiser und Frau Kaiser am 13. März 1983 in Tanis waren, hat uns Professor Jean Yoyotte, Direktor der französischen Expedition, freundlichst gestattet, das Monument zu photographieren, wofür er auch hier den Ausdruck wärmsten Dankes finden möge.

eben erörterten Bildzeichen in Tanis. Ich habe aber am Original in Karnak keine Spitzmütze als Kopfbedeckung beim Zeichen des hethitischen Königs gesehen. In der Kopie des Vertrages von W. Max Müller[9], die immer noch für "the most satisfactory" gilt[10], erscheint sie auch nicht, sondern eine Kappe oder ein Kopftuch, das in manchen Fällen mit einer Kordel zusammengehalten zu sein scheint, die am Hinterkopf zu einer Schleife gebunden ist.[10a]

Die in Ägypten bezeugten Darstellungen von Hethitern hat Wolfgang Helck sorgfältig zusammengestellt[11] und dabei betont, dass von Tuthmosis III. an bis hin zu Ramses II. eine deutliche Entwicklung schliesslich bis zur Wiedergabe des tatsächlichen Aussehens der Hethiter konstatiert werden könne. Das auch von ihm herausgestellte Bild Ḫattušili's III. in Abu Simbel und die hier zusätzlich gegebene Darstellung des gleichen Grosskönigs in Tanis zeigen deutlich genug, welcher Grad der Anpassung spätestens unter Ramses II. erreicht worden ist. Es kann kaum bezweifelt werden, dass den Ägyptern die Hethiter mit ihrer eigentümlichen Tracht damals sehr vertraut gewesen sind[12]. In Anbetracht der nahen Beziehungen, wie sie in jenen Jahrzehnten bestanden und schon allein äusserlich greifbar sind durch nicht wenige Gesandtschaften, die hin und her gingen, durch die dynastische Heirat zwischen den beiden Höfen und das gewiss nicht geringe Begleitpersonal höheren und niederen Grades, das bei dieser Gelegenheit—anscheinend sogar zweimal—in die ägyptische Residenz Piramessu kam und sicher zu einem nicht geringen Teil auch dort blieb, ist das ganz verständlich. Wenn es zutrifft, dass das "Hethiterfeld" bei Memphis zur Zeit des Eje eine

9. W. Max Müller, Der Bündnisvertrag Ramses' II. und des Chetiter-Königs (MVAG VII/5 [1902] 5. Heft).

10. James B. Pritchard, ANET 199 (Text von John A. Wilson).

10a. Vgl. Fig. Nr. 5.

11. Wolfgang Helck, Die Beziehungen Ägyptens zu Vorderasien im 3. und 2. Jahrtausend v. Chr. (Wiesbaden 1962) 342ff.

12. So fremd ist den Ägyptern vielleicht—bei allen Unterschieden in der wahren Bedeutung—die hohe hethitische Spitzmütze gar nicht erschienen, denn die oberägyptische Krone ist ihr nicht ganz unähnlich, und der syrische Reschef war ihnen während der 19. Dynastie ziemlich vertraut (z.B. Günther Roeder, Ägyptische Bronzewerke, Hildesheim 1937, Taf. 2 h–k), ganz abgesehen vom Seth (Sutech) auf der sog. 400 Jahr-Stele in Tanis, die diesen Gott mit konischer Mütze zeigt, an der vorn zwei Stierhörner angebracht sind und rückwärts ein langes Band herabhängt (Helck a.O. 484).

geschlossene Siedlung von Kriegsgefangenen gewesen ist[13], ging sogar vermutlich das Kennenlernen von Brauch und Sitte selbst auf niederer Ebene über die Ramessidenzeit zurück.

Soweit nimmt sich das alles ganz plausibel aus. Weiterreichende Überlegungen stellen sich aber ein, wenn man sich der hethitischen Seite zuwendet. Dort tragen die Könige oder Grosskönige gewöhnlich eine enganliegende, oben halbrunde Mütze, wie sie die Reliefs von Alaca Höyük, Sirkeli und Yazılıkaya zeigen. Darstellungen von Königen mit spitzer Mütze sind selten: Felsrelief Ḫattušili's III. bei Fraktin, Siegel Tutḫalija's IV. von Ugarit, Felsrelief am Karabel hinter Smyrna (İzmir), wenn der bewaffnete Mann dort ein König und kein Gott ist[14]. Sie alle haben Spitzmützen mit einem Horn oder mehreren Hörnern an der Vorderseite, die gewöhnlich für göttliche Attribute gelten, obwohl in Fraktin und Ugarit die Träger nach hethitischer Vorstellung gewiss nicht göttlicher Natur waren. Umgekehrt gibt es hethitische Bronzen von Göttern, die spitze Mützen, aber ohne Horn oder Hörner tragen. Die eine stammt vom Doğantepe bei Amasya, die andere aus der Gegend von Konya[15]. Man kennt aber auch Darstellungen, die den—oder einen—Sonnengott repräsentieren: in Yazılıkaya mit halbrunder Mütze und einem Mantel wie ihn oft auch die Grosskönige tragen[16], und auf einer

13. Recueil de travaux relatifs à la philologie et à l'archéologie égyptiennes et assyriennes 16,123 (Daressy) und 29,170 (Legrain). Hermann Kees, Kulturgeschichte des Alten Orients, Ägypten (HdA.III 1,3; München 1933) 239 Anm. 1; Ders., Das Alte Ägypten, eine kleine Landeskunde (Berlin 1955) 100. Wolfgang Helck, Urkunden der 18. Dynastie, Heft 22, Berlin 1958, 2109,16; Ders. Übersetzung, Berlin-Ost 1961 S. 402 Anm. 4 meint: "Kriegsgefangenensiedlung aus den Kämpfen gegen Šuppiluliuma beim Tod des Tutenchamun"; Ders., Lexikon der Ägyptologie II 1177/78, IV 135 (Militärkolonie ?).

14. Belege hierzu Anm. 2 und 3. Alaca Höyük: Bittel a.O. 191 Abb. 214. Siegel aus Ugarit: Ugaritica III (Paris 1956) 19 Fig. 24 und Pl. III. Bei Gâvurkale ist es nicht sicher, ob die von rechts her sich nähernden Adoranten Fürsten oder Gottheiten sind.

15. Doğantepe: Sedat Alp, Eine hethitische Bronzestatuette und andere Funde aus Zara bei Amasya, in: Anatolia VI 1961/62, 217ff. mit Taf. XXIII–XXVIII (ebenda 288: "Die Spitzmütze der Statuette von Zara hat keine Hörner"). Konya: Bittel a.O. (s. Anm. 2) 147 Abb. 147. Eine Bronzestatuette von Dövlek südwestlich von Sivas hat dagegen je ein Horn zu Seiten des Kopfes (J. Vorys Canby in: Hesperia XXXVIII 2, 1969 Pl. 41 a). Die kegelförmige Mütze hat in Anatolien eine alte Tradition, denn sie begegnet schon—mit Varianten—bei Bleifiguren vorhethitischer und bei Nagelbronzen älterhethitischer Zeit (Bleifiguren: Kutlu Emre, Anatolian lead figurines and their stone moulds, Ankara 1971, Tabelle bei S. 64; Nagelbronzen: Bittel a.O. 101 Abb. 92 und 93).

16. Boğazköy-Ḫattuša IX Taf. 22, 1 (Relief 34: "Sonnengott des Himmels", ebenda 174, wo Güterbock die Vermutung geäussert hat, die besondere Bedeutung des Sonnengottes für den hethitischen König sei "schon durch seine Kleidung ausgedrückt").

Zeremonialaxt aus Şarkışla, südwestlich von Sivas, mit einem gleichen Mantel, aber einer hohen Mütze, die vorn fünf Hörner übereinander hat[17]. Es fällt demnach schwer, aus den bisher bekannten Beispielen der hethitischen Königstracht, die freilich nicht gerade zahlreich sind, eine durchaus befriedigende Ordnung abzuleiten, was die Tragweise bei bestimmten Anlässen betrifft. Im Gange von Handlungen, in denen man sicher solche ritueller Art sehen darf, erscheint sowohl die niedere (Sirkeli und Yazılıkaya) als auch die hohe, spitze (Fraktin) Mütze.

Vielleicht ist es aber kein Zufall, dass Ḫattušili III. in beiden Fällen, die uns sein Bild noch erhalten zeigen (Abu Simbel und Tanis), mit der hohen Mütze erscheint, sich in Ägypten die Vorstellung dieser Kopfbedeckung zur Zeit Ramses' II. gerade mit ihm besonders verbunden hat. Wenn nämlich das allein durch die ägyptische Beschreibung überlieferte Siegel auf der Vorderseite des obenerwähnten Vertrages, das "ein Bild des Seth das Bild des grossen Fürsten von Chatti umarmend"[18], also Ḫattušili, zeigte, dem obengenannten, in Ugarit gefundenen Siegel Tutḫalija's IV. einigermassen entsprach[19], wäre Ḫattušili III. auf dem in Ägypten sehr wohl bekannten Vertragssiegel mit der hohen Mütze dargestellt gewesen. Leider lässt sich das an Originalen nicht nachprüfen, weil meines Wissens bis heute kein sog. Umarmungssiegel, in der Terminologie von H. G. Güterbock[20], von Ḫattušili gefunden worden ist[21]. Die Beschreibung im Vertrag zeigt jedoch, dass es auch diese Siegelgattung beim hethitischen Partner Ramses' II. gegeben hat.

17. Kurt Bittel, Beitrag zur Kenntnis hethitischer Bildkunst: Sitzungsberichte der Heidelberger Akademie der Wissenschaften, Philosophisch-historische Klasse, 1976, 4. Abhdlg., 23 mit Taf. VII–X. Bittel a.O. (s. Anm. 2) 299 Abb. 341.

18. John A. Wilson bei Pritchard a.O. (s. Anm. 10), 201.

19. S. Anm. 14.

20. Hans Gustav Güterbock, SBo I (1940) 19, 65 Nrn. 38A–41.

21. Thomas Beran, Die hethitische Glyptik von Boğazköy I: Boğazköy-Ḫattuša V, WVDOG LXXVI (Berlin 1967) 45f. und 79f. (dazu Taf. XII Nrn. 250a–253).

Fig. 1.

Fig. 2.

Fig. 3.

Fig. 4.

Fig. 5.-Karnak, aus dem Vertragstext

DIE 3. PERS. SING. DES POSSESSIVPRONOMENS IM LUWISCHEN

ONOFRIO CARRUBA

Pavia

Die Erforschung der Grammatik des Luwischen bietet immer wieder neue Probleme und interessante Ergebnisse. Das Gerüst der grammatikalischen Struktur ist in seinen allgemeinen Zügen schon einigermassen bekannt, viele kleine oder wichtige Einzelheiten werden neu ermittelt, herausgearbeitet und festgelegt.

Wir wollen hier einen kurzen Beitrag zur besseren Kenntnis der Personalpronomina Prof. Güterbock als Altmeister der Anatolistik vorlegen, in der Hoffnung, der verehrte Jubilar möge ihn als kleine Gabe gern entgegennehmen.

Das Hethitische gebrauchte als Possessiva* enklitische und flektierte Formen der Personalpronomina, die während der altheth. Zeit gut bezeugt sind (Friedrich HE §107; mit Otten-Souček, StBoT 8, 70ff.; Otten, StBoT 17, 35; Neu, StBoT 18, 65ff.). In den mittelheth. Texten erscheinen dann statt enklitischer Formen Syntagmata, die durch den Genitiv des betonten Personalpronomens und das regierende Substantiv gebildet werden (Friedrich, HE §106). Es stehen sich also folgende Typen gegenüber:

attas-mis und *ammēl attas* "mein Vater"
utne-met und *ammēl utnē* "mein Land"
pēdi-ssi und *apēl pēdi* "an seinem Platz"
kardi-smi oder *kartaz-mit* "in bzw. aus euerem Herzen" und
sumenzan É.ḪI.A DINGIR.MEŠ-*KU-NU* "euere Tempel"

Aus diesen Genitiva sind in den kleineren bzw. später belegten Sprachen regelrechte adjektivische Possessiva entstanden, welche normalerweise die gleiche Voranstellung des pronominalen Genitivs aufweisen (s. zuletzt Meriggi, Schizzo §§II 140ff. S. 319ff.).

Während für das Palaische die Frage nach den Possessiva wegen Mangel an ausreichenden Belegen nicht beantwortet werden kann, steht für das

*[Ed.: Cf. now also Neu, StBoT 26, 121, 165f., 170ff., 174, 197, and CHD 3, 215ff.]

Luwische das Problem noch ungelöst, weil einerseits Meriggi ein betontes Possessivum *tu-ú-is* (KUB 35.133 ii 27) nachzuweisen glaubte (WZKM 42 [1957], 220), das der gleichlautenden Form des Hier.-Luw., *tu-wa/i-*, entspricht (HhGl. s.v.; und Schizzo §141), andererseits Laroche (RHA XXIII/76 [1965], 44) alle Substantiva, die eine Form auf *-sa* (mit Variante *-za*, vgl. DLL §9, S. 133) zeigten, als Formen mit dem Possessivum der 3. Pers. Sing. n.gen. umdeutete.

Bis dahin aber war dieses *-sa/-za* als eine besondere Kasusendung angesehen worden (Laroche, DLL §28 S. 138), eventuell Plur. oder Kollektivum (Meriggi, WZKM 42, 204). *-sa* kann unmöglich nur in gewissen Substantiva einer ganzen Reihe das Possessivum bezeichnen, in allen übrigen nicht.

Andererseits sind solche Formen auch im Hier.-Luw. nachgewiesen worden, und zwar auch an Stellen, wo das adj., betonte Possessivum vorhanden ist, z.B. Kargamis A 11c 6 *á-ma-^{n}za a-tì-ma-^{n}za* (Hawkins et al. HHL, 174). Die Endung tritt schliesslich auch an die betonten Possessiva selbst, s. hier oben und z.B. Kargamis 18e 6 *á-ma-^{n}za* $_{)}$SAG-*ZÍ*$_{(}$*ta-ru-s*. Die Endung, die nur beim Nom.-Akk. n.gen. auftritt, scheint eine bestimmte, "personalisierende" Funktion zu haben, wonach die betreffenden Formen vom Unbelebten ins Belebte übergehen (Carruba, FsKronasser, 1ff.).

Ist also *-sa* (mit Lautvariante *-za*) eine Endung und kein Possessivpronomen, so müssen wir nach anderen Belegen suchen.

Interessante Beweise gibt uns KBo 13.260 ii 1–4 mit seinen ganz einfach gebauten Sätzen:

1 ha-at-ta-ra-am-ša-an a-[j]a-[ta]
mu-ha-at-ra-am-ša-an a-ja-t[a]
3 pí-iz-za-ar-na-am-ša-an a-ja-[ta]
tu-u-ri-im-ša-an a-ja-ta

Wegen des Vergleichs mit ii 16ff., wo sie wieder vorkommen, dürften die Substantiva im Akk. stehen, was auch die Satzstruktur bestätigt. Sie zeigen nun nach einem merkwürdigen—allerdings auch im Heth. belegten (*gimzu* statt *ginzu*)—anusvāra noch *-ša-an* gerade an der Stelle der im Luw. selten fehlenden Partikel(reihe).

Haben wir also mit einer neuen Partikel oder mit einem enklitischen Possessivum zu tun?

Eine andere Stelle desselben Rituals erweist sich für die Entscheidung als wichtig. Es handelt sich nämlich um den Satz iii 12–13, der für eine bessere Deutung in einem grösseren Zusammenhang gesehen werden muss:

5′ ku-i-in-zi zi-i-in-z[a]
ú-ša-an-da a-la-aš-ši-in-zi
7′ na-ah-hu-wa-aš-ši-en⟨-zi⟩ i-na-aš-ši-en-zi
pa-ri-ja-an šar-ha-mi-in-⌜zi⌝

9′ an-na-ru-um-me-en-zi ha-at-ta-in-zi
ha-at-ta a-da-an-du
11′ ši-e-hu-wa-en-zi še-e-wa
a-da-an-du pa-ri-ja-am-ša-at-ta
13′ tar-za-an-du a-at-ta a-ad-du-wa-an-za
pa-ri-ja-an ad-du-wa-li-ja-an
15′ wa-at-ta-ni-ja-an up-pa-an-na-an-du
(Ein Versuch für eine Gesamtdeutung folgt w.u.)

Wenn wir die zwei Sätze in iii 12–15 vergleichen, merken wir einen auffallenden Parallelismus in der Satzstruktur:

parijam-sa-tta   tarzandu
a-tta adduwanza parijan adduwalijan wattanijan uppannandu.

Wie *parijan* in 13–14 einen Akk. (vgl. heth. *parijan;* evtl. einen Dat.) Plur. regiert, so dürfte die Form Z. 12 ebenfalls einen Akk. (weniger wahrscheinlich einen Dat.), hier wohl Sing. regieren, nämlich *-sa-*, das sich als ein Pronomen entlarvt.

Dass die Form überdies Possessivfunktion hatte, zeigt die genaue Entsprechung des Syntagma *parijam-sa-* mit der bekannten altheth. Verbindung Adverb + Possessivum, *sēr-set* "für ihn" (wörtlich: "sein Oben/Dafür"); *pēra-sset* (aus **peran-set*) "vor ihm" (wörtlich: "sein Vorne"); *anda-se-* "in ihn/sie" usw.

Wir haben oben mit der Partikel *-tta* im letzten Teil des Syntagma gerechnet, weil sie auch im nächsten Satz erscheint und die Satzstruktur uns dazu zwingt. Die Annahme eines auch lautlich vollkommenen Parallelismus zum heth. Syntagma mit funktioneller Erhaltung des *-t* hätte in Analogie zur Entwicklung des enkl. Personalpronomens zu *-ata*—gegenüber heth. *-at*—ein luw. Possessivpronomen *-sata* (heth. *-set*) nicht *satta* ergeben.

Die Form *-sa* ist u.E. Nom.-Akk. n.gen., weil *parijan* den Akk. regiert; weil das Possessivum in diesen Verbindungen mit den Adverbien kongruierte, die ursprüngliche Neutra waren. Dazu ist zu sagen, dass *parijan* wohl das Neutrum des *-ija-*Weiterbildung eines **par-* oder von *pari* "pro-" (Carruba, FsNeumann, 43). Die Analogie zum Nom.-Akk. n.gen. des Demonstrativums *zā* bekräftigt die Annahme.

Was den Numerus betrifft kann *-sa* nur Singular sein, da eine Pluralform aus einem dem enkl. Personalpronomen (luw. *-mmas;* heth. *-smas* "euch; ihnen") ähnlichen Stamm gebildet worden wäre.

Der pronominale Bezug wird hier, wie oben ii 1–4, auf eine der beiden Hauptpersonen des Rituals, dem (Menschen)sohn (ii 30, 32, iii 17, 30) oder der Mutter (ii 30) hinweisen, da der "Herr des Rituals", EN SISKUR. SISKUR, unter ihnen zu suchen ist.

Ein Zusammenfall mit dem Nom.-Akk. n.gen. des Plur., der im Luw. ebenfalls *-sa* mit *-a*, wie bei allen Neutra, lauten dürfte, ist wahrscheinlich.

Unter Heranziehung der Form des in Z. ii 1–4 belegten Akk. c.gen. Sing. können wir vorläufig folgendes Schema für das luw. Possessivpronomen der 3. Pers. Sing. umreissen:

Sing.	Nom. c.	*-sis*(?)	Plur.	*-sa* (? vgl. *-ata*)
	Akk. c.	*-san*		
	N.-A.n.	*-sa*		*-sa* (? vgl. *-ata*)

Nun können wir uns zu dem Versuch einer Interpretation übergehen, wobei wir die Bearbeitung des gesamten Textes an anderer Stelle zu geben gedenken.

Die Sätze ii 1–4 lassen sich leicht unter einem Nenner bringen: "er machte/behandelte magisch/rituell s e i n e n Mörser/Spaten(?) s e i n e(n) *m.*, s e i n e(n) *p.*, s e i n e Lanze/Harke(?)" (s. Laroche, DLL 154f.; Meriggi, WZKM 42, 205 Anm. 33; Schizzo §II 210 S. 344).

Die zweite Stelle iii 5–15 dürfte ungefähr wie folgt lauten: "diejenigen, welche sie (c.gen. !) brachten, und zwar die *a.*, die Besorgten/Sorgvollen(?), die Fieberkranken(?), die *p.s.*, die Starken/Übermütigen, die *hattai*'schen sollen *hatta* essen, die *sehuwai*'schen sollen *se(hu)wa* essen, v o r i h m / a u f i h n z u sollen (immer wieder?) sprechen/knien(?), vor den Bösen/Gehässigen sollen schlechte(s) *w.* immer wieder bringen".

Das Vorhandensein des enkl. Possessivum im Luwischen zeigt, dass auch diese Sprache ein altes Sprachstadium mit ähnlichen Zügen wie das Althethitische durchgemacht hat, ein Sprachstadium, in dem die Urfassung des Textes KBo 13.260 geschrieben wurde.

Da die uns vorliegende Redaktion in sehr späten Zeit niedergelegt wurde (13. Jh.v.Chr.), ist die eventuelle Annahme der Nachahmung heth. grammatikalischer und syntaktischer Formen bzw. von Lehnbildungen aus dem Hethitischen ausgeschlossen, weil in dieser späten Zeit das Heth. weder das enkl. Possessivum noch vor allem die erwähnten Syntagmata *perasset, sĕrset* usw. verwendete (Carruba, OLZ, 1978, 249).

Darüber hinaus ist die Feststellung des enkl. Possessivpronomens im Luw. und seiner überraschenden Ähnlichkeit im Gebrauch bei den Adverbien in beiden Sprachen von grösser Bedeutung für die Geschichte der anatolischen Sprachen. Wir haben einen neuen, nicht nur grammatikalischen, sondern auch syntaktischen Beweis für die vorgeschichtliche Einheit der indogermanischen Sprachen Anatoliens.

LE NOM DE MATIWAZA SUR UN SCEAU HIÉROGLYPHIQUE

HATICE GONNET

Paris

En 1965, I. J. Gelb a publié onze sceaux hiéroglyphiques hittites et a proposé quelques lectures pour certains d'entre eux.[1]

Parmi ces sceaux, celui qui porte le n° 10 a attiré notre attention,[2] car le nom de personne qu'il porte pourrait avoir la même structure consonantique, *mtwz*, que le nom du roi du Mitanni. On sait que le premier signe cunéiforme notant ce nom peut avoir l'une des trois valeurs: kur/mat/šat, donc que le nom du roi du Mitanni peut être lu de trois manières différentes: Kur-tiwaza, Mat-tiwaza, Šat-tiwaza. Chacune de ces hypothèses a été soutenue.[3] Dans les textes de Boğazköy, le nom du roi du Mitanni n'apparaît que dans deux traités bilingues (akkadien-hittite), conclus entre le roi hittite et le roi du Mitanni,[4] qui ne permettent pas de trancher. Deux travaux récents, ceux de C. Zaccagnini[5] et de I. M. Diakonoff,[6] portant sur des textes de Nuzi, sont en faveur de la lecture Šattiwaza. Mais le sceau n° 10 de I. J. Gelb nous conduit vers une autre lecture.

Le sceau se trouve actuellement en Berlin. Nous ne disposons que des photographies (fig. 1a et 1b) et du dessin publiés par I. J. Gelb. Le dessin de Gelb étant reproduit d'après le moulage de l'original, nous republions ici son

1. I. J. Gelb, JKF 4 (1965) 223–226.

2. Le sceau n° 10 fait l'objet d'un court commentaire de M. Poetto (*La collezione Anatolica di E. Borowski* [= StMed 3], Pavie, 1981, 17 n. 24) qui signale de plus une republication du sceau par L. Jacob-Rost (*Die Stempelsiegel im Vorderasiatischen Museum,* Berlin, 1975, p. 23, pl. 5 n° 70 [b], avec p. 23, ouvrage que nous n'avons pu consulter) [Ed.—= VA 10942.].

3. Pour Mattiwaza, cf. E. Weidner, PD 2–37; J. Friedrich, AfO 2 (1924) 119–124; E. Laroche, NH n° 792 et Ugar. 6 (1969) 369, 371; pour Kurtiwaza, cf. H. G. Güterbock, JCS 10 (1956) 121 n. 18; A. Kammenhuber, *Die Arier im Vorderen Orient* (1968) 83; pour Šattiwaza, cf. B. Landsberger, JCS 8 (1954) 130; W. von Soden, ZA 60 (1970) 227; C. Zaccagnini, OA 13 (1974) 25–34; I. M. Diakonoff, AOF 3 (1975) 167–68.

4. E. Laroche, CTH n° 51–52.

5. Cf. C. Zaccagnini, OA 13: 25–34.

6. Cf. I. M. Diakonoff, AOF 3: 167–68.

dessin en l'inversant, c'est-à-dire en le présentant dans le sens qui aurait été celui de l'empreinte, les hiéroglyphes regardant vers la droite.

Le sceau est un sceau-bouton à deux faces. La face *a* porte une inscription; la face *b* représente un personnage debout,[7] de part et d'autre duquel sont disposés verticalement, soit les signes d'une inscription, soit des motifs de remplissage (la photo d'I. J. Gelb, 1b ne rend pas bien les détails et lui-même ne donne aucune explication à ce sujet). Nous nous intéresserons ici seulement à la face *a*.

I. J. Gelb commence la lecture de la face *a* avec la tête de bélier *L.110*[8] dont la valeur *ma* est certaine. Conformément à la règle, il lit le nom verticalement et continue sa lecture avec les deux signes qui sont au dessous, légèrement à gauche sur la fig. 1a, dont le premier rappelle à la fois *L.461* et *L.462* et dont le second est *L.376,* qu'il interprète comme idéogramme "I. STRONG." Pour I. J. Gelb, ces trois signes forment un groupe indépendant des trois autres signes qui sont situés à gauche, qu'il lit selon son syllabaire:[9] *ze-wa-i*. I. J. Gelb ne dit rien sur les signes qui figurent à droite du champ. Si l'on accepte l'ordre dans lequel il lit les signes, on aboutit à un nom inconnu, et peu vraisemblable, *Ma-ku(wa)lana,*[10] et les signes qui sont dans la partie gauche du sceau, sur la lecture desquels nous reviendrons, ne donnent pas de sens ici.[11] En revanche, si l'on adopte un ordre de lecture différent, on peut lire un nom et dégager un titre possible.

Disons tout de suite que dans la partie droite du champ, le groupe de signes *L.386–370* indique l'appartenance du sceau à un personnage masculin.[12] Le dédoublement du triangle *L.370* est à notre avis une fantaisie graphique du lapicide et ne doit pas créer de difficulté d'interprétation.

Pour nous comme pour I. J. Gelb, la lecture du nom commence par *ma L.110,* mais au lieu de continuer verticalement nous prenons comme deuxième signe le signe qui se trouve à gauche de la tête du bélier, *L.172*. La

7. Dans l'iconographie des sceaux hittites la représentation d'un personnage debout de profil est bien connue, cf. H. G. Güterbock, SBo II 20, 104, 106–115; I. J. Gelb, dans H. Goldman, *Excavations at Gözlükule-Tarsus II,* Princeton, 1956, 50; H. G. Güterbock dans K. Bittel, *Boğazköy V* 1975, n° 24, 25, 35.

8. E. Laroche, HH *1* (1960).

9. I. J. Gelb, HH *3* (1942) 1, 22, 31.

10. Dans un récent article (*Kadmos,* 21 [1982] 101–103) M. Poetto, à propos d'une empreinte de sceau hiéroglyphique inédit et du contenu de la tablette cunéiforme sur laquelle il figure trois fois, expose le problème de la lecture de l'idéogramme ARMÉE = *L.269, kuwatna/kuwalana* et dégage l'équation ARMÉE = *ku(wa)lana*.

11. M. Poetto (cf. note 2) lit les signes dans le même ordre que I. J. Gelb, et propose la transcription: *Ma-278* (= *L.461*)-*zi/za(-)tì-wa-zi/za* avec ce commentaire prudent: "forse un composto, oppure il nome del proprietario seguito da un attributo?"

12. H. G. Güterbock, dans K. Bittel, *Boğazköy V,* n° 37.

valeur *tì* de *L.172* a été proposée par E. Laroche, et acceptée par H. G. Güterbock;[13] J. D. Hawkins a proposé $ta_{(4)}$.[14] Puis, nous prenons comme troisième signe celui qui se trouve en bas du précédent, *L.439,* dont la valeur est en général *wa*. Enfin, toujours plus bas nous lisons comme dernier signe du nom, la flèche *L.376,* qui a la valeur *zi* selon *HHL,*[15] et qui, d'après E. Laroche, correspond sûrement à la consonne *z* du cunéiforme avec un vocalisme incertain. Nous obtenons ainsi le nom *Ma-ti/a*[16]*-wa-zi/a* qu'il est tentant de rapprocher du nom cunéiforme *Kur/Šat/Mat-ti-wa-za*. Si l'on accepte ce rapprochement, la lecture du nom cunéiforme serait donc *Mattiwaza*.

Quant aux deux signes situés au centre en-dessous de la tête de bélier *ma,* il s'agit probablement du groupe composé de deux signes *L.461/462* et *L.376,* qui forme parfois l'idéogramme ARMÉE = *L.269*. Ils sont ici disposés d'une manière inhabituelle: l'un au-dessous de l'autre, au lieu d'être l'un à côté de l'autre.[17] Mais, cette disposition verticale n'est pas le seul exemple qu'on ait; on la rencontre d'une part sur un sceau impérial de Boğazköy, SBo II nº 164, sur lequel c'est la flèche *L.376* qui surmonte *L.461/462,* d'autre part on trouve la même disposition sur notre sceau sur le monument rupestre de Suvasa-Gülşehir[18] où les signes en question sont entourés d'un ovale, *L.407* (fig. 2), qui indiquerait peut-être la valeur idéographique du groupe. A notre avis, malgré l'absence de *L.407,* il s'agit ici de l'idéogramme ARMÉE, *L.269* qui suggère que la fonction de notre personnage était une fonction militaire.

En bas à droite de la flèche *L.376,* on voit un signe à quatre branches, qui pourrait n'être qu'un motif ornemental. Toutefois, nous nous demandons si on ne peut pas l'interpréter comme une variante graphique du signe numéral pour le nombre "100," *L.399/302*. Dans ce cas, il pourrait indiquer le grade militaire de centenier (*LÚ *ME-E*) d'un certain *Ma-ti-wa-za*. Notons que

13. H. G. Güterbock, *ibidem*.

14. J. D. Hawkins et Anna Morpurgo-Davies, JRAS 1975; J. D. Hawkins, AnSt 25 (1975) 155.

15. J. D. Hawkins, Anna Morpurgo-Davies, Günter Neumann, *Hittite Hieroglyphs and Luwian: new evidence for the connection* (NAWG 1973 no. 6), Göttingen, 1974.

16. La lecture avec la valeur ta_4 de *L.172* (proposée par J. D. Hawkins, cf. note 14) rapprocherait le nom de ceux des textes de Nuzi sur lesquels, presque toujours, après la première syllabe, le nom continue avec *-ta-: -tawaza;* cf. C. Zaccagnini, OA 13: 27.

17. *L.269* figure soit sur des sceaux impériaux (H. G. Güterbock, SBo II, 19, 21, 87; Th. Beran, dans K. Bittel, *Boğazköy III,* 1957, pl. 31 no. 35; MDOG 93 [1962] 66f. 55b; I. J. Gelb dans H. Goldman, *Excavations at Gözlükule-Tarsus II,* Princeton, 1956, 54); soit sur des monuments rupestres impériaux tels que Hanyeri, Akpınar, Karabel, Taşçı et Beyköy.

18. B. Hrozný, ArOr 7 (1935) 516–522; P. Meriggi, Manuale II 283–285. Sur le monument de Suvasa-Gülşehir, ainsi que sur la stèle de Karkamiš A 4b et celle de Körkün (M. Kalaç, *Athenaeum,* 47 [1969] 160–163) notre signe est entouré d'un ovale = *L.407*. *L.407* ne figure jamais sur les sceaux.

dans les deux exemples hiéroglyphiques que nous possédons (fig. 3 et 4),[19] les signes qui indiquent les grades: "(chef de) 10" et "(chef de) 100" se trouvent à la même place que sur notre sceau.

L'ordre anormal des signes tels que nous proposons de les lire pourrait s'expliquer par une date tardive: la fin de l'empire.

19. Sur la fonction "(chef de) 10," cf. Th. Beran, dans K. Bittel, *Boğazköy III,* 23; E. Laroche, RHA XVI/63 (1958) 117; cf. un titre militaire en rapport avec "(chef de) 100," dans Th. Beran, MDOG 93, 66f. Dans les textes cunéiformes, parmi les grades militaires hittites nous connaissons LÚ PA 10 "chef de dix" (E. Laroche, NH n° 1414; R. Werner, StBoT 4, 4, 5, 16) et LÚ PA *LI-IM* "chef de mille" (S. Alp, *Belleten,* 11, 1947, 387–402). Le grade qui devrait être entre les deux n'est pas attesté. Notons toutefois, dans un texte de protocole militaire la succession des grades: chef de dix, LÚ DUGUD, chef de mille (S. Alp, *Belleten* 11: 387sqq.).

Fig. 1*a*.

Fig. 1*b*.

Fig. 2.

Fig. 3.

Fig. 4.

HITTITE FRAGMENTS IN PRIVATE COLLECTIONS

OLIVER R. GURNEY

Oxford

The fragments of Hittite tablets here published have been shown to me and to my colleagues C. B. F. Walker and I. L. Finkel over a period of some twenty years by persons returning from visits to Turkey. Since they would otherwise be lost to science, copies of them have been assembled here as a small tribute to Professor Hans Güterbock. Mr. Walker had already communicated nos. 3, 6 and 9 to H. Otten and A. Kammenhuber some years ago, but it was thought appropriate to include copies of them with the rest. They are arranged roughly in the order of Laroche's Catalogue.

Historical Texts

1

1. *n*]*a-aš* x *ši-*[. . . .
2.]-*wa-ar da-a-i*

---

3. ḪUL-*an*]x *ša-an-ḫa-zi zi-ga-at iš-ta*!*-ma-aš*[*-ti*]
4. [*nu ku-it ku-i*]*t me-ma-i*

---

5. [*nu-mu . . . a-pí-ni-eš-šu-w*]*a-an ut-tar ša-ku-wa-aš-ša-ri*[*-it* ZI*-it*]
6. [*ḫa-at-ra-a-i . . . . . .*] *nu-uš-ša-an a-pí-ni-e*[*š-šu-wa-an-ta-an* UN-*an*]
7. [*ma-a-an ša-an-na-at-ti nu-mu ḫu-da-a*]*k Ú-UL a-a*[*r-ti*]
8. [*na-an-mu pa-ra-a Ú-UL pí-eš-ti*]

"[If anyone . . . . . .] plots [. . . . .] and you (sing.) hear of it, [whatever] he is saying, [write] any such matter loyally [to me], and [if you conceal] any such [man] and do not [immediate]ly come [and hand him over to me] . . ."

This is clearly part of a treaty with an individual vassal. Parallel passages may be found in many of the published treaties, e.g. Kup. §18 55ff., Alakš. §11, Ḫuqq. §§4, 14–16, Šaušgamuwa iii 8–18, Madd. obv. 37–41, KUB

40.44, but none of these is identical, and short, 2-line sections are unusual. The small fragment KUB 23.96 has a similar section and might belong with this. All the suggested restorations are conjectural. For line 2 one might perhaps compare the Glossenkeil word *ku-ug-gur-ni-ia-u-wa-ar* (*appa anda udai*) in Šaušgamuwa iii 13.

2

(copy by C. B. F. Walker)[1]

This small fragment has in the right column references to a country (KUR-*e*) and the king of a country (LUGAL KUR ^{U}[^{RU}), and in the left column, twice repeated, the end of what appears to be the name Telipinuš (]-*nu-ša, -p*]*í-nu-uš*), presumably in this context the son of Šuppiluliuma, not the god. The fragment could be part of KUB 19.25. Elsewhere this man is usually referred to simply as "the Priest."

3

2′ EG]IR-*pa ku*-[
3′]x $^{\text{LÚ.MEŠ}}$UKU.U[Š
4′ ^{L}]$^{\text{Ú?.MEŠ}}$*du-ḫi-ia-*[*li*?*-eš*?
5′]x-*ša-a* GUD.ḪI.A-*ŠU u-*[*un*?-
6′]x *ku-it-pát IŠ-TU ša*-x[. . .
7′] *ku-iš-ki ú-iz-zi* A.Š[À

8′]x-*um-ma-na ar-ḫa da-a-*[
9′]x ÌR.MEŠ *a-še-ša-nu-ut* ÌR.M[EŠ
10′] *nu a-pu-u-uš-ša* ÌR.MEŠ *an-*[*da a-še-ša-nu-ut*?]

11′]^{MEŠ} É.DINGIR^{LIM} *A-BI* ^{d}UTU^{ŠI} *ut-*[
12′ (-)]UR.MAḪ *ku-wa-pí* ^{URU}x[
13′]x DINGIR^{LIM} EGIR-*an kat-t*[*a*
14′]*a* [

The nature of this piece is uncertain, but the troops called UKU.UŠ occur in historical texts and letters (references *apud* Güterbock, FsOtten, 76–7), and the phrases "he settled the subjects, . . . those subjects also [he settled there]" (9′–10′) suggest a historical context. UR.MAḪ (12′) could be part of a PN—possibly Piḫawalwi the prince, the writer of the letter RS 17.247 (*PRU* IV 191). Is this perhaps part of a letter touching on different topics?

1. This piece is believed to have been returned to Ankara.

Mythology (Anatolian)

4

1′ *-m]a-an iš-ta-ma-aš-t[a*
2′]UDU.ḪI.A EGIR-*pa u-un-ni-iš a-*[
3′ *-i]š ma-a-na-an a-ru-na-aš ú-*[
4′]*dam*?*-mi-e-li-it te-e-kán* [
5′]x-*an-kán a-ru-na-aš* x[
6′]x ^{d}*Te-li-pí-nu-ša* [

7′]*pár-na pí-en-ni-i*[*š*
8′]GAL ^{GIŠ}IG-x[
9′]*a*/˹*e*˺*-kán da-*˹*a*˺[-
10′]x-*ku-it* x[

This is evidently part of the myth about Telipinu and the Sea, CTH 322 (transliterated RHA XXIII/77: 79). Telipinu, sent by the Weather-god to rescue the Sun-god from captivity in the sea, takes the daughter of the Sea in marriage; the Sea demands the bride-price and the Weather-god, after consulting the Mother-goddess (^{d}MAḪ), gives him 1000 oxen and 1000 sheep. This fragment, with its reference to driving sheep, could follow shortly after the end of KUB 12.60. The script, however, is more archaic than that of KUB 12.60 and is not quite the same as that of the duplicate, KUB 23.81.

Epic of Gilgamesh

5

2′	^{d}GIŠ.GÍN.MAŠ-*aš* ^{d}x[	Gilgamesh the god/goddess . . .
3′	*ḫa-šir-mu-za ku-e-da*[*-ni* U_4*-ti*	On the [day] they engendered me . . .
4′	GISKIM-*az ša-ak-ka*$_4$*-aḫ-ḫ*[*i*	I shall know by a sign . . .
5′	*nu a-pí-e-da-ni* U_4*-ti* ^{d}[	On that day . . .
6′	1-˹*e-da-ni-ma*˺ *ḫa-a-l*[*i-*	to one cattle-pen(?) . . .
7′	*nu-za-kán* DINGIR^{LIM}*-IA* ^{d}[	And my god . . .
8′	*ša-a-it nu* ^{d}[	was angry, and the god . . .
9′	*ka-ru-ú za*?-[	formerly . . .
10′	4 *ME* MU.KAM.ḪI.A[	400 years . . .
11′	*ta*-x[	. . .

This piece presents a difficult problem. Gilgamesh is evidently addressing a god or goddess whose name is broken off in line 2′. The trace would fit ^{d}U[TU]. In the Akkadian epic Gilgamesh prays to the Sun-god before leaving

Uruk (end of Yale tablet col. v) and there is a reference to an omen; but if this prayer was included in the Hittite version, it would have occurred in a right-hand column of Tablet I, probably near the end of col. II, since at the beginning of col. II Gilgamesh and Šangašu are still seeking a wife for Enkidu, and by the end of col. III the heroes are already on their way to the Cedar Forest (see Kammenhuber, MSS 21 [1967] 49–50). Since this is a left-hand column, it cannot be placed here unless there was another recension of the epic, of which no trace has yet been found. A second prayer to the Sun-god is found near the end of Tablet I col. iv (Otten, IM 8 [1958] 114–6), but it is different from this.

A second possibility is that this is part of the dialogue with the goddess Ishtar. This name would also fit the traces in line 2′. A small fragment, KUB 8.58, is all that is preserved of this dialogue and its position in the Hittite series is unknown. It bears no resemblance to the present fragment in content, nor is there any contact between our fragment and the dialogue with Ishtar as we know it from the Akkadian epic.

The third possibility is that this belongs to the episode of Gilgamesh's encounter with the hero of the flood, named in the Hittite version (god) Ulluš or Ulluya. This name would also fit the traces, but the flood hero would hardly be addressed by Gilgamesh as "my god" and in this case it would be necessary to take *ILIYA* in line 7′ as the subject of *šāit,* alluding perhaps to an otherwise unknown incident (the god who was provoked was Enlil, but he was in no sense Gilgamesh's god). The episode is partly preserved in KUB 8.62, which is regarded by Kammenhuber (loc. cit.) as a separate composition. Gilgamesh does not appear until col. iv, where his role is to confer immortality on Ulluya. The present text could follow after the end of KUB 8.62. A point of resemblance is the division into short sections, and the shape of the edge (see cross-section) suggests that the preserved side might well be the reverse.

Magical Rituals (SISKUR)

6

The references to the "Old Woman of Ḫatti" and the "incantation of the goat" ([*ŠA*] MÁŠ.GAL *ḫu-uk-ma-in,* 6′) suggest that this is a magical ritual similar to the ritual of Tunnawi (cf. Tunn. §§11–13). The king, however, (line 1′) seems out of place in such a context. In 8′ perhaps [^{d}*Ḫa-an-t*]*a-ši-pu-uš,* but the reading is uncertain.

7

(copy by I. L. Finkel)

The reference to blue wool (3′) seems to indicate a magical ritual, but no other complete word (other than *anda*) is legible.

Official Rituals (EZEN)

8

This is a typical piece of a "Festritual" and comment is unnecessary.

9

Another typical piece of "Festritual": there is mention of the hearth, an Ishtar instrument and singing, and things are given to the king. Noteworthy is the reference to the men of Ankulla (Obv. 14′).

10, 11

Two further small fragments of "Festritual." No. 10 has references to an Ishtar instrument, the goddess [Ka]taḫḫa and the town of Zippalanda(?).

12

Part of a ceremony in honour of "Maliya of the male gods," parallel to KBo 11.32 obv. 19ff. On this goddess see now R. Lebrun in *Studia Paulo Naster Oblata,* II, *Orientalia Antiqua* (Orientalia Lovaniensia Analecta 13) 123–30.

Fragment of Uncertain Nature

13

(copy by C. B. F. Walker)

2′ [x P]A KI.MIN ^{URU}*Wa-lu-k*[*a*$^{?}$- . . .
3′ [x P]A KI.MIN ^{URU}*Ka*-[. . .
4′ [x +]x PA *ḫar-ša-ni*-x[. . .
5′ ⸢x x⸣ *ḫu-u-wa-eš-kir* [. . .
6′ ⸢*UL*⸣ *ḫu-u-kán-z*[*i* . . .
7′ [*n*]*u*$^{?}$ GU$_{4}$.[ḪI].A *te-ri-i*[*p*-

This fragment resembles KBo 5.5 (edited by V. Haas, KN 126–7), though the last three lines appear to be moving on to something different. Line 7′ provides further evidence that the activity *terip-* was performed with oxen (cf. H. Hoffner, AlHeth. 43). [Ed.: For *ḫaršanili-* of line 4′ cf. AlHeth. 66.]

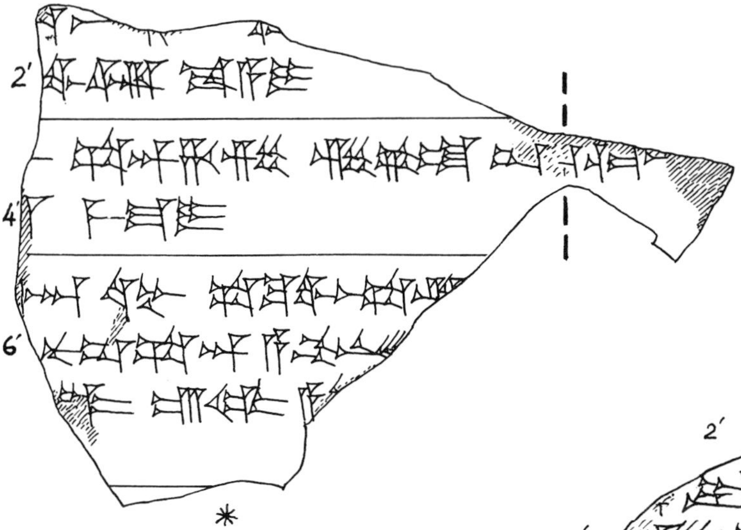

Fig. 1.

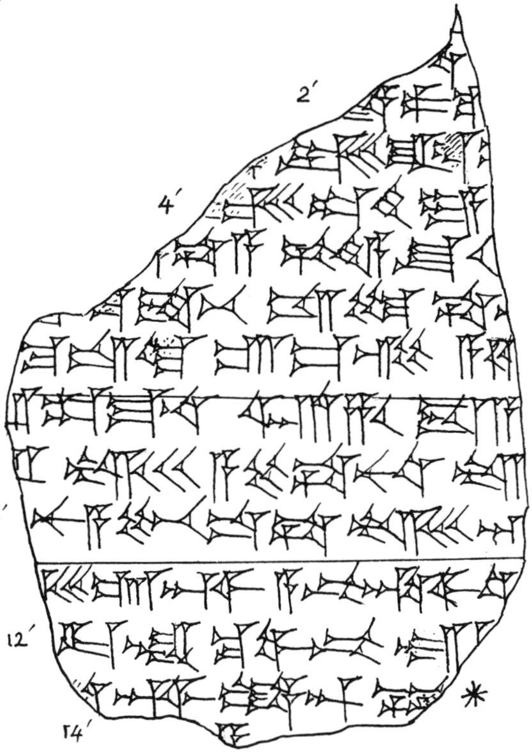

Fig. 3.

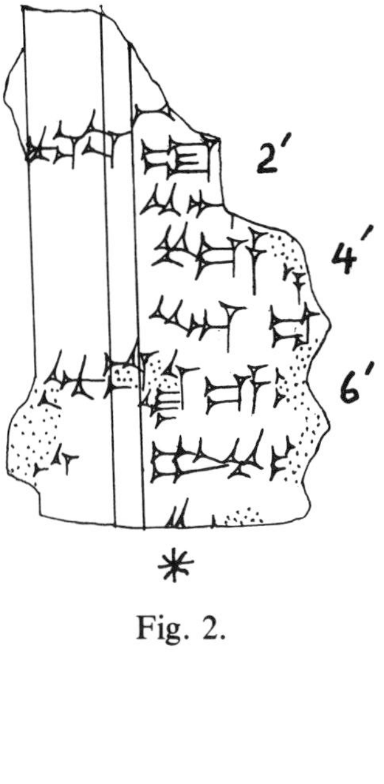

Fig. 2.

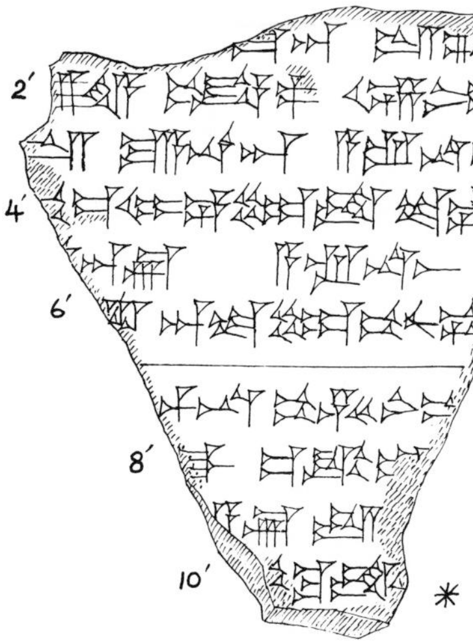

Fig. 4.

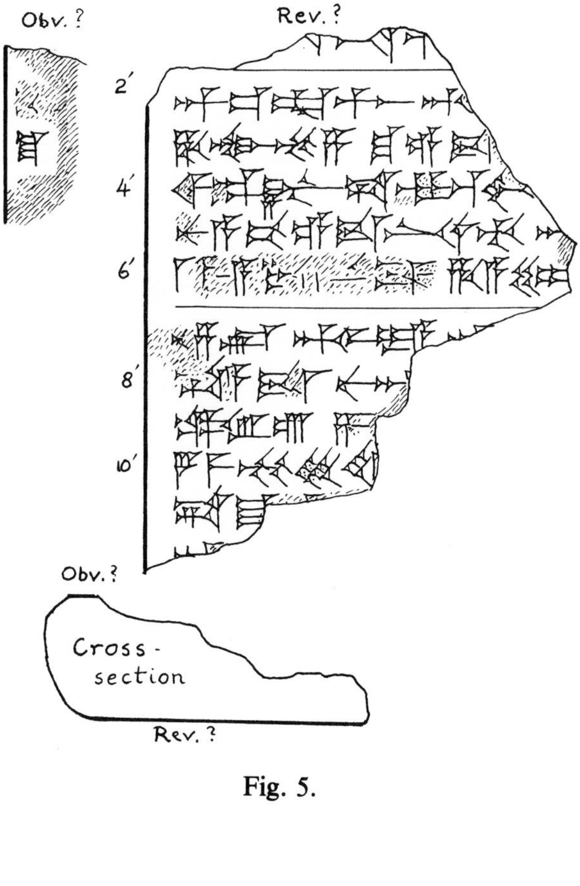

Fig. 5.

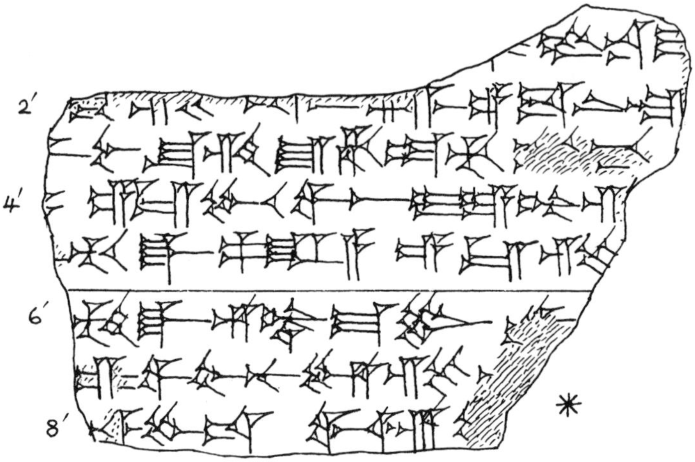

Fig. 6.

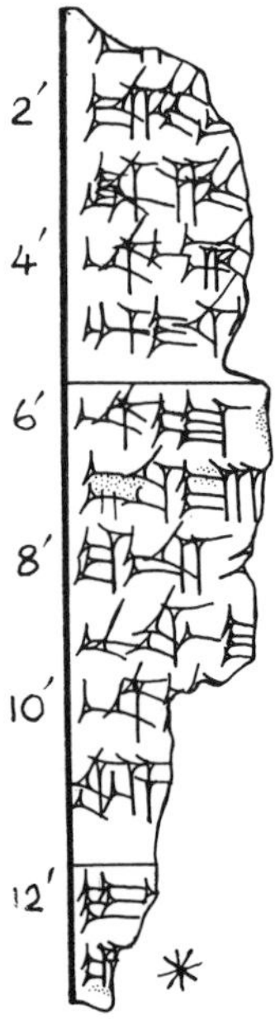

Fig. 7.

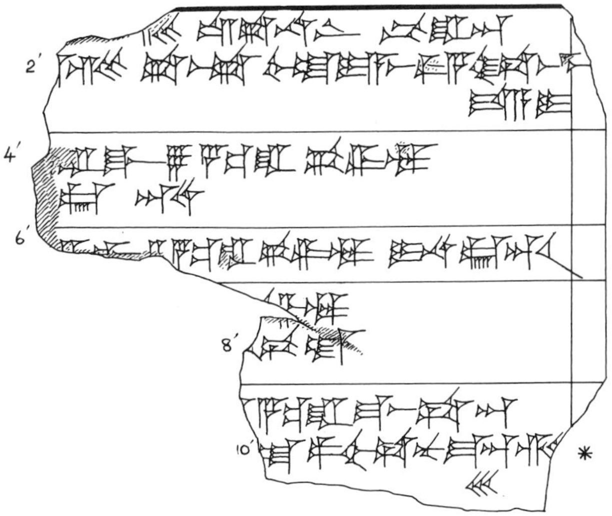

Fig. 8.

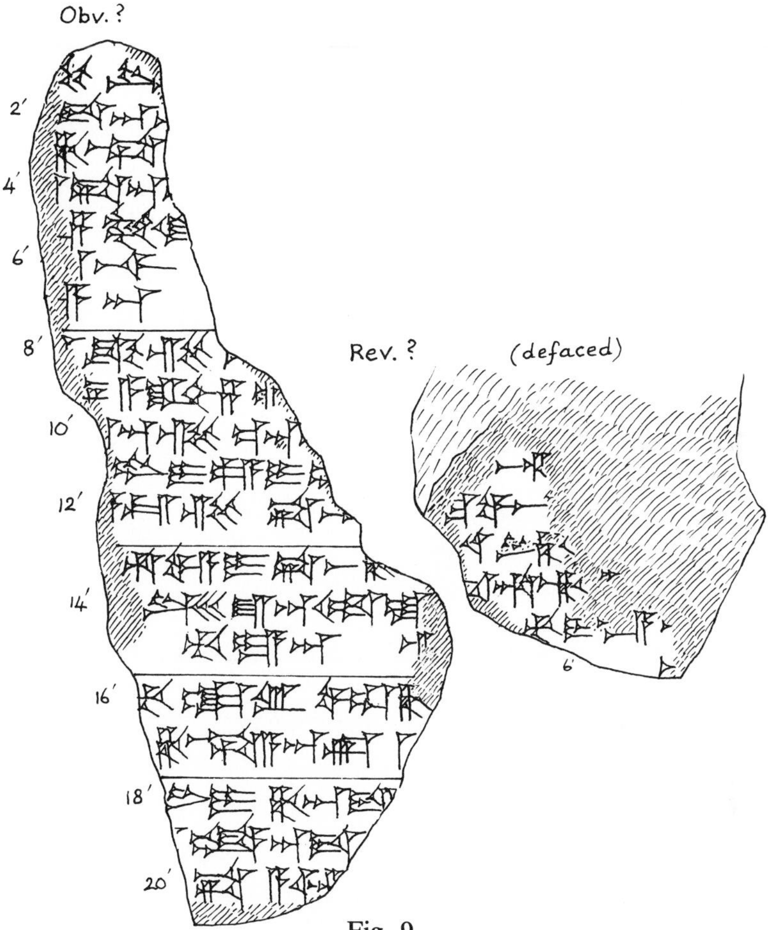

Fig. 9.

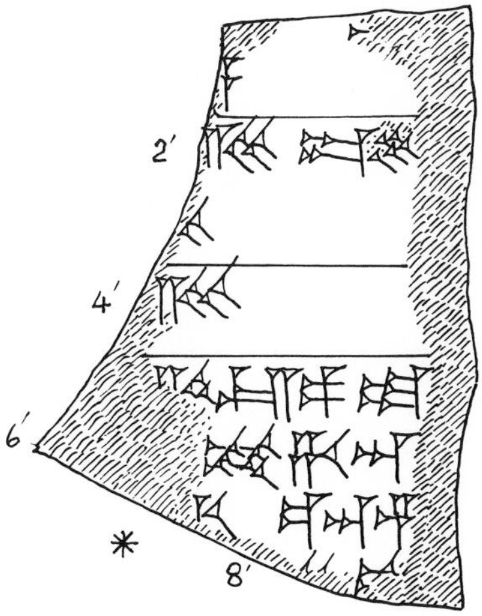

Fig. 10.

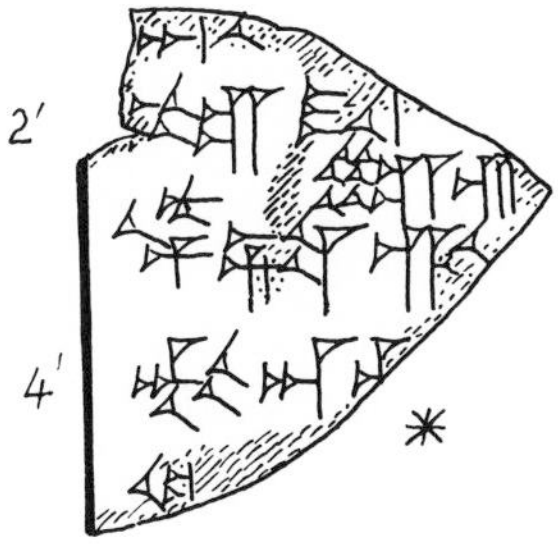

Fig. 11.

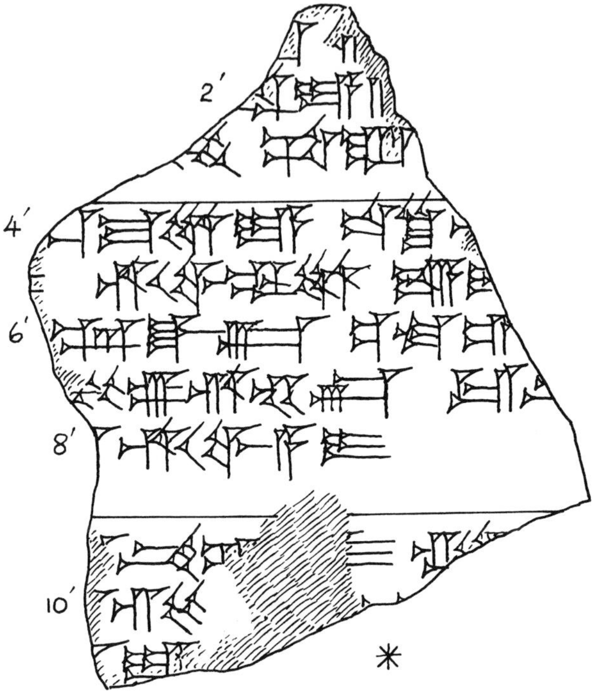

Fig. 12.

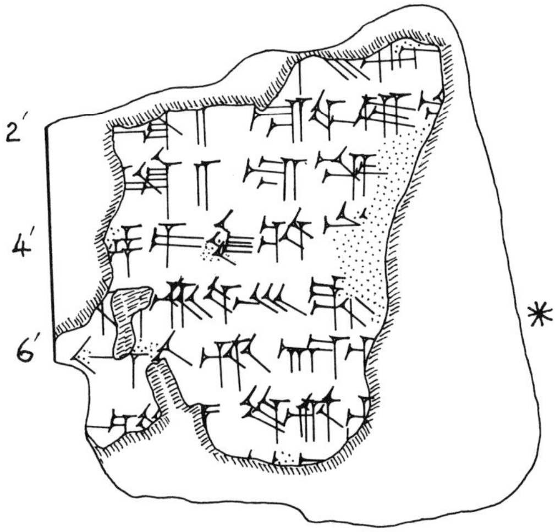

Fig. 13.

STUDIES IN HIEROGLYPHIC LUWIAN*

J. David Hawkins and Anne Morpurgo Davies

London and Oxford

The decipherment and understanding of the so-called Hittite Hieroglyphs was the achievement of a very few people, among whom the name of Hans Gustav Güterbock will always occupy an honoured place. In recognition of his pioneer work in this field, and in gratitude for his constant kindness and encouragement shown towards our own work, it gives us great pleasure to offer to him on this occasion some new interpretations of passages of some Hieroglyphic Luwian texts of the 1st millennium B.C.

1. KARKAMIŠ A 12

The block KARKAMIŠ A 12, bearing an inscription of Katuwas king of Karkamiš, must once have been impressive indeed, but has now lost almost all the sculpture which once surmounted it, as well as its left-hand side along with an indeterminate length of the text, and also its bottom part with a further unknown number of lines. In spite of these losses, it preserves a number of intelligible clauses containing some unusually interesting words, the interpretation of which we are now in a position to suggest, and which recur in various contexts in the other inscriptions. In particular here we shall consider: *walili-*, "field, plain"; *tanata/i-*, "empty, waste"; *titita/i-*, "brow?"; *warpi-*, "skill, knowledge"; and *piyatara/i-*, "giving, selling". Before tackling the contexts of each individually, it seems worthwhile to offer a transliteration and translation of the whole preserved text from which it may be seen that some outstanding problems remain. In general however, this text does offer the opportunity to draw together threads of some previously partially argued interpretations as well as to advance some new ones.

*While in Chicago, Hawkins had the welcome opportunity of discussing with H. A. Hoffner some of the problems raised by passages in this contribution and is much indebted to him and to the files of the CHD for a number of valuable references and suggestions.

Text

1, §1 EGO-wa/i-mi-i ^{I}ka-tú-wa/i-sa IUDEX-ní-i-sa DEUS-ní-ti
(LITUUS+)á-za-mi-sa kar-k[a]-m[i-si-za-sa (URBS) REGIO].
DOMINUS [. . .] ^{I}su-h[i- . . .
[. . . ||]

2, §2 [. . .]-ti-[zi]-ha |NEG$_2$ (PES$_2$)REL$_2$.REL$_2$-sà-ta-si
§3 mu-pa-wa/i-´ (DEUS)TONITRUS-sa (DEUS)kar-hu-ha-sa
(DEUS)ku-AVIS-pa-sa-ha |PRAE-na |PES$_2$(-)wa/i-sà-i-ta
§4 wa/i-tá-´ (CURRUS)wa/i+ra/i-za-ní-na à-tá [|]PES$_2$(-)wa/i-[z]a-ha

3, §5 [. . . ||] |CAPERE-ha
§6 *318(-)sa-pi-si-za-pa-wa/i(URBS) AQUA-pa-ti-na (*245)tá-na-ta-ha
§7 á-wa/i-ia-na-wa/i-na-pa-wa/i(URBS) "CASTRUM"-sa 100
CURRUS(-)ku-sa-ti |INFRA-tá "PUGNUS"-sá-ha
§8 wa/i-mu-tá-´ |("*273")wa/i+ra/i-pi |*275-i-ta
§9 à-wa/i [. . .
[. . . ||]

4, §10 m[u$^{?}$-pa-wa/i]-tú-tá-´ mi-ia-ti-´ |IUSTITIA-ni-ti-i (LITUUS)
ti-ti-ti-i |PES$_2$(-)[. . .]
§11 wa/i-tú-[ta]-´ ("*350")á-sa-ha+ra/i-mi-sà |PES$_2$(-)pa-za-ha
§12 |(*273)wa/i+ra/i-pi-ha-wa/i-tú ("SCUTUM")hà+ra/i-li-ha
|*257(-)pi-ia-[ta]ra/i-[. . .] |PES$_2$(-)pa-za-ha
§13 wa/i-tú-wa/i-na-´ PRAE-na |"*30"(-)ri+i-nu-wa/i-ha
§14 à-w[a/i] pi-[. . .

Translation

§1 I am Katuwas the ruler, beloved by the gods, the Country-Lord of Karkamis, [son of] Suhis [. . .]

§2 . . .
[To those fields my fathers] and [grandfath]ers had not marched,

§3 but the gods Tarhunzas, Karhuhas and Kubaba *walked*(?) before me,

§4 and I ——ed the chariot,

§5 [and . . .] I took.

§6 I wasted the river-land of the city (-)Sapis(-)

§7 and the walls/fortresses of the city Awayana I ——ed down with 100 . . .

§8 One/they ——ed me for skill,

§9 and [. . .

§10 By my righteousness [I] we[nt] before(?) him . . . ,

§11 I went to him (as) an *offering*,

§12 I went to him for skill and defence ("shield") and profit ("selling"),

§13 And it before him I caused to . . .
§14 and [. . .
. . .

Notes

§2. This passage has long been restored from the parallel KARKAMIŠ A 11b, 1.3; cf. also KARKAMIŠ A 25 a 3, 1.1, for another fragmentary occurrence of the same passage. For an elucidation see Hawkins, AnSt 25 (1975), 136f. cit. 32 a–b. For the association of (TERRA+LA+LA)*walilita-* with Hitt.(-Luw.) *ulili-*, "field", see below, with contexts.

§3. See Hawkins, AnSt 30 (1980), 161 cit. 11.

§4. See AnSt 25 (1975), 126 cit. 2b.

§6. AQUA-*patin* = *hapatin*, "river-land", following the elucidation by Laroche, including this passage, in FsOtten (Wiesbaden, 1973), 181.

(-)sapisiza(n)(URBS), now clearly recognizable as an ethnic adj. formed with suffix *-iza-*, as *Karkamisiza-*, "Karkamišean".

(*245)*tanata-*, "empty, waste", cognate with Hitt.(-Luw.) *dannatta-*, factitive *dannattaḫḫ-*, see below, with contexts.

§7. *awayanawana*(URBS), clearly acc. pl. neut. of an ethnic adj. in *-wani-*. The order of reading the place name, as against a possible *ayawana-*, has been chosen because of the resemblance to the Hittite PN *Awayana* (Laroche, NH, no. 214).

"CASTRUM"-*sa:* acc. pl. neut. of *harnisa(n)za*, understood from the KARATEPE alternative equivalents of *qrt*, "fortress" (203, 288, 305, 353, describing Karatepe itself); *ḥmyt*, "wall(s)" (95, 122); *ʾrṣt*, "place(s)" (130).

Sense: the verb is of unknown reading and interpretation, and *(-)kusati* a hapax legomenon but presumably to be interpreted by reference to the accompanying logogram. "I *broke* down the walls of the city Awayana by 100 *rams*" seems likely.

§8. *275-*i-ta:* the verb is firmly concealed behind the logogram attested only here. For (*273)*warpi-*, "skill, etc.", see below with contexts. The context here suggests the interpretation: "They (the gods?) *commended* me for skill".

§§10–12. (PES$_2$)*pazaha:* verb in all three clauses, though partially restored in §10, is best taken as an intrans. verb of motion perhaps cognate with Hitt. *pai-* "go"; see Hawkins, in FsLaroche, 153f.

-tu: enclitic pronoun, 3 sg. dat., appears contextually in each case to refer to a god.

§10. LITUUS(-)*ti-ti-ti-i:* following Hawkins' examination of the logogram LI=TUUS (in Kadmos 19 [1980], 123–142), which was shown to alternate with a sign "eye", OCULUS, and normally to determine verbs of perception, it seems worthwhile to examine the possible identification of this Hierogl. *hapax legomenon* with Cuneiform Luwian *titit-*, and Hittite ^{UZU}*titita-*. The latter had been identified by Friedrich, Sommer (HWb, s.v.) and Alp (Anatolia 2 [1957], 3, 42–5) as "nose", but this was rejected by Laroche (RHA XVI/63 [1958], 106f.) on the basis of the Cuneiform Luwian context where the word is determined by *tawassati* or *tawassan=zati* "of the eye(s)"; he proposed instead "pupil", i.e. a part of the eye not already accounted for by the words Hitt. *laplapa-*, Luw. *lalpi-*, "eyelash", and Hitt. *enera-*, "eyebrow(-hair)". If the contrast between *-t-* and *-tt-* spellings is ignored this interpretation runs against a Hittite context noted by Riemschneider (KUB 43.60 I 18–20) which reads as follows:

MÁŠ.GAL-*ša-an ša-ap-pu-it wa-al-aḫ-du* UDU.NITÀ [Ed.—sic; expected sign NITÁ]-*ša-an* SI.ḪI.A-*an-da wa-al-aḫ-du an-na-ša-an* UDU-*uš ti-it-ti-it-te-et wa-al-aḫ-du*,

"Let the he-goat strike him with (his) *šappu-*, let the ram strike him with (his) horns, let the mother sheep strike him with (her) *tittitta-*". See now Poetto, AIΩN, Ann. Sem. Studi Mondo Class. Sez. Ling. 1 (1979), 117ff.

Yet it still seems likely that the Hitt. and Luw. words are to be identified. The problem is thus what is the part of the body which can be qualified as "of the eyes" (Luw.), and with which a ewe can "strike" (butt?) (Hitt.). "Eyebrow ridge", "brow", "forehead" seem to be possible candidates; *enera-* may simply refer to "eyebrow" or more closely to "eyebrow-hair"; *ḫant-* has a more generic meaning of "forehead".

In our context two possibilities are open. The Hierogl. *titita-* may have acquired a generic value parallel to that of Hitt. *menaḫḫanda*, Akk. *ana pānī, ana putī;* if so our sentence would mean: "I *went* in front of him because of my righteousness". Alternatively, *titita-* may have retained its special meaning and if so the sentence would mean: "Because of my righteousness I *went* to him, to his brow".

§11. ("*350")*asharmis:* apparently defined as an "offering" by the passage KAR=KAMIŠ A 11b, §18 (see AnSt 31 [1981], 150f., cit. 1 [vi–xi]), where it refers to periodic sacrifices of bread and animals. Although the sense here may be strange, attempts at alternative renderings run into further difficulties: e.g. to interpret (PES_2)*paza-* as a transitive verb, and *asharmis* as object. We may suppose that our passage refers to a dedication of Katuwas to his god: compare Ḫattusili's dedication to Ištar of Šamuḫa.

§12. (*273)*warpi-*, ("SCUTUM")*harli-* and (*257)*piyatar*[. . .]: since the interpretation of (PES_2)*paza-* as an intransitive verb of motion is preferred, these forms are taken as dat. sing., although it would also be possible for them to conceal acc. sing. masc./fem.

(*273)*warpi-*, "skill, etc.", see below with contexts.

("SCUTUM")*harli-:* interpreted by reference to KARATEPE, 49–50 = Phoen. *mgn* (so Laroche, HH, no. 272). Here the word is probably not to be understood literally as "shield", but by extension as "defence, protection".

(*257)*piyatar*[. . .]: following our proposal to recognize in *257 ("silver?") + "giving hand" the verb *(arha) piya-*, "sell" (FsNeumann [1982], 91–105 esp. 95 and note 3), we would wish to recognize here a derivative, meaning "selling" or the like. Since we envisage a dative, some such restoration as *piyatar*[*i-ha*] seems called for (only one or two signs are missing). In the absence of a complete reading and exact parallels, the nature of the suffix must remain uncertain. It could be compared with Hitt. *-(a)tar*, but we should expect an *-n-* form in the indirect cases; or we may think of an original **-trom* (cf. Hitt. *šawitra-:* Oettinger, Heth. und Idg., 197ff.). An extended sense of "selling" suitable for grouping with "skill" and "defence" as goods for which one goes to a god, is perhaps "profit, trade"; i.e. one would hope for one's divine sponsor to provide acumen, security and commercial success. [Ed.—Compare Hitt. *ḫappar* "trade, sale price", *ḫappar iya-*, *ḫapparai-* "to sell".]

§13. "*30"*(-)i+ra/i-nu-wa/i-* or "*30"*-ri+i-nu-wa/i-* seems to offer the possibilities of interpreting *ir(a)nuwa-* or *-rinuwa-*. The otherwise unattested logogram does not help. Meriggi's identification with Hitt. *arnu-* is of course to be discarded.

wa+tu+an: "it (acc. sg. masc./fem.) to him . . ." must apparently refer back to *warpi-*, which would be easier if *harli-* and *piyatar*[. . .] could in some way be understood as subsumed under *warpi-*.

2. (TERRA+LA+LA)*walili-*, ETC.

The Hierogl. contexts examined in AnSt 28 (1978), 106, show that the compound logogram TERRA+LA+LA stands for apparent phonetic variants of a basic **walili-:* namely, *walilita-*, *walirita-*, *wariri-*, and *wari(za)*. The general sense is indicated by the logogram and confirmed by the KARATEPE equivalents *wariza* = *ʾrṣ ʿmq*, "land of the plain (of Adana)" (23, 200), and *wariri* // *tas*REL+*ra/i* = *ʾrṣ*, "earth, land" (62). The extended form in *-t* or *-nt-* presumably has a similar sense.

A comparison with the Hittite root *ulili-* is useful both in reestablishing the Hitt. meaning, about which there has been some doubt, and in defining more closely the range of the Hierogl. Luw. word.

Sommer pointed out that Hitt. *ulili-* corresponds to Akk. *ṢĒRU* "plain, steppe, country" (AS, 85), but this was discarded by Güterbock on the grounds of the difficulty of interpreting the verb *ulilišk-* in the light of this recognition (RHA VI/43 [1942–43], 104). The HW meanings "greenery, plant growth" and "be green, sprout", followed by most scholars, go back to the observations of Güterbock. Lately see Poetto, Ist. Lombardo (Rend. Lett.) 107 (1973) 25f.

Yet the original bilingual evidence for the meaning of *ulili-* was clear enough. The bilingual KUB 4.4 obv. 10–12 [cf. edition by Laroche, RA 58 (1964), 69f.] has the following:

Akk. "You create the herb of the field (*šammi ṣēri*) for the sustenance of the beasts."

Hitt. "[You] create the *uliliyaš kikla-* for the beasts of the field to eat."

Thus *uliliyaš kikla-* (the latter a hapax legomenon) = *šammi ṣēri*, "herb of the field", is paralleled in the Hittite by LÍL-*aš* (i.e. *gimraš*) *ḫu*[*itni*], "beasts of the field" (= Akk. *kurummat būli*). Already here we observe a close parallelism between *ulili-* and LÍL/*gimra-*, which is further evidenced by the attestation of a *ŠA* [*L*]*abarna uliliyaš* ^{d}KAL (KUB 2.1 ii 43) equated by Laroche with ^{d}KAL *ṢĒRI* (Rech., 70), parallel to the other gods of the LÍL. Compare also KBo 10.45 ii 24–25, "with it/him (*katti=šši*) Ištar came to me from the *ulili-*", and Otten's remarks on the passage explicitly associating the reference with "Ištar of the Field" (ZA 54 [1961], 149f.).

KUB 29.1 i 52 has the instructions to the eagle: "Spy out in the *ulili-*(and) the forest", where "field (and) forest" seems more meaningful (so Goetze, ANET, 357) than simply "in the green forest". Laroche again seems to favour this interpretation of *ulili-* when it occurs as a nominal element (NH, 322, "prairie?"). The existence of a form *uliliyašši-* as the name or epithet of a deity points to the existence of the root in Luwian.

Thus a body of evidence and opinion has continued to favour the equation *ulili-* = *ṢĒRU,* and the link with the Hierogl. attestations which points in the same direction should serve to confirm this. The outstanding problem remains the verb *ulilišk-* in the following context, KUB 29.1 i 28f., an address to great trees: *nepišaš kattan uliliškiddumat* UR.MAḪ-*aš*⟨*maš*⟩ *kattan šeškit* "You *ulilišk*-ed under the heaven, and the lion lay down under you".

Since *ulilišk-* is to be taken as a denominative verb (iterative form) of *ulili-*, "field, meadow, plain", its meaning may perhaps be taken without undue strain as "spread out, extend".

The Hierogl. attestations then distribute themselves as follows: KARATEPE V: Hu. ("TERRA+x")/Ho. (TERRA+LA+LA)*wá/í+ra/i-za* "I extended the *plain* of Adana (here to the west, and here to the east)."

KARATEPE XXXVII (Hu.): TERRA+LA+LA-*za* "Peacefully dwelt Adana and the Adanean *plain.*"

KARATEPE XII: Ho. (TERRA+LA+LA)*wa/i+ra/i-ri+i* // Hu. (TERRA) *ta-sà*-REL+RA/I "The evils which were in the *land*".

KARKAMIŠ A 11 b, 3 // 12, 2 // 25a 3, 1: (TERRA+LA+LA)*wa/i-li-li-tà-za* "To those *regions* my fathers, grandfathers, and *ancestors*(?) had not marched." See AnSt 25 (1975), 136f. cit. 32(a–b).

ANDAVAL, 1.2: ⌜*à*⌝-*wa/i* (TERRA+LA+LA)*wa/i-li-ri+i-ta-ti* | REL *ARHA* (PES)*u-sa-wa/i à-wa/i* |(EQUUS)*á-sù-wa/i-za* |*za-ti la-pa-ni-wa/i* "When I bring (them?) away from the *plain(s),* I shall summer-pasture the horse herd(?) here." [Ed.—Cf. CHD sub *lapana-*.]

It would be interesting to see if this statement could be compared with known patterns of transhumance in the Niğde area (ancient kingdom of Tuwana).

3. (*245)*tanata-*

The interpretation of the logogram 245, on the basis of its appearance and its resemblance to 244, as a "wall" goes back to Meriggi's original *Glossar* (1934), and is maintained in the works of both Meriggi and Laroche as the interpretation of the noun *tanata-* (*Glossar*², "Mauer"; HH, "édifice");

similarly the verb *tanata-* (*Glossar*[2], "(um)mauern"; HH, "édifier"). Curiously Laroche seems to have abandoned an earlier interpretation, in which he identified *tanata-* with Cuneiform Hitt. *dannatta-*, "empty, waste" (RHA XI/52 [1950], 51), on the basis of the following comparison: Hatt. ii 66: *nu-za ke-e* KUR.KUR.MEŠ *dan-na-at-ta* . . . EGIR-*pa a-še-ša-nu-nu-un* "I myself resettled these devastated lands." MARAŞ 1, 4: | *à-wa/i* | (*245)*ta-na-ta-´* ("SOLIUM")*i-sà-nu-wa/i-ha* "I settled the devastated (places)."

This is surely correct. The appropriateness of this identification of *tanata-* in the contexts in which it occurs certainly outweighs any conclusions which might be drawn from the logogram, the meaning of which is far from self-evident. Thus the equation Hierogl. *tanata-* = Hitt.(-Luw.) *dannatta-* should be readopted. It is interesting to note that Friedrich registered it in HW basing himself on Laroche's original proposal (see s.v. *dannatta-*).

We may add the following Hierogl. attestations:

KARKAMIŠ A 31/32, 6: *245-*tá-pa-wa/i* LOCUS-*ta*$_4$-*ta*$_5$ [. . .]-*i-ha* "I [repair]ed(?) the devastated precincts." See AnSt 31 (1981), 155f. LOCUS-*ta*$_4$-*ta*$_5$ presumably stands for **pedanta*, an *-ant-* suffixed form of **peda-*, "place".

KARKAMIŠ A 11 b, 4 (// KARKAMIŠ A 25r): *à-wa/i pa-ia-´* | REGIO-*ni-ia* (*245)*ta-na-tá-ha* "I devastated those countries."

Laroche, RHA XI/52:51, compares the Hierogl. verb *tanata-* with the Hittite factitive form *dannattaḫḫ-*, "empty, devastate". Parallel Hittite statements are common, e.g. in the Annals of Šuppiluliuma and Muršili (cf. AM, p. 78 iii 44; p. 80 iii 65). Compare also above, KARKAMIŠ A 12, §6.

The forms of this stem identified in Hierogl. are thus:

(1) *tanata*, nom./acc. pl. neut. of the adjective;
(2) *tanata-*, verb stem, factitive.

There is no indication in the former of the stem vowel, whether the adjective is an *-a-* or *-i-* stem. The following passage may be relevant here (KARKAMIŠ A 11 b, 2): *wa/i-sa-´* *245-*ti-i-sa ARHA* MANUS+RA/I(-) *ia+ra/i-ia-ta*. Since *245 cannot at present be shown to determine a root other than *tanat-*, we must consider whether we should recognize the word here too. The verb *arha (-)yari(ya)-* is nowhere unequivocally transitive (but cf. AnSt 29 [1979], 159f. n. 52), though it is not understood. On the other hand it is difficult to interpret *245-*ti-i-sa* as any form of accusative, so it is possible that it represents the nom. sg. masc./fem. *tanatis*, which would give the sense: "And he ——ed away empty(-handed)." [Collation by Hawkins of MARAŞ 8 after the submission of this paper has yielded a probable (*245)*ta-na-ti-na*, "empty", acc. sg. masc./fem., which would confirm the *-i-* stem.]

4. (*273)*warpi-*

Hoffner's (Finkelstein Mem. [1977], 107) and Weitenberg's (Hethitica 2 [1977], 47–52) short studies on the root(s) *warpa-* show the difficulty of drawing all the attestations together. Hierogl. passages including the noun *warpi-* have been considered by Hawkins (AnSt 25 [1975], 150f.; AnSt 29 [1979], 159 and note 49), and it was noted that the Hierogl. attestations needed further consideration. This is attempted here. The view taken is that the Hierogl. contexts taken together do permit a reasonably clear idea of the semantic range of *warpi-*. Unfortunately the Cuneiform Luw. attestations of the root as listed in DLL are all fragmentary and contribute little to further elucidation. The much more complicated question of the association of the Hierogl. and Hittite roots is not pursued here.

SULTANHAN stele, 1.3 (+new fragment): | *à-wa/i* | *tu-wa/i+ra/i-sà-sa* | (DEUS)TONITRUS-*hu-za-sa* ⌜| *wa/i*⌝*-su-SARMA-ma-*[. . . . . .]*-ti-i* | [x-*w*]*a/i-ta-li-na-´* | *wa/i+ra/i-pi-na* | *pi-ia-ta* "Tarhunzas of the Vineyard gave to Wasusarmas . . . a *mighty*(?) *warpi-*." Cf. Hawkins, AnSt 25 (1975), 151; Poetto, FsNeumann, 278 note 11.

The translation "mighty" is based on a restoration [*muw*]*atalin*. If the physical connotations of *muwatali-* turn out to be inappropriate to *warpi-*, the alternative restoration [*tiw*]*atalin* proposed by Poetto could be considered; the meaning of this word is not well established, but clearly could be expected to begin with "appertaining to the sun" or the like.

In any case "a mighty (or sun-like) *warpi-*" is here the attribute of a ruler; cf. here the phrase MARAŞ 1, 1.2: *muwatalisis warpalis hamsukalas* "great grandson of the *warpali-* Muwatalis".

KARKAMIŠ A 15 b, 11.3–4: "I brought up Kamanis as successor, and because I *displayed*(?) *warpi-* in preeminence over kings, I brought up his younger brothers. . . . I knew twelve languages, and to me my lord *gathered*(?) every country's son by (means of) travelling for (the sake of) language, and he caused me to know every *warpi-*." See the discussions in AnSt 29 (1979), 159 note 49; AnSt 25 (1975), 150f.

In the first case *warpi-* is again a ruler-like quality exhibited by the author Yariris in his treatment of Kamanis and his brothers, the children of his lord. The emphasis here would seem to be on the moral qualities of loyalty and faith, hence the translation previously chosen, "virtue".

In the second instance, where the context deals with literacy and the knowledge of languages, *warpi-* seems to refer to intellectual attainments, thus generally "knowledge, skill".

KARKAMIŠ A 12, §8 (see above): "They (the gods(?)) *commended*(?) me for *warpi-*."

Whatever the exact connotations of the logographically written verb, *warpi-* apparently refers back to the qualities displayed by the author Katuwas in the preceding sections of military exploits; thus "skill, valour".

KARKAMIŠ A 3, 1.1: | *za-ti-pa-wa/i* | *kar-ka-mi-si-za* (DEUS) TONITRUS-*ti-i* [I]*ka-tu-wa/i-sa* | REGIO-*ni-ia-si* DOMINUS-*ia-sa* REL-*i-zi* ("*273")*wa/i+ra/i-pa-si* | DOMINUS-*ia-zi-i pi-ia-tá*

ma-wa/i-sa | (CAELUM.*286.x)*sa-pa-tara/i-i-sa*

| *ma-pa-wa/i-sa* | (*265)*mi-zi-na-la-sa*

| *ma-pa-wa/i-sa* | (SA_4)*tu-ni-ka-la-sa*

ma-pa-wa/i-tà | (*69.OVIS)*ku-ki-sa-ti-zi*

"The masters (lords) of *warpi-*, whom Katuwas the country-lord gave to this Karkamisean Tarhunzas,

whether the one (was) a *sapatari-*,

or whether the other (was) a *mizinala-*,

or whether the other (was) a *tunikala-*,

or whether the others (were) *kukisati-*s . . ."

The passage further defines *warpi-* as a quality possessed by non-royal persons who are of sufficiently low status to be given to a god by a ruler, i.e. craftsmen and artisans. Their actual trades are denoted by four terms of which only two occur elsewhere: *tunikala-* recurs in ASSUR letter g, i as ("PANIS.SA_4") *tunikara-*, perhaps in view of the logogram to be taken as a maker of NINDA *tunik;* and *kukisati-*s are found in the KULULU lead strips, where they appear to have some connection with sheep. In any case here "masters of *warpi-*" must be masters of "skills" or "crafts"; in a treatment of the KULULU lead strips, to appear in *Belleten,* Hawkins compares them to the [LÚ.MEŠ]*BĒL QĀTI,* the craftsmen given by Ašmunikkal to the Stone-House in KUB 13.8.

KÖRKÜN, 1.2: *wa/i-ti ku-ma-na á-sa-ti-ru-sa* REX-*ti-sá wa/i+ra/i-pa-si* DOMUS-*na* AEDIFICARE "When king Astirus built himself the houses of *warpi-*."

In view of the previous contexts defining *warpi-* in terms of "skill, craft, knowledge" etc. it is hard to resist the conclusion that a *warpi-* house would be a school or training institution of some kind.

Finally in KARKAMIŠ A 12 §12 (see above), we have seen *warpi-* linked with "shield" (metaphorically of "defence, protection") and "selling" (perhaps "commerce, trade, profit"), as goods apparently in the gift of a god. In this context the sense already postulated for *warpi-* on the basis of the other attestations seems sufficiently appropriate.

5. KARKAMIŠ A 11 a, 6–7

In AnSt 25 (1975), 143, Hawkins discussed KARKAMIŠ A 11 a, 6–7 *wa/i-tú-ta-´* (PANIS)*tú+ra/i-pi-na* (LIBARE)sa_5*+ra/i-la-ta-za-ha* NEG_3*-sa AR=*

HA | *tà-ti-i* and translated it "(with him may the gods be angry) and for him may they not take up bread and offerings!"

The worrying point was the meaning of *ARHA ta-* in the sense of 'receive' rather than 'take away', but this meaning had to be postulated to make sense of the negative which precedes the verb. It is now possible to quote two parallels, one fairly close, one more remote, which confirm that interpretation.

An Assyrian statue found in Syria at Tell Fekherye and tentatively dated to the middle of the ninth century B.C. has recently been published.[1] The statue carries two inscriptions, one on the front in Assyrian cuneiform and one on the back in Aramaic; essentially it is a bilingual text with differences of detail between the two texts. It contains a dedication to Adad, name and titles of the dedicator, and a lengthy curse against anyone who removes the name of the dedicator.

The first part of the curse in Assyrian reads (lines 28–30): ^{d}IŠKUR *be-li* NINDA-*šú* A-*šú la i-ma-ḫar-šú* ^{d}*Ša-la be-si* NINDA-*šú* A-*šú* KI.MIN "(Celui qui effacera mon nom du mobilier de la maison de Adad, mon seigneur), que Adad mon seigneur n'accepte de lui ni sa nourriture ni sa boisson. Que Shala ma dame sa nourriture (et) sa boisson *ditto*."

The Aramaic has parallel sentences (lines 16–18). We could not have asked for a closer parallel to the KARKAMIŠ inscription nor for one in a more similar chronological and cultural context.

A more remote comparison comes from a Greek text. Aeschines, *Contra Ctesiphontem* 109ff. reports the oath pronounced by the Amphiktyones of Delphi after the first sacred war (early sixth century B.C.). The oath, we are told, was accompanied by a prayer and a curse against anyone who would violate it.

It has been pointed out more than once that the curse is very close to the curses which we know from Near Eastern documents: the earth should not bear fruit, women should not give birth to children similar to their parents but to monsters etc. The final clause states:

καὶ μήποτε . . . ὁσίως θύσειαν τῷ Ἀπόλλωνι μηδὲ τῇ Ἀρτέμιδι, μηδὲ τῇ Λητοῖ μηδ' Ἀθηνᾷ Προνοίᾳ, μηδὲ δέξαιντο αὐτοῖς τὰ ἱερά.

"and let them never sacrifice piously to Apollo or to Artemis or to Leto or to Athena Pronoia, nor let (these gods) accept offerings from them" (ibid., 111).

1. A. Abou-Assaf, P. Bordreuil, A. R. Millard, La statue de Tell Fekherye et son inscription bilingue assyro-araméenne, Paris 1982.

6. KARKAMIŠ A 6, 5

KARKAMIŠ A 6 is one of the texts put up by Yariris and as noted by Meriggi can serve as an introduction to, or a conclusion of, the whole set of sculptures near which it is carved. In line 5 Yariris notes that after (or behind) Kamanis he made his brothers, and then continues:

(i) | *à-wa/i* | REL-*i-zi* | ("*314")*ka-tú-na-sa* | *i-zi-i-sa-ta+ra/i*
(ii) *wa/i-ma-za* || *zi-la* | ("*314") *ka-tú-ni-zi* | (MANUS) *i-sà-tara/i-i* ("PONERE")*tú-wa/i-há*
(iii) REL-*zi-pa-wa/i-ma-za-´* | ("*382")*tara/i-pu-na-sa* | *i-zi-i-sa-ta+ra/i*
(iv) *wa/i-ma-za* | *zi-la* | ("*382")*tara/i-pu-na-zi-i* | (MANUS)*i-sà-tara/i-i* "PONERE"-*wa/i-ha-´*

The division in sentences is that traditionally adopted and the standard translation would read:

"and those whom the *katunas* honours,
to them then/here I put *katuninzi* in the hand;
those whom (for them) the *tarpunas* honours,
to them I put then/here *tarpunanzi* in the hand."

The discussion has concentrated on the meaning of *katunas* and *tarpunas*. Do these words refer to the toys held in the hands of the children in the monumental carvings? No certain conclusion is possible, but another problem ought to be discussed.

In (i) *katunas* is not the expected nominative singular; given the nominative plural *katuninzi* we would expect **katunis*. As it stands, *katunas* is either a mistake or a genitive singular. A second problem concerns the verb *izistari;* the stem *izista-*, "to honour" is frequently attested. In particular we know a 3rd person sg. *izistai* attested in A 1 a, 5, A 1 b, 3. As a general rule *-i* forms of 3rd person sg. and *-ti* forms also of 3rd person sg. are not attested for the same verb (cf. A. Morpurgo Davies, *Festschrift Szemerényi* [Amsterdam 1979], 577ff.), which would oblige us to take the verb here as a third person sg. past, i.e. *izistara* < **izistata*. However, it is a noticeable feature of *-i* verbs in Cuneiform Luwian and Hierogl. Luwian that their third sg. past persons seem regularly to have *-tta* (and not *-ta*) forms in Cuneiform Luwian, and non-rhotacized *-ta* forms in Hierogl. Luwian (cf. A. Morpurgo Davies, "Dentals, Rhotacism and Verbal Endings in the Luwian languages," KZ 96 [1982], 245–270. Hence if *i-zi-i-sa-ta+ra/i* were really a third person singular preterite, the conjugation of the verb *izista-* would be entirely exceptional.

Two grammatical oddities are enough to give pause. Do we understand the text correctly? A closer look shows that between the two occurrences of *i-zi-i-sa-ta+ra/i* in (i) and (iii) and the particle chains which start (ii) and (iv) there are no word dividers. It is open to us to read *i-zi-i-sa-ta+ra/i* in both cases as the first word of the second clause (i.e. of (ii) and (iv)) with attached relevant particles. If so we would have:

(i) | *à-wa/i* | REL-*i-zi* | ("*314")*ka-tú-na-sa*
(ii) | *i-zi-i-sa-ta+ra/i-wa/i-ma-za* | *zi-la* | ("*314")*ka-tú-ni-zi* | (MANUS)*i-sà-tara/i-i* ("PONERE")*tú-wa/i-há*
(iii) REL-*zi-pa-wa/i-ma-za-´* | ("*382")*tara/i-pu-na-sa*
(iv) *i-zi-i-sa-ta+ra/i-wa/i-ma-za* | *zi-la* | ("*382")*tara/i-pu-na-zi-i* | (MANUS)*i-sà-tara/i-i* | "PONERE"*-wa/i-ha-´*

"and those who (are) of *katuni,*
to them then/here I put in the hand *katuni*'s with/for honour;
and those who (are) of *tarpuna,*
to them then/here I put in the hand *tarpuna*'s with/for honour.

In (i) and (iii) we have a nominal construction parallel to that of KARKAMIŠ A 1 a, 5:

à-wa/i REL-*i-sa* | OVIS(ANIMAL)*-si*
à-wa/i za-à-ti-i | STATUA*-ru-ti-i* | OVIS(ANIMAL)*-na* | (LIBARE)*sa*$_5$*+ra/i-li-i-tú*
REL-*i-sa-pa-wa/i* | (PANIS)*tu+ra/i-pa-si-i*
wa/i-tú-´ (PANIS)*tu+ra/i-pi-na* (LIBARE)*sa*$_5$*+ra/i-la-ta-za-ha* PES$_2$*(-)pa(-)* PES$_2$*-ia-tú*

"and who (is) of sheep,
let him sacrifice a sheep to this statue;
but who (is) of bread,
let him bring bread and libation to it.

In (ii) and (iv) above *izistari* must be a noun in the ablative put in the first position in the clause for emphasis. The noun is obviously an abstract related to the verb *izista-* in the same way in which the noun *wariya-,* "help" (SULTANHAN, 4) is related to the verb *wariyaya,* "he helps" (BOHÇA, 3, 5).

7. KULULU 1, line 6

In Meriggi's edition (*Manuale* II/1, 48ff.) the end of KULULU 1 is not clear. The last clause is extraordinarily short and Meriggi assumes that the text continued on a stone now lost. The sentence which immediately precedes it is treated as obscure. Yet, nothing proves that the text is incomplete and it is possible to make sense of it as it stands.

The author is Ruwas, servant of Tuwatis, and in the first part of the inscription we are told that he built houses or temples (DOMUS-*na*), settled there the god Tarhunzas and instituted yearly sacrifices. We then have a curse against anyone who does harm to the houses (or temples) followed by a prayer that the gods may "come well" for Tuwatis. The final part reads:

(i) | *á-mu-pa-wa/i* |REL-⌊*i*⌋| DEUS-*na-za* | *ta-wa/i-ia-na* | ARHA | *i-wa/i* |
^{I}*tu-wa/i-ti-sa-ti* | *tara/i-u-na-ti*
(ii) | *za-ia-pa-wa/i* DOMUS-*na zi-ti*

"When/as I shall go off into the presence of the gods through the justice of Tuwatis,
(then) these houses (will be) here."

The first clause obviously refers to Ruwas' death; suitably enough in a newly found inscription (M. Kalaç, *Anadolu Araştırmaları* 9 [1983], 167ff.) the same Ruwas speaks of himself as dead: "I was Ruwas . . .". The second clause is a nominal sentence: *zi-ti* may be a mistake for, or a by-form of, *za-ti,* "here". The verb "to be" is not required and it is interesting to observe that in a language with no formal mark of the future it is possible to have nominal sentences even when semantically a future verb is required; in contrast it is well known that the past verb cannot be omitted.

In (i) the verb *i-* 'to go' and the adverbial *tawiyan,* "towards, in the presence of" are well known. The phrase "go off into the presence of the gods" seems to take a mid-place as a euphemism for "dying" between the Hittite "to become a god", viz. to die, said of kings and queens, and the standard Hierogl. word for "to die" *ARHA wal/r(a)-* (cf. Hawkins, KZ 94 [1980], 109ff.). The preverb *ARHA* is common to both Hieroglyphic expressions (cf. also Hitt. *arḫa akk-,* "to die"). [Ed.—For *arḫa akk-* "die off" cf. HW^{2} 51.]

The Hieroglyphic passages which refer to death have been collected by Hawkins in KZ 94:109ff. and in *Death in Mesopotamia,* ed. B. Alster (XXVI R.A.I., Copenhagen 1980, 213ff.). We may now add KULULU 1, 6, the new inscription edited by Kalaç, and perhaps KARKAMIŠ A 3, 3–4 where the final curse against the malefactor states: "When he *sa-ti-´ pa-la-sa-ti-i,* let him not behold the faces of Tarhunzas and Kupapas" (Kadmos 19 [1980], 130). The temporal clause may well refer to the malefactor's death, even if we do not recognize the verb, while the main clause implies that the final reward, that of being admitted to the presence of the gods, is denied to the accursed man.

STUDIES IN HITTITE GRAMMAR

HARRY A. HOFFNER, JR.

The University of Chicago

Hans Güterbock has contributed more than any other living scholar to the elucidation of Hittite grammar. It is an honor for me to offer this small study to him on his seventy-fifth birthday, when his insight into the Hittite language has never been greater.

A. ON THE NEGATIVE *natta*

1. BIBLIOGRAPHY

Hrozný, SH (1917) 184 ("nicht", wr. also *Ú-UL* and NU; erroneously added *ne-et-ta*); Zimmern, OLZ 1922:297; Sommer, AU (1932) 41, 98, 384f. (mostly concerned with the meaning "nein" and the use in questions); Götze, AM (1933) 255 (wr. *na-at-ta* once in Murš. II); Friedrich, HE (1940) par. 285, 288–90 (= HE² 279, 281–83) (excellent summary of usage); Carruba, ZDMG Suppl. 1 (1968, printed 1969) 235 (on diachronic distribution of *na-at-ta* and *Ú-UL* writings); Houwink ten Cate, Records (1970) 49 (on the vacillation between *na-at-ta* and *Ú-UL* in MH texts); Kammenhuber, KZ 83:269, 278 (denying validity of writings *na-at-ta* and *Ú-UL* as a criterion for text dating); Mauer in THeth 9 (1979) 163 (repeating Kammenhuber's point of view).

2. THE WRITING OF *natta*

a. Syllabic writings

It is agreed by all that pronounced *natta* underlies the ideographic writings. That the same spoken word underlies all writings does not, however, alter the fact that in the vast majority of instances scribes writing in the earliest period (all OS texts and most MH/MS ones) wrote that word syllabically (*na-at-ta*), while with a mere handful of exceptions scribes writing new compositions in NH wrote either *Ú-UL* or *UL* (so already Carruba 1968). The spelling *na-at-ta* in a new NH composition was first noted by Götze (AM

255, noting KBo 5.8 i 21). Other examples are StBoT 16 obv. 5, 11 (Tudḫ. IV), KBo 18.28 iv 7 (NH letter), KUB 28.80 iv 11 (NH colophon with archaizing writings like *da-i-e-er* [iv 6] and *ku-u-ru-*..), KBo 1.30:5, 7 (NH vocab.). Examples from pre-NH/NS texts prove only that the NH scribe followed the convention of his pre-NH original in writing the word syllabically.

The writing *na-at,* which occurs once in OS (KBo 6.2 iv "55") and twice in OH/NS (KBo 3.28:19, KUB 12.63 i 32), may be a mistake for *na-at-ta*. KBo 6.2 iv "55" (OS, law 98) was read "*na-at* 'ne - pas'!" by Hrozný (Code Hittite 76). Friedrich (HG 48 n. 4) read *na-at-*[*ta*], but the spacing of signs on the tablet does not permit the assumption that the last sign of *na-at-ta* was separated from the rest of the word, since there was apparently another word which followed it on this line. For further discussion of law 76, utilizing the wording of its duplicate KBo 6.3 see the article by E. Laroche in this volume.

Yet the fact that this same writing *na-at* occurs three times, all in texts originally written in OH, makes one wonder if such a strange writing might be evidence for a rare variant of this word. It is understandable how *na-at* "not" might have been avoided in order to prevent confusion with *n=at* "and it". The writing *na-at-ta* could only be confused with *n=at=ta* "and they/it (to) you", a combination which never occurs, being replaced by *ne-et-ta* (*n=e=ta*) KBo 4.10 rev. 12.

b. Akkadographic Ú-UL *and* UL

Mauer (THeth 9:163) claimed that the writing *UL* (versus *Ú-UL*) provides a criterion for dating a text to the 13th century, but gave no evidence to support this assertion. Kühne (StBoT 16:26 n. 17) gave 'einige Belege' but claimed that scribes already in the mid-14th century occasionally wrote *UL*.

The writing *UL* (with one sign) occurs in late NS copies of texts whose originals date from OH. Thus, it is found in a copy of the Telepinu myth (KUB 33.4 and KUB 33.8, CTH 324). It can also be found in a late copy of the MH *BĒL MADGALTI* instruction (KUB 40.57 iv 8). It occurs regularly in copy A (KUB 13.4) of CTH 264 (instructions for the temple personnel, pre-NH/NS), contrasting with *Ú-UL* in the other copies. It is found twice in copies of Muršili II annals (KUB 14.17 iii 6 [written over onto the obverse, where cramped space dictated the shorter *UL*], KBo 16.6 lower edge 3), and in a copy of Muršili II's prayer to Telepinu (KUB 24.1 iii 20). But it first occurs with any frequency in texts composed after the reign of Muwatalli. The Muwatalli texts CTH 76, 171, 381 and 382 have 34 examples of *Ú-UL,* and none of *UL*. The writing *Ú-UL* continues either exclusively or along with *UL* in the following texts composed after Muwatalli: (Numbers separated by a colon express the ratio of occurrences of *Ú-UL* to *UL*.) The Apology of Ḫattušili III (CTH 81) 35:2. Puduḫepa's letter to Egypt (CTH 176) 30:5. Ukkura inquest (CTH 293) 34:0. KUB 5.1 (CTH 561: oracles on campaigns of Ḫatt. III) seems to use *UL* exclusively, while the similar text KUB 5.3+ (CTH 563.1) has 4:5. KBo 4.10 (CTH 106: Ulmitešup) 5:0. One Tudḫ. IV instr. (CTH 255.2) uses *Ú-UL* exclusively, while the other (CTH 255.1) prefers *Ú-UL* to *UL* by a 19:6 ratio. The Šaušgamuwa treaty has 7:0 and 2 examples of *na-at-ta*. Cult inventories of Tudḫ. IV (CTH 525) about 3:12. Šuppiluliyama II: KBo 12.38 (CTH 121) 0:4. KBo 4.14 (CTH 123) 12:9. KUB 26.32++ (CTH 124) 0:6. From the foregoing evidence it could be concluded that the writing *UL* (versus *Ú-UL*) first appears in copies made in the reign of Ḫattušili III and becomes common only in Šuppiluliyama II texts. But it should be noted that, even after *UL* appears in the reign of Ḫattušili III, it is only preferred by scribes of certain texts, usually oracle texts or cult inventories. The Šuppiluliuma I oracle text cited by Kühne (StBoT 16:26) contains only a single example of *UL* (KUB 18.2 ii 17), and since oracle texts were sometimes recopied (cf. CTH 562.2 and 568), one cannot be absolutely certain that KUB 18.2 was a 14th century original.

c. NU *and the negation of* GÁL

The NU which in oracle texts occurs in the combinations NU.SIG$_5$ and NU.ŠE does not stand for a separate negative word (*natta* or *lē*). Rather NU.SIG$_5$ and NU.ŠE represent a single verb which means "to be unfavorable" (Sommer, HAB 91 n. 1).

In DUMU-*miš=a* NU(.)DUMU-*aš* KBo 3.27 (BoTU 10β) 14, it is extremely unlikely that NU.DUMU stands for a noun meaning "no son". More likely the NU represents *natta* (Sommer, HAB 212).

Another example of NU standing for *natta* is GIM-*anmamu ABU-KA* ^{LÚ}*LIṬŪTI* . . . NU SUM "But when your father didn't give me the hostages . . ." KUB 19.55 + KUB 48.90 lower edge 4 (Milawata letter, 13th century). Here it is very unlikely that NU.SUM stands for a negative verb ("withheld"). Much more likely is the assumption that this stands for *natta pešta* (Hoffner, AfO Beiheft 19:134).

NU.GÁL stands for *natta ēšzi/ašanzi* "do(es) not exist". OS: *kāni* ^{LÚ}ŠU.GI-*eš=a* NU.GÁL "Are there here no old men?" KBo 22.1:6, cf. CHD sub *miyaḫuwant-*; OH/post-OS: *šarnikzel* NU.GÁL Laws 21, 37, 38, 42, 49, 90; *ḫarātar=šet* NU.GÁL Law 197; *takku* URU-*aš* NU.GÁL Late parallel version to law 6; [*takk*]*u INA LÌB-BI* NIM.LÀL NU.GÁL Law 92; *takku* IN.NU.DA [*a*]*nda* NU.GÁL Law 100; *takku=at ēšzi takku=at* NU.GÁL (= *natta ēšzi*) KUB 1.16 ii 54 (OH/NS); *takku* DUMU.LUGAL *ḫantezziš* NU.GÁL . . . *mān* DUMU.LUGAL-*ma* DUMU.NITA NU.GÁL KBo 3.1 ii 36–7 (OH/NS); MH: ERÍN.MEŠ.ḪI.A=*ma=wa=kan* ANŠE.KUR.RA.ḪI.A *anda* NU.GÁL Maşat 75/15:11–12 (MH/MS); *kā=wa* NU.GÁL *kuiški* Maşat 75/104:16 (MH/MS). Sometimes *natta ēšzi* is written *UL* Ì.GÁL or NU Ì.GÁL: [*nu ku*]*edani ANA* DINGIR-*LIM* LÚ É DINGIR-*LIM* Ì.GÁL [*kue*]*dani=ma ANA* DINGIR-*LIM* LÚ É DINGIR-*LIM* NU Ì.GÁL KBo 13.72 rev. 4–5; [. . .]*UL* Ì.GÁL KBo 12.64 iv 5 (treaty fragment, 13th Cent.); [*kuitki*] Ì.GÁL *kuitki=pat* NU Ì.GÁL KUB 40.88 iii 9 (deposition, NH), ed. StBoT 4:22f.; *mān ANA* É.GAL É dUTU-*aš maršaštarreš UL kuiški* Ì.GÁL KUB 5.9 obv. 9 (oracle, 13th Cent.).

It is not necessary to use a syllabically written form of *eš-* to specify the present tense in this construction. To express the past tense, however, it is necessary to do so: *nu=ššan kappuwawar* NU.GÁL *ēšta* KBo 3.4 ii 43–4, iii 35, 54, KUB 14.15 iii 52 (all AM); URU BÀD EGIR-*pa appannaš AŠRU* NU.GÁL *kuiški ēšta* KBo 5.8 ii 24–5 (AM); *nu=mu=kan* ŠÀ KUR URU*Ḫatti* SAL-*TUM* NU.GÁL *ēšta* KUB 21.38 obv. 52 (Pud.); GIM-*an wātar* NU.GÁL *ē*[*šta*] KUB 14.3 i 42 (Taw.).

3. The Position of *natta* in the Clause

a. The normal position

The normal position of *natta* in the verbal clause is before the verb (HE 281). OS: *takku šumeš natta šaktēni* KBo 22.1:5, cf. ibid. 25, 26, 30; *luzzi natta karpīezzi* KBo 6.2 ii 40; *šaḫḫan natta iššer* ibid. iii 15; *š=uš* LÚ-*aš natta aušzi* StBoT 8 iv 22; *nikuš=šmuš natta ganeššir* KBo 22.2 obv. 18 (cf. 17) (StBoT 17); [*takku n*]*atta=ma uwaši* KBo 7.14 obv. 5; MH/MS: *ŪL šanḫuanzi* KBo 15.10 ii 76; *ŪL dammišḫaizzi* Maşat 75/113:17 (FsLaroche 30); NH: *ŪL takšulait* KBo 5.6 ii 10 (DŠ frag. 28); NUMUN *ŪL annieškir* Ḫatt. ii 16 (= B ii 1).

b. natta, lē, nawi *and the preverbs*

natta usually comes between the preverb and the verb (Friedrich, HE 281), but there are many examples of the reverse order. The same is true for the negative *lē*, but all known examples of *nawi* follow the preverb. The following examples, listed by preverbs, will supplement the few examples given by Friedrich. By "preverb" I mean here such words as *anda, andan, āppa, āppan, arḫa, katta, kattan, parā, šarā*. I am well aware that some Hittitologists prefer to call these adverbs. Members of this group, however, are more closely associated with the finite verb than are such other adverbs as *kinun, apiya, ḫūdāk*, etc.

anda: *našta andaya ŪL kuinki tarnai* IBoT 1.36 i 73 (MH/MS); *andatkan lē*

IGI-*wantarinuškanzi* KUB 13.2 iii 7 (MH/NS); *anda ŪL uit* Alakš. B i 11; *anda ŪL dalaḫḫun* Alakš. A i 76; *anda ŪL kuiški peššiškit* KUB 13.35+ i 20 (StBoT 4:4); *anda ŪL kuiški* KAR-*zi* KUB 15.1 ii 32–33 (Ḫatt. III); *anda ŪL tiyami* KUB 26.32 + 23.44 + 31.106 iii 13–14; but: *ŪL kuitki anda ešun* KUB 21.19 (+ KUB 14.7) i 19, KUB 14.7 i 15; *ŪL anda ešun* KUB 21.19 i 35, ii 5; *nukan ŪL-ma anda šalikmi* KUB 5.1 i 29, cf. ii 10, 54. ***lē*** and ***nawi*:** mostly *anda* + *lē* + vb.—[(BÀD-*ešni)=ya=kan a*]*nda lē kuiški warnuz*[(*zi*)] KUB 31.86 ii 28–29 w. dupl. KUB 31.89 ii 16–17 (MH/NS); *puruttiyaššan* (var. *puruttešni*) GUD UDU . . . *anda lē tarniškanzi* ibid. ii 24–25 w. dupl. KUB 31.89 ii 12; *araḫzenaš=a=kan anturiyaš=a* [(*ANA* AN.ZA.G)ÀR] . . . GIŠ*zup=paru anda lē kuiški dāi* ibid. ii 26–27 w. dupl. KUB 31.89 ii 14, etc.; but rarely reversed (2x in Muw.): *ANA* KUR-*TI-matkan lē anda šanḫti* KBo 11.1 obv. 39 (contra rev 8!); *tapa*[*riyawamu*]*zakan lē anda kištati* KUB 14.3 i 20–21; ***nawi*:** *andaššan parna nawi paizzi* law 93. The subject of word order of *anda(n)* with the negatives was not raised in Kammenhuber, FsOtten 141–160 or in HW² 105b (IV 4. Präv.).

***āppa(n)*/EGIR-*pa*/EGIR-*an*:** [*ūk idalu āp*]*pa ŪL iyammi* KUB 1.16 iii 24 (OH/NS); [*aruna*]*n tarmami nu āppa natta laḫui* KUB 31.4 + KBo 3.41:14 (OH/NS); GUD-*unašta ḫāliaz āppa ŪL kuššanqa karšun* KUB 30.10 obv. 15 (OH/MS); *zig=aš āppa Ū*[*L paitta*] KUB 14.1 rev. 35 (MH/MS); *karū=za šumenzan* É.DINGIR.MEŠ-*K*[*UN*]*U* EGIR-*an anzel* [*iwar*] *ŪL kuiški kap=pūwan ḫarta* KUB 17.21 i 7–8 (MH/MS); cf. ibid. i 12, 17; *numukan* IGI.ḪI.A-*wa* LÚKÚR EGIR-*pa ŪL kuiški nāiš* Ḫatt. i 68–69; but: *nuwašmaš* KASKAL.ḪI.A *ŪL* EGIR-*pa ḫišwandari* ABoT 60 obv. 17 (MH/MS). With *lē* the word order is always *appa(n) lē*, never the reverse: *tat āppa šarā lē uēzzi* StBoT 8 iii 12–13 (OS); d*Telepinuwaš=a* . . . *šāwar āppa QĀTAMMA lē uizzi* KUB 17.10 iii 26f., cf. iv 19; *n=at=apa* EGIR-*pa lē uizzi* KBo 15.10 ii 16, iii 58 (MH/MS); *nušmaš kī uttar NĪŠ* DINGIR.MEŠ EGIR-*an lē tarnanzi* KBo 5.3 ii 7, cf. 50–51. HW² 149 does not list a preverbial function for *āppa* and only suggests a possible one for *āppan* ("Vielleicht schon Präv."), referring to VI 2b (pp. 153f.), where however only an adverbial function is mentioned. No mention is made of word order with *natta* or *lē*.

***arḫa*:** *arḫawa* LÚ.MEŠSIPA.GUD . . . *ŪL dališkizzi* ABoT 60 obv. 12–13 (MH/MS); *iktaš=ma=du=ššan irḫaz ŪL naḫšariyawanza arḫa ŪL uizzi* KBo 3.21 ii 17–18 (OH?/NS); *nu namma arḫa ŪL tarnāi* KUB 13.4 ii 23–24 (pre-NH/NS); *nu ḫurpaštanuš arḫa ŪL išḫuwai* KUB 29.1 iv 18–19 (NH); *nu=šši=ššan* dUTU-*ŠI* URU*Iyaruwattan* URU-*an arḫa ŪL daḫḫi* KBo 3.3+ i 31–32 (NH); no counterexamples known. With *lē* only *arḫa lē* is attested: *zikka=war=ašta* GIŠ*luttan*[*za*] *arḫa lē autti* KUB 17.6 i 19–20; *našta arḫa lē kuitki* (var. *kuiški*) *ḫarkzi* KUB 31.86 ii 15; *natkan ziladuwa ŠA* m*Ulmitešup* :*war*[*watni*] *arḫa lē kuiški dāi* KBo 4.10 rev. 22–23. ***nawi*:** *kuitmanwa ḫanneš=*

šar arḫa nawi ariyaweni KBo 16.47:16–17. HW^{2} 259–287 makes no reference to the syntax of the negated *arḫa* + vb.

katta, kattan, kattanta*:** GAL-*yaz* KÁ.GAL-*az katta ŪL paiškanda* IBoT 1.36 i 60 (MH/MS); *numu namma kattan ŪL kuiški uizzi* ABoT 60 rev. 6–7 (MH/MS); *INA* KUR ^{URU}*Alminawarankan kattanta ŪL kuwatka tarnummeni* KBo 5.6 i 4–5 (DŠ frag. 28); but *ŪL-wa kuššanka katta ēpta* KUB 24.8 i 28–29, 33–34 (pre-NH/NS). ***lē and ***nawi*:** *našta* . . . GUD UDU [URU]-*az katta lē tarnanzi* KUB 13.2 i 7f.; *našta kuitman ḫaliaz* $^{\text{LÚ.MEŠ}}$*ḫaliyatalleš katta nawi uwanzi* KUB 13.1+ i 6–7. There are no examples of *lē katta(n)* or *nawi katta(n)*.

***parā*:** *nankan parā ŪL kuiški tarnai* laws 34 and 36; *nat ANA* ^{d}UTU-*ŠI parā Ū*[*L paitta*] KUB 14.1 rev. 23 (MH/MS); *parā ŪL pīe*[*zzi*] IBoT 1.36 i 31, (MH/MS); ZI-*itmaškan parā ŪL paizzi* ibid. i 47; *kuiš ŠA* KUR ^{URU}*Ḫatti* NAM.RA.ḪI.A *parā ŪL pāi* Ḫuqq. iii 69; cf. iii 71; *nat* DINGIR.MEŠ-*aš* ZI-*ni parā ŪL arnutteni* KUB 13.4 i 51 (pre-NH/NS); *nuwamukan parā ŪL iyašḫatta* KBo 5.6 iv 3 (DŠ frag. 28 A); no counterexamples are known. In the imperative most examples are *parā lē*: *apušmakan parā lē uwanzi* KUB 13.8:8 (MH), *parāmaškan lē kuiški tarnai* ibid. 9, *parāmakan . . . lē kuiški pāi* ibid. 14–15; [*nuza*] *memian parā lē kuedanikki* [*mem*]*atteni* KUB 26.8 ii 6–7, but *lēwaranzan kuedanikki* [*parā*] *mematti* KUB 26.1 i 58–59 (same text, restored by von Schuler, Dienstanw. 11).

***šarā*:** *našta namma šarā ŪL uizzi* KUB 17.10 iv 16–17 (OH/MS), cf. Myth. 37; *nušmaš* . . . EZEN.ḪI.A *kiššan šarā ŪL kuiški tittanuwan ḫarta* KUB 17.21 i 21–23 (MH/MS); *mān* 12 $^{\text{LÚ.MEŠ}}$*MEŠEDI-ma šarā ŪL arta* IBoT 1.36 i 11–12 (MH/MS); [*nat*] *wetinanzama šarā ŪL arnuzi* KUB 31.86 ii 11 (MH/NS); no counterexamples are known. Also w. *lē: naškan šarā lē uiškitta* KUB 1.16 ii 36.

***edi*:** ḪUR.SAG-*an tarmaemi tašta edi natta neyari* KUB 31.4:13 + KBo 3.41:12; but in a rhetorical question *ŪL* DUMU.MEŠ-*ŠU edi nāir* KUB 1.16 iii 41 (OH/NS).

c. natta *and indefinite pronouns and adverbs in* -ki, -ka

kuiški, kuitki, kuwapikki, kuezka, kuššanka, and *kuwatka* regularly follow *natta* immediately. Usually they come between *natta* and the verb. **OS:** [*i*]*dālu natta kuedanikki takkišta* KBo 3.22:8 (StBoT 18:10f.); *kušanna natta kuiški iē*[*zzi*] KBo 6.2 iii 17 (law 55); *kinuna natta kuwapikki pāun* StBoT 8 iv 13; **OH/MS:** *natta/ŪL kuššanka* KUB 30.10 obv. 12, 13, 15, rev. 21; *natta/ŪL kuwapikki* ibid. obv. 16, 17; *ḫuišnuzzi ŪL kuiški* ibid. rev. 24–25; **OH/NS:** LUGAL-*š=a ŪL kuitki* [*š*]*aggaḫḫi* KUB 1.16 iii 5, cf. iii 26; [*n*]*atta=šta kuitki kuedanikki daḫḫun* KUB 31.4 + KBo 3.41 (= BoTU 14β) 4, cf. 5, 6; **MH/MS:** *anzel* [*iwa*]*r ŪL kuiški kappūwan ḫarta* KUB 17.21 i 7–8; *namma arḫa ŪL* *kuēzka uwanzi* ibid. iii 20; cf. ibid. i 12–13, 17–18, 20, 22–23; *ŪL kuinki tarna*[*i*] IBoT 1.36 i 73(bis), *ŪL kuiušga ūḫḫun* KUB 23.72 obv. 20; **NH:** *nuwa ŪL kuitki šakti* KUB 19.29 iv 16 (AM 18); *numu ŪL kuiški aušta* KBo 4.4 iii 35 (AM 126); *nuwa damēdaniya* KUR-*e ŪL kuedanikki AŠPUR* KBo 5.6 iv 8–9; *numu* :*ḫuwappi* DINGIR-*LIM*-*ni* :*ḫuwappi* DI-*ešni parā ŪL kuwapikki tarnaš* Ḫatt. i 40–41; cf. ibid. i 49–55; *numukan* ḪUL-*lu uttar katta ŪL kuitki āšta* ibid. i 62; *numukan* IGI.ḪI.A-*wa* LÚKÚR EGIR-*pa ŪL kuiški nāiš* ibid. i 68–69; *nušmaškan ŪL kuezqa kuit ḫaptat* ibid. ii 76; *naš ŪL kuitki* DÙ-*nun* ibid. iii 27–28.

This order is observed with *lē* and *nawi* as well: *URRAM ŠĒRAM kī* [*tuppi l*]*ē kuiški ḫulliezzi* KBo 3.22 34 (OS); *nu* LÚ*ḫippari ḫāppar lē* [(*ku*)]*iški iezzi* KBo 6.2 ii 49–50 (law 48, OS); *nušši* EGIR-*an nawi kuitki tekkuššiyaizzi* Mşt 75/113:12–14 (MH/MS); *kinunawa* ANŠE.KUR.RA.ḪI.A *nawi kuiški uizzi* Mşt 75/15:15–17 (MH/MS); *nu ANA* KUR LÚ.KÚR *nawi kuitman kueda=nikki pāun* KBo 3.4 i 20–21 (AM 20); *nāwi kuwapik*[*ki*] SIxSÁ-*at* KUB 19.23 rev. 6–7; *nāwi kuitki ēšta* KUB 42.100 iv 15. With transposition of the verb to the head of the clause for emphasis: *ḫuišnuzzi ŪL kuiški* KUB 30.10 rev. 24–25 (OH/MS), *iyawe*[*n=ma*]*=war-at ŪL kuitki* KBo 22.6 iv 12 (OH/NS).

d. natta *and the adverbs* manqa *and* imma

***manqa*:** All examples of negated *manqa* are either *UL manqa* or *nūman manqa* (cf. CHD sub *manqa*). No *lē manqa* or *nawi manqa* is attested. Neither is the sequence *manqa UL/natta* found.

***imma*:** Cf. below under 4 c.

4. *natta* IN QUESTIONS

a. Previous studies

In 1932 Sommer observed that, when *natta* occurs in rhetorical questions, it often takes a clause initial position (AU 54 n. 4). Although not all clauses with initial *natta* are rhetorical questions, the clause initial position serves to show emphasis, which is appropriate in rhetorical questions. Sommer did not say if rhetorical questions with non-initial *natta* existed. In a lecture at the 1983 Midwest Regional Meeting of the American Oriental Society to be published soon, Güterbock noted several examples of rhetorical questions with non-initial *natta*.

This new evidence prompted me to reexamine the subject in a comprehensive manner, in order to determine what role was played by word order in negative sentences. In the corpus of Hittite texts which I examined, out of 48 examples of clause initial *natta* in adequately preserved contexts, 15 were rhetorical questions and 33 were not. This demonstrates the validity of

Sommer's remarks. Clause initial *natta* obviously functions in most cases merely to emphasize the negative, without any implication of a question. In the following paragraphs I give a selection of negative rhetorical questions, choosing for inclusion those not already cited by Güterbock, whose paper will soon be available in published form.

b. Rhetorical questions with initial natta

natta=šamaš LÚ.MEŠDUGUD *tuppi ḫazzian ḫarzi* "Has (my father) not inscribed a tablet for you dignitaries?" KBo 22.1 obv. 23 (instr., OS); *natta* LÚ.MEŠ*NAŠI ṢIDIDI=KUNU* ibid. 17–18; *ŠA* LÚGAL.GAL-*TIM* É-*ŠUNU kuwapi ŪL-at ḫarker* "Where are the houses of the grandees? Have they not perished?" KUB 1.16 iii 45 (edict, OH/NS), ed. HAB 14f.; *natta ūk* ÍD.MEŠ-*uš* ḪUR.SAG.MEŠ-*uš arunuš=a* [EGIR-*p*]*a tarmaīškimi* "Do not I . . . the rivers, mountains and seas?" KUB 31.4 + KBo 3.41:12–13 (OH/NS); *ŪL-wa* LUGAL-*waš araš=miš zik* "Are you not the friend of me, the king?" KUB 29.1 i 35 (myth and rit., OH/MS); [*Ū*]*L-war=aš gimraš* DUMU-*aš* "Is he not a son of the steppe?" VBoT 58 i 28 (missing god myth, OH/NS), ed. Myth 24; *ŪL* SAL.SUḪUR.LAL *iyattat* "Didn't a harem woman go by? (And he gazed at her.)" Ḫuqq. iii 54; *UL=at=kan A-NA* DAM-*ŠU* . . . [*š*]*anḫzi* "Will (the offended god) not (also) require it of his (the offender's) wife . . . ?" KUB 13.4 i 36–37 (instr., pre-NH/NS), ed. Chrest. 148f.; *nuza kuēl walliyatar ŪL-za ŠA* dU *piḫaššašši* EN-*YA walliyatar* "And whose praise will I be? Will I not be the praise of the Stormgod *p.*, my lord?" KUB 6.45 iii 48–49 (prayer, Muw.); *ŪL-at ŠUM*[-*n*]*i ḫandaš iyanun* "Did I not do it for the sake of (my good) name?" KUB 21.38 obv. 52 (letter of Pud.), ed. Stefanini, Pud. 12; (Don't the parents give him the fee of the nurse?) *ŪL=ma=an=za=an=kan duškiyazi* "And don't they (*attaš annaš* takes sg. verbs here) rejoice in it?" KUB 14.7 iv 12–14 (prayer, Ḫatt. III); *ŪL=war=an=kan tuetaza memiyanaz kuenni*[*r*] KUB 8.48 i 12 (Gilg., NH); *ŪL=wa ŠA* LUGAL ÚŠ *išiyaḫta* KUB 14.4 iv 26 (Murš. II); [*Ú-U*]*L-at=za kikkištari* KBo 4.14 ii 4 (Šupp. II).

c. Rhetorical questions with non-initial natta

To Güterbock's list of six examples we may add a further sixteen: [*takk*]*u=wa=šmaš=šta išḫar=ma šiyati ūk=ma=šmaš* [IGI-*a*]*nda zaḫḫiya kuwat ŪL pāimi* "But if their blood has spurted forth, why should I not go against them in battle?" KBo 3.16 obv. 16–17 (Naramsin, OH/NS), ed. Güterbock, ZA 44:54f., 63 (deciding against reading the var. in B as a rhetorical question); (If a mortal were to live forever, the unpleasant illness of the man would also continue;) *man=at=ši natta kattawatar* "Wouldn't it (then) be a grievance for him?" KUB 30.10 obv. 23 (prayer, OH/MS); *man zik ŪL aršanieše* "Wouldn't you be upset?" ABoT 65 rev. 6 (letter, MH/MS), cf. HW² sub *aršaniya-* and CHD sub *man; nuwata ŪL imma peḫḫi peḫḫi=ta* "Shall I not indeed give it to you? I will give (it) to you!" VBoT 2:8–9 (letter to Amenophis III); *ug=a=wa=z ŪL imma* LÚ-*aš* "Am I not indeed a man?" KUB 23.72 obv. 40 (Mita text, MH/MS); *nušši attaš annaš ŠA* SALUMMEDA *ŪL imma pāi* KUB 14.7 iv 12–13 (cf. above); (He whom we will indeed take up for ourselves:) *nuwann[aš apaš] ŪL imma* DUMU EN-*E=NI* "Is he not indeed the son of our lord?" KUB 26.1 i 22–23 (instr., Tudḫ. IV); *ammuqqa=wa=za ŪL* DUMU! EN-*KA* "Am I not also a son of your lord?" KUB 21.42 i 17 (cumulative line count 24); probably also *našmu ŪL imma* LÚ*ḪA-⟨DA⟩-NU* KUB 14.3 ii 75 (Taw.), despite contrary argument of Sommer, AU 138f.; *nu* DINGIR.MEŠ *ŪL [šekteni k]uel=aš dammešḫaš* "Do you gods not know whose is the injury?" KBo 4.8 iii 3–4 (prayer of Murš. II), ed. Hoffner, JAOS 103:188; *nutta ŪL imma peḫḫi* VBoT 2:8–9, *ANA* ŠEŠ-*YA* SAL-*TUM ŪL imma ēšta* KUB 21.38 obv. 53 (Pud.); *nu šumeš* DINGIR.MEŠ *ŪL uškatteni* KUB 14.4 ii 3–4 (Murš. II), cf. ibid. ii 8; *natmu ANA* LÚ.MEŠ KUR URU*Ḫatti piran ŪL imma walliyatar ŪL kuit ēšta* KUB 21.38 obv. 48; *nat ŪL imma walliyatar* ibid. 51; URU*Niḫiryaza=kan ŪL* 1-*aš arḫa unnaḫḫun* KBo 4.14 ii 9 (Šupp. II), cf. ibid. ii 11.

d. natta *in non-rhetorical questions*

The following examples show that negative questions which are not rhetorical always employ *natta* in non-initial position: *nuwaran kuit ḫanda ŪL wemiya[nzi]* "Why do they not find him?" VBoT 58 i 23 (missing god myth, OH/NS); TÚG-*ŠUNU* TÚG*išḫialšemetta kuit natta ešḫa[š]kanta* "Why are their garments and their sashes not bloodied?" KBo 3.34 i 20 (anecdotes, OH/NS); *kuwat=war=an parā ŪL pe[šti]* "Why will you not extradite them (i.e., *arnuwalan*)?" Ḫuqq. iii 71, ed. SV 2:130f.

5. *natta* Negating the Predicate of a Nominal Sentence

a. An adjective or participle

ūk=wa a[tti]=m[i natt]a āššuš KBo 22.2 rev. 4–5 (OS) with NS dupl. *ūk=wa atti=mi ŪL āššuš* KBo 3.38 rev. 20; *takku kuššan piyan . . . takku kuššan=a natta piyan* KBo 6.2 ii 28–29 (OS); *dandukišnaš=a* DUMU-*aš ukturi natta ḫuišwanza* KUB 30.10 obv. 21 (OH/MS); *ekunaš=aš n=aš ŪL g[enzuwalaš]* KUB 1.16 ii 7 (OH/NS); *nutta⟨⟨ma⟩⟩ mān* SAG.DU dUTU-*ŠI QĀTAMMA ŪL nakkiš* KBo 5.3 i 19–20 (Ḫuqq.) (note: Contra Houwink ten Cate, FsOtten 133 n. 77 the emendation is necessary. *nu* and *-ma* can indeed stand in the same clause, but not in the same chain of introductory sentence particles. The example *nu*[*-uš-m*]*a-aš-ma* in KBo 5.3 iv 34 after collation must be read *š*[*u-um-m*]*a-aš-ma*.); *kuieš* *ŪL* *daranteš* KUB 6.45 iii 6 (Muw.); *am=mukmaškan ŪL anda malanza* KUB 21.38 obv. 26 (Pud.); [*ANA PANI* ^LÚ^*MUTI=ŠU=y*]*a=ši kue ŪL a-a-ra ēšta* KUB 14.4 i 13 (Murš. II); *takku atti=ma anni ŪL āššu* Law §28, late version.

b. A noun

natta GUD.MAḪ-*aš* . . . *apaš* GUD.MAḪ-*aš* KBo 6.2 iii 23–24 (OS); *natta* ANŠE.KUR.RA.MAḪ-*aš* . . . *apaš* ANŠE.KUR.RA.MAḪ-*aš* ibid. 27, 28; *man=at=ši natta kattawatar* KUB 30.10 obv. 23 (OH/MS); *ŪL* DUMU-*YA apā*[*š*] KUB 1.16 ii 14 (OH/NS); *ŪL-wa* LUGAL-*waš araš=miš zik* KUB 29.1 i 35 (OH/NS); [*Ū*]*L-waraš gimraš* DUMU-*aš* VBoT 58 i 28 (OH/NS); *ug=a=wa=z ŪL imma* LÚ-*aš* KUB 23.72+ obv. 40 (MH/MS); *nuwaratmu :šallakartatar :kupiyatišmawarašmu ŪL* [*kuiški*] KUB 13.35 i 25 + KUB 23.80 obv.! 11 (Ḫatt. III); ^LÚ^*TARTENU-ma ŪL ANA* LUGAL *ayawalaš* KUB 14.3 i 11–12 (Taw.); *nuwaratmu ŪL waštul* KUB 26.1+ iii 30–31 (Tudḫ. IV); *ammukkawaza ŪL* DUMU EN-*KA* KUB 21.42 i 17 (Tudḫ. IV); *mān teši* LUGAL KUR ^URU^*Karanduniyaš=wa ŪL* LUGAL.GAL KUB 21.38 obv. 55–56; *n=at=mu ANA* LÚ.MEŠ KUR ^URU^*Ḫatti piran ŪL imma wal=liyatar* ibid. obv. 48; cf. obv. 51. Cf. also other examples sub 4 b and c.

c. Adverbs or other predicates

^d^*Telepinušwa* DUMU-*YA andan* NU.GÁL "T., my son, is not there" KUB 17.10 i 21–22 (Tel. myth, OH/NS) cf. above under 2 c; *nat ŪL kā* ABoT 65 obv. 7 (MH/MS); ^URU^*Maraššantiya=z* [*Ū*]*L MAḪAR* ^d^UTU-*ŠI ešun* ibid. 12–13; *kī=ma AWATE*^MEŠ^ *ŪL kuitki* 1-*edaz* 1-*edaz IŠTU* ^URU^*Ḫatti=at* Alakš. A. iii 76–77 (Muw.); *UL-yawa kuit iyawaš nuwarat iya* KUB 21.38 obv. 39 (Pud.); *n=an punuš mān kišan mān ŪL kišan* ibid. 12 (cf. 24); *ŪL anda* Ḫatt. iii 22, KBo 3.4 iv 47.

6. *natta* Negating an Element Other than the Predicate

Other Hittite negating words (*lē, nawi, nūman,* etc.) are unsuited to this task. In this use it is possible for there to be still another word negating the predicate. *numu* LUGAL-*an āški* DINGIR-*YA ŪL aššanuwandan anduḫšan lē iššatti* KUB 30.10 rev. 22–23 (OH/MS); *kāšašmaškan parkuin mišriwantan ḫarkin* ^GIŠ^PA *ŪL walḫantan* UDU-*un šipandaḫḫun* KBo 15.10 ii 8–10 (MH/MS); *iktaš=ma=du=ššan irḫaz ŪL naḫšariyawanza arḫa ŪL uizzi* KBo 3.21 ii 17–18 (OH?/NS).

In another type of sentence *natta* negates the subject for emphasis. Here one should translate with an English cleft sentence ("It was not . . . who . . ."): *natta=an ūk tarnaḫḫun* LUGAL-*š=an* SAL.LUGAL-*š=a tarnaš* "It was not I who released it. The king and queen released it" StBoT 8 iii 4–5 (OS); cf. *natta ūk* ÍD.MEŠ-*uš* ḪUR.SAG.MEŠ-*uš arunuš=a* [*āpp*]*a tar=maiškimi* KUB 31.4:12 + KBo 3.41:11 (OH/NS); URU*Niḫiryaza=kan ŪL* 1-*aš arḫa unnaḫḫun* KBo 4.14 ii 9, cf. ii 11; *n=aš ŪL* 1-*aš aki* KUB 13.4 i 33; *n=e āppa ŪL* SIG_5-*in uiškanta* TelPr. ii 3–4; cf. also exx. under 3 c.

B. ON THE DATIVE-ACCUSATIVE ENCLITIC PRONOUN

Friedrich (HE pp. 147f., sec. 288) noted that the usual order of sentence enclitics seems to admit exceptions in the case of the dat.-acc. personal pronouns. But these are not exceptions, since they conform to a simple rule. When the dat.-acc. pronoun is plural (i.e., -*šmaš* or -*naš*), it always precedes the third person enclitic pronoun -*a*-. But when the dat.-acc. pronoun is singular (-*mu, -ta, -ši*), the pronoun -*a*- may follow only in the case of -*ši* and only if it has also preceded (i.e., it is represented twice; *n=at=ši=at,* etc.; examples in HW^2 sub -*a*-[2]).

Examples of the plural dat.-acc. pronoun followed by the pronoun -*a*-: *nu=šmaš=an karipten* Tel.pr. ii 73 (OH/NS); *linkiya=naš=at kattan kittaru* KBo 16.50:20–21 (oath of Ašḫapala, MH/MS); *nu=šmaš=at=kan piran ḫal=ziandu* Mşt 75/13:24–25 (MH/MS), ed. Alp, Belleten 44:45ff.; *ŠA* KUR-*TI=wa=naš=at išḫi*[*ul*] . . . KUB 14.1 obv. 86 (Madd., MH/MS); *nu=šmaš=a*[*t piran walluškitten*] KUB 23.68 + ABoT 58 obv. 17 (Išmerika treaty, MH); *nu=šmaš=at ḫanni* KUB 13.2 iii 32 (*BĒL MADGALTI,* MH/NS); *zik=a=š*[*ma*]*š=at mān paitti* EGIR-*pa me*[*mat*]*ti* Ḫuqq. iii 23, cf. ii 8; *nu=šmaš=at=kan anda ēppir* KBo 5.6 (DŠ frag. 28 A) i 20; *nu=šmaš=at* KUB 13.4 i 51, ii 68, iv 8, 22, 33, 46, 66 (instr., pre-NH/NS); *nu=šmaš=an uwatteni* EGIR-*zian arḫa šarratteni* ibid. iv 20; *našma=wa=naš=an uššaniyawen našma=war=an=kan waḫnumen* ibid. iv 73–74; *nu=šmaš=aš* LÚ*EMI=ŠUNU kuit* KUB 14.3 i 64; *nu=šmaš=at* KUB 13.3 iii 15 (NH), KBo 11.1 obv. 36 (Muw.), KBo 4.12 obv. 28 (Ḫatt. III); *nu=šmaš=at=kan* KUB 21.27+ iv 7 (Pud. prayer); *nu=šmaš=aš lē šekteni* KUB 21.42 iv 18 (instr., Tudḫ. IV); *nu=naš=aš karū* GIM-*an* ÌR-*DUM kulawanieš ē*[*šta k*]*inun=n*⟨*aš*⟩*=aš* (text: *ki-nu-na-aš*) *QĀTAMMA* ÌR *kulawanieš ēšdu* KUB 19.55 + KUB 48.90 rev. 45–46 (Milawata letter, 13th century), ed. Hoffner, AfO Beiheft 19 (1982) 131f.; *nu=šmaš=an* d*IŠTAR šarlaimmin šipanzakanzi* Ḫatt. iv. 74.

There is one possible example of -*naš* flanked by doubly written pron. -*a*-: *nu=war=an=naš=an anzel* ZI-*ni piyawen* KUB 13.4 iv 72–73. This cannot be read *nu=war=naš=an,* because there would be no reason for the *r* in -*war*-. It is also possible that one should read: *nu=war=an=naš=šan*. The only other exception is: *tet=war=at=naš iyaweni=war=at* "Tell it to us; we will do it" KUB 12.63 obv. 24 (OH/MS).

The conditions governing the position of the pl. dat.-acc. pron. (*-šmaš*, *-naš*) in the chain of introductory particles seem not to have changed from OH through the 13th century. The doubling of the pron. *-a-* before and after the sing. dat.-acc. pronouns, on the other hand, is a phenomenon which first appears in late NH.

BRIEF COMMENTS ON THE HITTITE CULT CALENDAR: THE OUTLINE OF THE AN.TAḪ.ŠUM FESTIVAL

PHILO H. J. HOUWINK TEN CATE

Amsterdam

1. In two highly important articles published in the Journal of Near Eastern Studies volumes 19 (1960) and 20 (1961) Professor Hans Gustav Güterbock, dedicatee of this volume and discoverer of the phenomenon of Outline Tablets, first published the Outline Tablet of the AN.TAḪ.ŠUM^{SAR} Festival of the spring.[1] Later, in his major review article on the reconstruction of the geography of the north-central area of Hittite Anatolia, he presented the evidence available at that time on the parallel Outline of the *nuntarriyašḫaš* Festival of the autumn.[2] These two articles will always remain exemplary for the manner in which the study of a specific festival should be undertaken. At that time thirty years had already passed since Güterbock published in 1930 a large group of festival texts in KUB 25 (Festrituale). While the subject of this contribution to a volume dedicated to him on the occasion of his seventy-fifth brithday may thus seem appropriate, since his work on this important and perhaps most numerous genre of Hittite texts now already spans more than half a century, the choice has its risks, too, for it will always remain his own special field.[3]

1. JNES 19 (1960) 80–89 and NHF 62–68.

2. JNES 20 (1961) 85–97 (review article on J. Garstang and O. R. Gurney, Geogr) and especially 90–92 together with notes 27–38.

3. Usually I ask Professor Güterbock for advice before attempting to formulate a final draft. Actually on this occasion I was fortunate enough to have asked his opinion in an initial phase and he helped me not only with bibliographical matters, but in response to a question about Bo 2438 also sent me a copy of his transliteration of it, inspired by a marginal note in Hans Ehelolf's personal copy of KUB 25, in which Ehelolf had noted at KUB 25.27 iii 9–16 and 14 that Bo 2438 iv 4′ff. and 8′ was relevant at both points. Afterwards I received permission from Professor Klengel to use Professor Güterbock's transliteration for this or any other publication. I am deeply indebted to both Professor Güterbock and Professor Klengel and hasten to add that Professor Klengel informed me that publication is foreseen for 1985 in KUB 55, currently under preparation by Dr. H. Freydank. [Ed.—now KUB 55.5]

2. I have two aims: first, following hints given by Güterbock, I should like to stress that the problem of the cult calendar needs to be placed in a historical perspective;[4] secondly, I should like to argue, again in his footsteps,[5] that in such a historically oriented approach three sources are likely to be particularly relevant, the two outlines CTH 604 and 626 I, as mentioned above, CTH 568, characterized by Laroche as a report on an inquiry about the manner in which a number of festivals should be celebrated, and CTH 629 = KUB 25.27, used by Güterbock in his editio princeps of the Outline of the AN.TAḪ.ŠUM^{SAR} Festival as in part parallel (copy S), although dealing with EZEN.MEŠ SAG.UŠ, 'the regular festivals'.

a. CTH 604:

A = KBo 10.20, even after the subsequent publication and recognition of additional pieces of B still by far the best preserved copy, certainly a 13th century copy and possibly even dating from the second half of that century. The copy may have been written from dictation. It is Güterbock's main manuscript in his text-edition.

B = KUB 30.39 + KBo 24.112 + KBo 23.80, a considerably older, presumably 14th century copy which, however, does not seem to have been the tablet underlying A's hyparchetype of an earlier period (see below sub 7).

C = KUB 10.94, a very small piece, which with respect to those lines for which it duplicates A and D resembles A instead of D. I do not dare to express an opinion on the date of the copy itself, but, as far as the contents go, it could be related to the same hyparchetype as A.[6]

D = 438/s, not yet published in text-copy, but mentioned in passing in Güterbock's treatment of the text in NHF, 62–68 and now available in transliteration and translation in Sedat Alp's recent book Tempel (TTKY VI/23) 146–149.

E = KUB 44.39, presented in transliteration by A. Margherita Jasink-Ticchioni in SCO 27 (1977) 183 n. 3.

In Güterbock's editio princeps, based on the recent find of KBo 10.20, the then available part of B (KUB 30.39) as well as C are fully incorporated. Fortunately the two more recent manuscripts D and E duplicate approximately the same parts of A, while C also overlaps a part of the Outline, as

4. JNES 20 (1961) 91–92 and especially NHF 63: "Da einige der Einzelrituale in Ausfertigungen Tudḫaliyas IV. vorliegen, ist es möglich dass ihm auch eine Revision der Gesamtverlaufe zuzuschreiben ist, doch sind die erhaltenen Übersichtstafeln leider undatiert." See, too, below sub 7 together with notes 34–36.

5. See below b and c notes 11 and 15.

6. Only C ii 2′ may now also be restored after D ii 9′ (SAL.LUGAL-*ma-kán I-NA* É.SAL.LUGAL AN.TAḪ.ŠUM^{SAR} *da-a-i*), but even this is at most a theoretical possibility.

given by A and D. This offers an opportunity to study the relationship between the various copies as far as their factual contents are concerned (see below sub 5).

b. CTH 568:

A = ABoT 14 + KBo 24.118 (= 515/b + 413/c + 2380/c).

B = KUB 22.27 (cf. Laroche, RA 42 [1948] 216).

C = VBoT 131 (cf. Laroche, CTH 568; formerly D, but the earlier C = 515/b, quoted by Otten, FsFriedrich 358–359 has since then in combination with other pieces been joined by Otten to ABoT 14).

D = KBo 24.119 (= 91/b, formerly E), first mentioned by Otten, BiOr 8 (1951) 229.

E = JCS 24 (1972), 176 n° 78 (cf. Laroche, CTH Premier Supplément, RHA XXX [1972], 114 n° 568).

F = KUB 50.82 (see Archi, Inhaltsübersicht, V).

G = KUB 50.32, H = KUB 50.33 and I = KUB 50.34 (each of these new duplicates may form part of copy B).

J = 239/f (first mentioned by Otten, BiOr 8 [1951] 229; Otten quoted a line from the tablet in ZA 53 [1959] 182, which shows another example of EZEN *ḫad/tauri* for the composition. It must belong in the first part which ends at B I 31′).

K = KBo 30.22 (= 2001/f, mentioned by Singer, StBoT 27:134f. as duplicating A iii 5–19).

L = KBo 30.23 (= Bo 69/101, cf. Singer, StBoT 27:134f.; it duplicates A iii 7–10).

As far as the format of the copies is concerned, there is a marked difference between A, which shows three columns on obverse and reverse, and B, which has only two columns on each side. The result is that one line of B equals approximately two lines of A. In this respect copy D agrees with A, while copies C, G–I and presumably also K seem to have a line-width comparable to that of B. F needs more lines than B and fewer lines than A for the same amount of text. E, probably a very late copy, is too small to be judged in this respect. Moreover, I do not yet know where it belongs; mentioning again a *ḫad/tauri* Festival, it probably duplicates a part of the text before B i 31′ (in the gap between A i 20′ and B i 1′). The beginning of the composite text can be restored as follows: (1) KUB 50.33 (= H) i 1–15 (over ll. 9–14 duplicated by A + i 2′–9′), followed by A i 10′–21′: beginning of the treatment of the *ḫad/tauri* Festivals of the spring and the autumn; (2) gap where E and J may possibly belong; (3) B i 1′–31′ (over ll. 6′–18′ duplicated by A ii 1–27 and over ll. 26′–31′ by D iii 1–10); (4) B i 32′ = D iii 11–13: end of the treatment of the *ḫad/tauri* festivals of the spring and the autumn. After a treatment of festivals of the presumably early autumn, beginning with the

KI.LAM Festival,[6A] the latter part and certainly more than a fourth part of the whole text deals with journeys and "side-trips" of the Divine Fleece or Shield, i.e., often clearly Zitḫariya.[7] The long passage referred to in the "note," added to the colophon of both copies A and B of the AN.TAḪ. ŠUM^{SAR} Outline, could have formed the beginning of this second major subject of the oracle inquiry.[8] As set forth sub 4, the treatment of the *ḫad/ tauri* festivals of the spring (and the autumn) links the oracle inquiry to the AN.TAḪ.ŠUM^{SAR} Outline. Clear references to events taking place during the *nuntarriyašḫaš* Festival and in winter-time with regard to Zitḫariya are to be found in the last part of the text. The most important of these is the separate journey of Zitḫariya, as described in the main recension of the Outline Tablets of the *nuntarriyašḫaš* Festival, (CTH 626 I) copies A and B as well as in the oracle inquiry.[9] Professor Güterbock, elaborating on earlier remarks made by Goetze and Otten, interpreted the version of CTH 568 as a variant of the "side-trip" of the god, as described in the Outline. I wonder whether the two may not be reconciled by translating (CTH 626 I A) KUB 9.16 i 9–11

6A. [Ed.: This would be the only evidence for the date of the KI.LAM Festival. Cf. I. Singer, StBoT 27 (1983) 132–5, who interprets ABoT 14 differently.]

7. The remainder of the text, which will be dealt with more fully elsewhere, can be restored as follows: B i 33′–34′ = D iii 14–17, followed by D iii 18 = KUB 50.34 (= I)ii 1, KUB 50.34 ii 2–5 = A iii 1–7, A iii 8–24 (over lines 8–9 duplicated by KUB 50.34 ii 6 and over lines 22–24 by C: 2′–3′; see, too, above sub K and L) followed by C: 4′–9′; gap; KUB 50.32 (= G) ii 1′–iii 1 (duplicated over lines ii 4′–iii 1 by A iv 1′–4′), followed by A iv 5′–27′ (duplicated over lines 5′–20′ by KUB 50.32 iii 2–10) and possibly continued by KBo 24.119 (= D) iv 1′–5′; gap; B iii 13′–19′ (practically useless); gap; B iii 26′–44′ (over lines 40′–44′ duplicated by A v 2′–11′), followed by A v 12′–20′; gap (?); B iv 1–41 (duplicated over lines 22–39 by A vi 3′–30′ and over lines 22–36 by KUB 50.82 (= F): 1′–18′); end missing.

8. A minor indication in favour of the conjectural hypothesis that Zitḫariya' separate journey during the Festival of the Spring would have been dealt with in the oracle inquiry may perhaps be found in the vague similarity between CTH 629 = KUB 25.27 i 1′–4′ (for this tablet 2nd day of the AN.TAḪ.ŠUM^{SAR} Festival) and B iii 30′–32′, as well as between ibidem i 25′–27′ (6th day) and B iii 33′–35′, ibidem i 28′–32′ (8th day) and B iii 36′–39′, but I confess that this similarity may be misleading. Perhaps it is safer to surmise that the long passage referred to in the "note" added to the colophon of the copies A and B (see below sub 4) would have occurred somewhere in the very badly preserved earlier parts of B iii (= the missing beginning of A v ?).

9. After the visit of Zitḫariya to his own temple in Ḫattuša before his separate journey during the *nuntarriyašḫaš* Festival (2nd day according to [CTH 626 i A] KUB 9.16 i 4–6 = (B) 34/t + KBo 3.25 + KUB 10.48 i 4–5) has been alluded to in A v 12′–20′ and at least one other 'secondary Festival,' possibly not mentioned in the Outline Tablets, has been referred to in the broken passage B iv 1–3, his separate journey is described in B iv 4–13 and more vaguely alluded to in iv 14–17.

= (B) 34/t + KBo 3.25 + KUB 10.48 i 8–9 as follows: "Zitḫari[ya] goes to Ḫakmara/Ḫakkura, but he goes out to Tatašuna."[10]

It should be mentioned at this point that CTH 568 twice refers to an "earlier" or "former" tablet of presumably similar contents: once it seems to say that this tablet was unclear in its wording (see below sub 4), while the second time it mentions that it maintains a regulation, as set forth in the former tablet.[11] Finally, it was clearly considered an important text, since it is an oracle text which has been preserved in a surprisingly large number of copies.

c. CTH 629 = KUB 25.27:

This short text, which is poorly preserved, deals according to the colophon with the manner in which, "when the king celebrates the 'regular festivals'," these must be performed *šakuwaššar(a)-*, "correct" or "complete"(?). In this respect the main emphasis lies on the party responsible for the goods, the food and the drink, to be used in their performance. In addition to governmental agencies, specific institutions ("houses"), connected with various types of personnel, apparently were made responsible for certain 'regular festivals.'[12] Up to a point the type of tablet represented by KUB 25.27 may be said to reflect the results of an oracle inquiry like CTH 568, since that text also deals with the question of cult deliveries. But insofar as the Outline Tablets have the character of a cult inventory as well as that of an outline,[13] these likewise show connections with texts like CTH 568 and 629. As far as the contents of KUB 25.27 are concerned, one may now conclude that, while from its specific point of view the first part of the text deals with 'days,' known from the Outline of the AN.TAḪ.ŠUM^{SAR} Festival (i 1′–32′ offers material for the second up to the seventh day of the festival), the latter part

10. Cf. Güterbock, JNES 20 (1961) 90–91; for the proposal to emend *Ḫakmara* into *Ḫakkura*, see Otten, RlA 4/1 (1972) 49 and del Monte, RGTC 6: 67–68; the passage reads [9]. . . [(^{d}*Zi-it-ḫa-ri*)*-i̯a-a*] [10]^{URU}*Ḫa-ak-ma/ku-ra pa-iz-zi pa-ra-a-m*[(*a-aš*)] [11]^{URU}*Ta-ta-šu-na pa-iz-zi* UD.3 [.KAM]; see Zuntz, Ortsadv., 63–64 for the meaning "hinausgehen" in addition to "weitergehen." Copy B of CTH 568 (KUB 22.27) was first used by Goetze on account of its geographical implications in an article devoted to "The Roads of Northern Cappadocia," RHA XV/61 (1957) 91–103, in which Goetze took his starting-point from the itinerary of the *nuntarriyašḫaš* Festival, one would now say from the Outline of that Festival (ibid. 90f. 100 n. 13). It was mentioned by Otten, FsFriedrich 356 and 358–359 regarding its relevance for the cultic journeys of ^{d}*kurša-*, the Divine Fleece or Shield. Finally Professor Güterbock defined its proper framework when he both related it to and contrasted it with the Outline Tablets of the *nuntarriyašḫaš* Festival in JNES 20 (1961) 90–92 and NHF 68.

11. *an-na-la-az* [19]*tup-pí-an-za QA-TAM-MA i-i̯a-an* (A iii 18–19), cf. Laroche, RHA XI/52 (1950) 40 and Singer, StBoT 27:135.

12. Cf. Archi, OA 12 (1973) 209–226, especially 217–226.

13. Cf. Güterbock, JNES 19 (1960) 87.

of the text and especially iii 9–16 may be compared with 'days' of the *nun=tarriyašḫaš* Festival (the text spreads over three days celebrations mentioned in the Outline Tablets IBoT 2.8 iv$^{?}$ 4′–8′ = Bo 2438 iv 6′–10′ for two, namely the sixteenth and seventeenth days of the festival).[14] The tablet thus deals with 'regular festivals' which were celebrated throughout a whole calendar year from spring to spring.

3. The evidence of CTH 568 would seem to corroborate Güterbock's inference from CTH 629 (NHF 64) that there were 'secondary festivals' or subsidiary ceremonies during both festivals. Not all of them were necessarily mentioned in the concise descriptions of the Outline Tablets. To my mind this category could encompass the *ḫad/tauri* festivals, as mentioned not only in the Outline Tablets of the AN.TAḪ.ŠUM^{SAR} Festival (no less than five examples, see below sub 4), but also preserved for the *nuntarriyašḫaš* festival (one example so far; cf. KBo 14.76 i 7′–8′ = KBo 22.228: 8′–10′: it is performed in the temple of the Stormgod by a prince or a bodyguard sent for that purpose by the king on the ninth day of the festival in question).[15] I should also like to place in this category the visits of Zitḫariya to his own temple (in Ḫattuša) before his "side-trips" during the festivals of the spring and the autumn.[16] Possibly in particular these "secondary festivals" or subsidiary ceremonies were liable to be shifted to a different day in the schedule: Professor Güterbock already discerned that according to KUB 25.27 i 9′–11′

14. It appears from a marginal note in Professor Ehelolf's personal copy of KUB 25 that Ehelolf had already discerned the similarity between KUB 25.27 iii 9–16 and Bo 2438 iv 4′–10′ (see note 3). As has been remarked above, Professor Güterbock recognized the relevance of i 1′–32′ for the AN.TAḪ.ŠUM^{SAR} Festival. Passages of Bo 2438 iv have been quoted in recent years by Professor Otten, StBoT 15: 9 and 20 and by Starke, ZA 69 (1979) 110 n. 151. Laroche was the first to recognize in Bo 2438 an Outline Tablet of the *nuntarriyašḫaš* Festival (CTH Premier Supplément, RHA XXX [1972] 115, nº 626), while it has been used as such by Košak, Linguistica 16 (1976) 55–64.

15. $^{7'}$[(*I-NA* É ^{d}IM-*ma* LUGAL-*uš*) *m*]*a-a-an* DUMU.LUGAL [*m*]*a-a-an* ^{LÚ}*ME-ŠE-DI* $^{8'}$[(*u-i-ia-zi nu* EZEN) *ha-t*]*a-ú-ri* [*i*(*-ia*)]-*zi*.

16. These visits clearly were 'secondary Festivals': in respect to the AN.TAḪ.ŠUM^{SAR} Festival it is not mentioned in the summary description of the 2nd day in A i 19–23 = B obv. 14–17, although the "note" (see below sub 4) refers to it. This also happens in the tablets describing the day in question, which, moreover, allude to the oracle inquiry: KUB 10.17 ii 5′–8′ (= KUB 10.18 ii 7–9) $^{5'}$*nu ki-iš-ša-an ḫa-an-da-it*[*-ta-at*] $^{6'}$*nu* ^{d}*Zi-it-ḫa-ri-ia-aš* $^{7'}$*A-NA* EZEN AN.TAḪ.ŠUM^{SAR} *I-NA* É-*ŠU i-ia-at-ta-ri*. Apparently the same procedure was followed during the *nuntarriyašḫaš* Festival: (CTH 626 i A) KUB 9.16 i 4–5 = (B) 34/t + i 4–5 should be restored as ^{4}*lu-uk-kat-ti-ma* ^{d}*Zi-it-ḫa-ri-ia-aš I-NA* É[*-ŠU*] ^{5}*pa-iz-zi*, cf. (CTH 568) A v 12′–14′, $^{12'd}$UTU-*ŠI-ma ku-ua-pí* $^{14'}$*la-aḫ-ḫa-az ne-ia-ri* $^{13'}$*nu* ^{d}*Zi-it-ḫa-ri-ia-an ku-ua-pí* $^{14'}$*I-NA* É-*ŠU tar-na-an-zi*. Both the parallelism as such and the reference to the oracle inquiry strengthen the case for the unity between CTH 604, 626 i and 568. There are more examples which prove that the redaction of the tablets for the individual days is related to the Outline or vice versa.

the *ḫad/tauri* Festival in the temple of Zababa took place on the 4th instead of on the 16th or 15th day of the festival (cf. JNES 19 [1960] 82 n. 20 and below sub 4 and 6), and according to KUB 25.27 i 14′–19′(?) the *ḫad/tauri* Festival in the temple of the Sungod(dess) on the 5th instead of on the 12th or on the 11th day of the festival in question (cf. JNES 19 [1960] 82 n. 18 and below sub 4 and 6). These remarks are partly based on my admittedly tentative restoration of the first "transition" of CTH 568 when the text begins to deal with festivals presumably of the early autumn: "[This] *ḫad/tauri* Festival one performs in the autumn (and) in the spring. When [His Majesty] celebrates the festivals of the autumn, the festivals which one (then) begins to [perfor]m for His Majesty, in each [year in which His Majesty] celebrates the festivals, they shall perform [those festival]s strictly correctly (complete?), while one shall not make up for them at a later moment."[17]

4. The previous subsections devote so much attention to the possible relationship of CTH 568 to the Outline Tablets of both the AN.TAḪ.ŠUM^{SAR} and the *nuntarriyašḫaš* Festivals mainly because the beginning of CTH 568 seems to refer to precisely the oracle investigation which is mentioned in (CTH 604 A) KBo 10.20 ii 18–24, 34–39, 43–51; iii 14–18. Unfortunately the passages in question are to be found in the middle part of this Outline Tablet, which has not yet been recovered for the older copy B. This is the more unfortunate since both copies A and B refer in the "note" attached to the colophon to either the same or an earlier oracle inquiry. The wording of the colophon is highly remarkable in its own right, since it remarks that the tablet records "how the Festivals of the AN.TAḪ.ŠUM^{SAR} are performed for the first time."[18] This vaguely suggests that both copies describe, to use an irreverent expression, a "first performance," which is likely to have needed royal authorization. After the totals of the days involved, 35 (B) and 38 (A), the latter according to Professor Güterbock's beautiful text-restoration based on a computation of the days treated after the 22nd day (A iii 25), the colophon of both copies continues with "(being the days) which they devote to the festivals of the AN.TAḪ.ŠUM^{SAR}." Perhaps one

17. Cf. KBo 24.119 (= D) iii 11–18 (duplicated over lines 11–16 by B i 32′–34′ and for line 18 by KUB 50.34 [= I] ii 1), followed by KUB 50.34 ii 2–3 (duplicated over lines 2–3 by A iii 1–4); restorations between parentheses inside the square brackets are derived from the duplicates; I maintained D's line-numbering for the missing part of the tablet; for the free restorations see A iii 8–15: [11][*ki-i(-ma* EZ)]EN *ḫa-da-u-ri* [12][(*zé-e-na-an-t*)]*i ḫa-me-eš-ḫa-an-ti* [13][(*e-eš-ša-an-z*)]*i* [14][^{d}UTU-*ŠI(-za ku-ṷa-pí* EZ)]EN.ḪI.A [15][(*zé-e-na-an-da-aš i*)]*-i̯a-zi* [16][(*nu* EZEN.ḪI.A *ku-e-uš A-N*)]*A* ^{d}UTU-*ŠI* [17][*e-eš-šu-u-ṷa*]*-an ti-an-zi* [18][*nu-za* ^{d}UTU-*ŠI* (EZEN.ḪI.A *ma-ši-i̯a-a*)]*n-di* [19][MU.KAM*-ti i-i̯a-zi a-pu-u-uš-ma* EZEN(.ḪI.A)] [20][(*ša-ku-ṷa-aš-ša-ru-uš-pát e-eš-ša-an-zi*)] [21][(*Ú-UL-aš-kán ḫa-pu-ša-an-z)i*]. [Ed.: Cf. CHD sub *mašiyant-*.]

18. Cf. Güterbock, JNES 19 (1960) 84–85 and 87.

may even translate *an-da ḫa-an-da-a-an-zi,* as used in this passage, as "(being the days) which they arrange" or "subsume" to the Festivals of AN.TAḪ.ŠUM^SAR^. I feel tempted to conclude that in the course of redactional work festival days were grouped and perhaps regrouped differently from an older tradition. The difference between 35 (B) and 38 (A) days does strengthen the likelihood that this may have happened. Then follows the "note": "To remember: for the AN.TAḪ.ŠUM^SAR^ Festival of Zitḫariya one goes to his own temple (that is) to his own temple (in Ḫattuša). The wording that was determined is too long (var.: It was thus determined by the god; the wording is too long)."[19]

These four *ḫad/tauri*-passages in A are rather uniform. I shall quote the first in Güterbock's translation; in each of the four examples in which the oracle inquiry is referred to, an adversative *-ma* indicates that the celebration may have had the character of a "secondary festival," as described above sub 3; a last and fifth example of a *ḫad/tauri* Festival in A (iii 19–22) is slightly different itself (see below), but in this respect identical: "(But in the temple of the Sungod(dess) they perform the *ḫad/tauri* Festival.) (18) They slaughter [ten] sheep. (19) [And] they take the meat and cook it (20) [and] put it before the deity. A[ll] the sheep (21) they take back [t]o the palace, (22) but [one] sheep they leave in the temple. Just as the singer (23) and the bodyguard have set up (the cups) in the temple of the Stormgod, in the same way (24) they set (them) up i[n the temple of the Sungod(dess)]; thus [it was determined] by the deity."[20] In each case the god and thus the temple referred to differs, first the temple of the Sungod(dess) (ii 18–24; 12th—or perhaps 11th day, see below sub 6), the temple of Zababa (ii 34–39; 16th or 15th day; actually the name of the festival is broken off, but Güterbock, JNES 19:82 n. 20, restored it after S i 9′–10′), the temple of the Stormgod (ii 43–52; 17th or 16th day) and finally the temple of the Protective Deity (iii 14–18; 20th day). It is of importance to note that practically all the key words of the first passage recur in the beginning of the oracle inquiry: *ḫuek-, šuppa da-, dala-/dali(ia)-,* ^LÚ^NAR, ^LÚ^*MEŠEDI*. In the first line reference is made to the fact that this inquiry takes place, "because the EZEN *ḫad/tauri* [is being] chan[ged] with respect to (lit.: away from) the tablet," adding, as I understand it, that on the tablet mention had been made of ten sheep (followed by a quotation), but that "it [contained no instructions (?)] (on the manner in which) the eating and the setting up (or: the providing for) of the cups" was to be arranged, i.e. that it did not make clear who had to take care of the necessary provisions. Then follows the first question: "Shall they offer those

19. See above sub 3 note 16.
20. Cf. Güterbock, JNES 19 (1960) 82, 86.

nine sheep to the Stormgod, [and shall they] of[fer] one [sheep to Šerri] and to Ḫurri?" After a broken passage which mentions the bodyguard and the singer, the inquiry continues: "[Of those sheep] which they slaught[er] shall they take the meat from all of them [and] shall they assign [it to the palace], but shall they leave (behind) one sheep?"[21]

In the continuation of the Outline Tablet follows one last reference to a *ḫad/tauri* Festival, this time without quotations from the oracle inquiry: (19) "Next day ⟨(the king [go]es)⟩ [t]o the temple of the Stormgod of Aleppo. [(But)] in the temple of the [(Mother)] Goddess (20–21) they perform the *ḫad/tauri* Festival for Ka[tta]ḫḫa, Nergal, Ḫašameli and [(Ea)], (22) and they offer ten sheep in (each?) temple."[22] Perhaps a few additional remarks may be made. Assuming of course that the two texts have rightly been compared with one another, it may be of importance to note that, after an unfavourable answer has been received on the generally formulated question, "Shall the *ḫad/tauri* Festival be performed for [a]ll those temples, for which it takes place, in the same manner as they performed it in the temple of the Stormgod for (this) temple?",[23] CTH 568 starts out its investigations more in detail with the one in respect to the temple of the Protective Deity (A i 21′) and that after the first gap in the text "the small (?) temples of Šulinkatti and Ḫašam(m)eli (É.MEŠ DINGIR.MEŠ-*i̯a ku-e* TUR-*RU-TI ŠA* ^{d}*Šu-li-in-kat-ti Ù ŠA* ^{d}*Ḫa-ša-*

21. See KUB 50.33 (= H) i 1–11 (restorations between parentheses inside the square brackets are derived from the duplicate A i 1′–6′ = H i 9–15): ^{1}EZEN *ḫa-ta-u-ri ku-it IŠ-TU ṬUP-PÍ ú-e-e*[*ḫ-ta-ri* . . .] ^{2}*nu-kán A-NA ṬUP-PÍ* 10 UDU *i-i̯a-an* 10 UDU-*u̯a-kán* [. . .] ^{3}*a-da-tar-ma* GAL.ḪI.A *aš-nu-mar Ú-UL ku-it-ki* [. . .] ^{4}*u-ni* 9 UDU *A-NA* ^{d}U *ši-pa-an-da-an-zi* 1 [UDU-*ma A-NA* ^{GUD}*Še-er-ri*] ^{5}*Ù A-NA* ^{GUD}*Ḫu-ur-ri ši-pa-a*[*n-da-an-zi* . . .] ^{6} ^{m}*Ša-pu-ḫa*-LÚ-*iš ma-aḫ-ḫa-an* x[. . .] ^{7}*AŠ-RA* ^{LÚ}*ME-ŠE-DI ku-in IŠ-T*[*U* . . .] ^{8} ^{LÚ}NAR-*ma iš-ḫa-mi-iš*[*-ki-u-u̯a-an* . . . *ma-aḫ-ḫa-an*] ^{9}*zi-in-na-i a-pa-a-aš-ma* [. . . 10 UDU.ḪI.A *ku*(*-i-e-eš ḫu-u-k*)*án-zi*] ^{10}*nu ḫu-u-ma-an-da-aš š*[(*u-up-pa da-an-zi*) 9 UDU.ḪI.A *I/A-NA* É.GAL-*LIM* (*ma-ni-i̯a-aḫ-ḫa-an-zi*)] ^{11}1 UDU-*ma-kán da-li-i̯*[(*a-an-zi* DINGIR)-*LUM-za QA-TAM-M*(*A ma-la*)*-a*(*-an ḫar-ti*)]. With respect to *aššanu-/ašnušk-* see A ii 21–26 (= B i 16′–18′) ^{21}*nu* EZEN *ḫa-da-u-ri I-NA* É ^{d}U ^{22}*ma-aḫ-ḫa-an i-e-er* ^{23} ^{LÚ}*ME-ŠE-TUM-i̯a-kán* ^{LÚ}NAR-*i̯a* ^{24}*ma-aḫ-ḫa-an aš-nu-uš-kán-zi* ^{25}*I-NA* É ^{d}*Ka-taḫ-ḫa-i̯a-an-kán* ^{26}*QA-TAM-MA aš-nu-u̯a-an-zi,* as compared with (CTH 604) A iii 17–18, ^{17} ^{LÚ}NAR-*i̯a-kán* ^{LÚ}*ME-ŠE-DI I-NA* É ^{d}U GIM-*an* ^{18}*aš-ša-nu-e-er I-NA* É ^{d}LAMMA-*i̯a-kán QA-TAM-MA aš-ša*[*-nu-u̯a-an-zi*] (see A i 21′ for É ^{d}LAMMA-*i̯*[*a-an* in the oracle inquiry).

22. A iii 19–22, as restored after D iii 8′–11′ and E iii 7′–10′; 21st day; the last sentence occurs in both A iii 22 and D iii 11′ (see now Alp, Tempel 148–149); cf. Güterbock, JNES 19 (1960) 83, 86; all the necessary adjustments were made by Güterbock, NHF 65.

23. Cf. A i 10–16: $^{10'}$*I-NA* É ^{d}IM *ma-aḫ-ḫa-an* EZ[E]N *ḫa-da-u-ri* $^{11'}$*i-e-er nam-ma-i̯a ku-e* É[.MEŠ] DINGIR.MEŠ $^{12'}$EZEN *ḫa-da-u-ri-iš ku-e-da-aš A-N*[*A*] É.MEŠ DINGIR.MEŠ $^{13'}$*i-i̯a-an-za na-an A-NA* É ^{d}U *m*[*a-aḫ-ḫa*]*-an* $^{14'}$[*i*]*-e-er a-pé-e-da-aš-ša-an A-NA* É[.MEŠ DINGIR.M]EŠ $^{15'}$[*ḫu-u*]*-ma-an-da-aš QA-TAM-MA i-i̯a-a*[*n-zi*] $^{16'}$[DINGIR-*LIM*]*-za QA-TAM-MA ma-la-an ḫar-ti*.

am-mi-li in B i 9′–10′ = A ii 8–10)[24] and the temple of Kattaḫḫa are the subject of the inquiry. It is certainly possible that Šuli(n)katti takes the place of Nergal in the Outline Tablet.[25] Again in the last passage, in which it seems to paraphrase the results of the oracle inquiry without actually referring to it (iii 14–18), A mentions the singer and the bodyguard, presumably a high-ranking one, since in the third passage (ii 43–51) a prince takes his place, and the temple of the Stormgod. For this fourth example D iii 6′–7′ only says: "But [(in)] the temple of the Protective Deity they perform the *ḫad/tauri* Festival. They slaughter [(ten)] sheep." It clearly is a later and abridged version. On the basis of both CTH 604 A and CTH 568 an oracle question in respect of the proceedings in the temple of the Stormgod must have formed the starting-point of the investigation, but there is no complete correspondence, since the Outline Tablet refers in its third passage with regard to the temple of the Stormgod to a prince instead of to a bodyguard. In this respect the *ḫad/tauri* Festival mentioned by two Outline Tablets of the *nuntarri=yašḫaš* Festival fits somewhat better. It leaves at least one choice between a prince and a bodyguard (see above sub 3 together with note 16). But this resemblance is counterbalanced by the fact that the text-restorations ^{LÚ}NA]R-*ma-az* SÌR-*ki-iz-zi* (A ii 49) and *zi-e*]*n-na-i* (A ii 50) would reinforce the connections between A ii 43–51 and the beginning of the oracle inquiry, rendering it more likely that the 17th or 16th day of the AN.TAḪ.ŠUM^{SAR} Outline formed the starting-point for the oracle inquiry. The most important point, possibly to be derived from a fully proven identity in background, rests on the fact that, since CTH 568 deals with events from both the spring and the autumn festivals, the modernization or the renewal of the cult calendar, to which it seems to be related, must have affected both festivals. This would seem to indicate that the evidence for Muršili II's role with respect to the *nuntarriyašḫaš* Festival, as put forward by Professor Güterbock, would also be valid for the AN.TAḪ.ŠUM^{SAR} Festival of the spring, this under the proviso that the description of Zitḫariya's "side-trip" in CTH 568 may be reconciled with the relevant evidence of the Outline Tablets of the festival of the autumn (see above sub 2 together with note 10).

5. Concentrating my remarks in this subsection on a comparison of the factual contents of the various copies, I should like to offer the following comments. In view of the fact that B obv. 23 mentions the preparatory measure "A[nd] the palace-intendant of the palace of (or: at) the right side pre-

24. But see, too, B i 21′–31′ where their temples are mentioned again without such an epithet.

25. Cf. Güterbock in Bittel, Yaz² 176 together with the literature referred to in note 42: Šulinkatti is the Hattian equivalent of ^{d}U.GUR = Nergal, the Babylonian god of war and plague.

sent[s] [the storage vessel of the Stormgod of Zi]ppalanda" (see, too, A i 30–31),[26] it certainly is striking that the opening of the vessel is not mentioned in B obv. 24–29, this in contrast to the passage A i 37–39 where the day as such is stressed by the addition of the particle *-pat* (i 39). I feel inclined to interpret this as a second indication that B does not yet represent the final version of its redaction (see my earlier remark on the colophon sub 4). With respect to the rather obscure distinction between what happens on the 6th and on the 7th day, E's main contribution is, at least if one accepts the highly likely text-restoration *[lu-uk-kat-t]i-ma* for E ii 4′ as proposed by A. Margherita Jasink Ticchioni, SCO 27 (1977) 183 n. 3, that it corroborates what Güterbock surmised, namely that the visit of the king and the queen (B obv. 30 and A i 44, this in contrast to E ii 4′ and S i 28′ which only refer to the king) to the temple of the Sungod(dess) in Ḫattuša took place early in the morning of a new day, before the king left for Arinna by way of Matella, cf. Güterbock, NHF 64. Consequently one may now read B obv. 24–29 and presumably A i 32–43 as well as the description of one single day. In the abridged version of the Outline represented by E and D the order of A's components in i 37–43 has apparently been changed, but E ii 1′–3′ refers to both the preparations for the consecutive days and the opening of the storage vessel of the Stormgod (of Zippalanda?).[27] And, what is actually more important, D iii 12′–16′ reflects an important editorial change, cf. Güterbock, NHF 65: instead of referring to the *mugauwar* of Ištar of Ḫattarina (CTH 615), on three consecutive days, 22nd–24th days, after which follow offerings to the same Ištar on the following days), D seems to refer to CTH 617. A first offering to the Goddess or spring Kalim(m)a is in fact already mentioned for the 20th day by D iii 5′ and E iii 4′. In combination with the fact that Alp's presentation of D has made it abundantly clear that in general E ii 7′–12′ and iii 1′–10′ may be restored after D ii 2′–8′ and iii 3′–11′ respectively, this results in a secure chronological ordering of the various copies as far as their factual contents are concerned: B precedes A (and C), while D and E follow on A.

6. A's "And for three days they perform a Festival" (A i 40) may now be taken to apply to the passage i 44 up to ii 10, to the three days described in

26. $^{\mathrm{L[\acute{U}]}}$*A-BU-BI-DU* ZAG-*aš-š[a* ^{DUG}*ḫar-ši ŠA* ^{d}U ^{URU}*Zi-i]p-pa-la-an-da* ⸢*ḫi*!⸣-⸢*ik*⸣-*z[i]* (^{DUG}*ḫar-ši* instead of ^{DUG}*ḫar-ši-i̯a-al-li*, A i [30] after i 38, for reasons of space; the restoration of the verbal form in A i 31 is even more problematical).

27. I wonder whether one could read and restore A i 40–41 as follows: ^{40}[*nu*] *I-NA* UD.3.KAM EZEN *e-eš-ša-an-zi* 8 GUD.ḪI.A.ŠE$^{?}$7$^{?}$ UDU.ḪI.A ^{41}[*ḫal*]-⸢*ku*⸣-⸢*e*⸣-⸢*eš*⸣-⸢*šar*⸣ *ŠA* É.GAL $^{\mathrm{L\acute{U}}}$*A-BU-BI-TI-pát da-aš-kán-zi*. The reading at the end of line 40 would be based on the first legible signs of E ii 1 (ŠE 7 UDU).

i 44–ii 4 (7th day), ii 5–7 (8th day) and ii 8–10 (9th day) respectively, which include the highlights of the proceedings in Matella, Arinna and Ḫattuša.[28] Thus it becomes advisable to emend UD.10.KAM in A ii 10 to UD.9.KAM. This emendation is desirable in any case, since the full recognition of the third *ḫad/tauri*-passage, which again refers to the oracle inquiry, makes it highly likely that an extra day should be added for A iii 1–3: the description of the preceding day ends with *ḫandaittat* (actually *-at* at the end of the line is preserved), as also happens in ii 24 (restored by Professor Güterbock) and in ii 39. In the fourth *ḫad/tauri*-passage the scribe omitted the reference to the oracle inquiry, although he paraphrased its results (A iii 14–18; see, too, above note 21). Reckoning backwards from the 22nd day in A iii 25, an extra 17th day should be added for A iii 1–3, while I should like to propose that the day-numbers between ii 5 and ii 51 (days 9–17) should all be lowered by one. A i 40–43 should be explained, I believe, as an example of what also happens elsewhere in both outlines: at the end of the description of a day the preparations for later events are recorded.[29]

7. In NHF 66 note 55 Professor Güterbock proposed emending ^{D}U ^{URU}*Ḫur-ša-an-na-aš-ši-in-na mu-u-ga-an-zi,* as partly preserved in A iii 43 and 45, to ^{D}U *ḫar-ša-an-na-aš-ši-in-na mu-u-ga-an-zi* on account of D ii 7′ (= E ii 12′) and D ii 11′. As a mistake it indicates in my opinion that at least this part of A was written from dictation, since the scribe actually must have thought that the derivative was built on one of the place-names, mentioned under the heading Ḫuršanaša in del Monte, RGTC 6: 128–129. There are more indications that the text was dictated: twice A interchanges the sequence of words, as given by B (i 20, as compared with B obv. 15 and iv 12–13, as different from B rev. 7′); in i 22 LUGAL-*uš* of B obv. 16 is lacking and in iii 19 LUGAL-*uš* and *pa-iz-zi,* as compared with D iii 8′–9′. In view of A's sign forms I should like to suggest that this dictation of A from an older hyparchetype may very well have taken place at a comparatively late date in

28. In all likelihood the 8th day on which the king "placed" the AN.TAḪ.ŠUM^{SAR} in Arinna while the queen did the same in the É.SAL.LUGAL in Ḫattuša was the most important of these days. The parallelism to the description of the 5th day of the *nuntarriyašḫaš* Festival is very striking: both days mention the main activity, from which the Festival of the Spring even derives its name, and in both cases the king and the queen officiate separately, in the spring in Arinna and Ḫattuša, in the autumn in Arinna and Taḫurpa, cf. Güterbock, NHF 68–69; Hoffner, AlHeth 49 n. 237, where the expressions as such for both festivals (*tai-/tiịa-* instead of *da-*) are explained; Košak, Linguistica 16 (1976) 57. Also this parallelism strengthens the unity of conception alluded to in note 16.

29. See with respect to the AN.TAḪ.ŠUM^{SAR} Festival A i 30–31 = B obv. 23 (note 26); B obv. 28–29 (actually a part of A i 40–43, thus offering a third indication that B does not yet represent the final version of its redaction); A ii 28–29, cf. Gurney, Schweich 35–36.

the 13th century, probably in its second half.[30] In respect to such a late date for the actual copy it may be useful to note that after one example of the old form (i 15) *li* is always written with the young form of that sign. With regard to other distinctive signs (*ik*/GÁL, KÙ, URU and to some extent also *šar* and *Ù*) copy A usually shows the youngest forms. In respect to *šar* and *Ù* some young forms, not always the youngest forms of the sign in question, may be encountered. As far as the usage of the syllabary is concerned, it may be mentioned that, while B consistently gives a syllabic Hittite rendering of the place-name ^{URU}*Ḫattuša-*, A, which starts out with such syllabic renderings (i 3, 4, 18 and 22), later uses ^{URU}KÙ.BABBAR-*ši* (ii 3, 6 and 8) and ^{URU}KÙ.BABBAR-*TI* (ii 15). All this displays a marked contrast to B, which in every respect is written like texts which stem from the first and second decade of the reign of Muršili II, KUB 14.4, KBo 4.8 (+), KUB 36.81, KUB 48.106 and KUB 31.121 (+ 121 a) + KUB 48.111. Moreover, I believe that from a linguistic point of view copy B is likely to be older, or rather is likely to preserve more old material than A, or rather A's hyparchetype. Instead of *lukkatti* or even *luk(k)at,* B consistently uses *lukkatta* and A *lukkatti*.[31] Instead of *andan,* B everywhere shows *anda* in combination with terminative verbs in order to designate direction towards a point. In three passages B uses the older 'preferred' word-order *anda* place-name *pai-* (obv. 8, 32–33; rev. 6′). In the two preserved cases A (and its hyparchetype?) have applied the usual modernization to *andan*: i 10, iv 10–11; see, too, for other examples of this modernization A i 16 = B obv. 12, i 19 = obv. 14. But it should be added that these examples of *lukkatta* and *anda* are, as it were, counterbalanced by a few variants in A where this tablet or again its hyparchetype shows an older form than the one preserved in B: *ta-aš-ta* (A i 13) as opposed to *na*[*-aš-t*]*a* (B obv. 10), *ta* (A i 17) as compared with *nu* (B obv. 13) and—most important of all—*ta-aš-še* (A iv 15) instead of *nu-uš-ši-za* (B rev. 9′; in combination with *peran ed-*/*ad-*). These counterexamples render it highly unlikely that A could have been copied or dictated from B, but nothing precludes that A is a 13th century copy, dictated from an hyparchetype which constituted a modernization from an intermediary period of a tablet in many respects similar to B, but in others different and for some passages preserving an older form than B. In other words A may reflect the final version of the redaction referred to above sub 5. Perhaps I should refrain from pronouncing an opinion on the date of D and E, since D, the larger one, has

30. See Kammenhuber, Materialien, Lfg. 2 Nr. 3 *ta* (1973) 109 and THeth 9 240 in her treatment of the *-še*/*-ši* variation, but I do not believe that *-še* formed part of the living language of this late period. See, too, below.

31. Cf. the treatment of this adverb in CHD 3/1: 76–77.

not yet been published in text-copy. Taken by itself E shows young forms of *li* and URU. But for both D and E an orthographic argument can be marshalled to date these copies and by implication the revision which they embody to a late period: D iii 9′ and E iii 8′ write ᵈ*Ḫa-at-tág-ga* instead of ᵈ*Ka-a*[*t-ta*]*ḫ-ḫa* (A iii 20). For the former rendering of this divine name Otten and Kühne, StBoT 16:49–50 offer as comparative material from historical texts their own starting-point, copy B of the Šaušgamuwa Treaty rev. 16′ (ᵈ*Ḫa-at-tág-ga-aš*), KBo 4.10 rev. 2 (idem) and ABoT 56 ii 23 (ᵈ*Ḫa-at-ta-k*[*a*-). They reconstruct a phonetic development: *Kataḫḫa* > *Kataḫga* > *Ḫataḫḫa* > *Ḫataḫga* > *Ḫatagga* with historical and religious texts from the latest phases of the Hittite Empire period representing this last stage. CTH 629 = KUB 25.27 is likely to be a young tablet because of the mixture between *lukkatti* (ii 8′, 13′, 26′; iii 9, 12 and 13) and *luk(k)at* (i 12′, 20′; iii 17 and 20; see for this criterion note 32). Since KUB 25.27 also shows ᵁᴿᵁPA-*ši* (i 1′ and 21′), it may very well be a very young tablet indeed. The same authors refer for this rendering of ᵁᴿᵁ*Ḫattuša-* to the Šaušgamuwa Treaty, left edge 1 and KBo 12.38 i 6 and thus again to historical texts from the time of Tudḫaliya IV and Šuppiluliuma II respectively.[32] Reckoning backwards it seems as if a case can be made for a dating of both the dictation of A and of the origin of D and E as well as of CTH 629 to the time of Tudḫaliya IV. This would be in perfect accordance with the cult reform, ascribed to this king since Güterbock KUB 25 (1930),[33] and also with the fact that copies of festival texts describing individual days of the festivals of the spring and the autumn stem from the reign of Tudḫaliya IV.[34]

Mainly on the strength of Güterbock's argumentation that the main recension of the *nuntarriyašḫaš* Festival Outline is likely to stem from the time of Muršili II,[35] but also because it is historically unlikely that royal attention

32. Cf. Otten and Kühne, StBoT 16:33–36. KUB 25.27 shows in every respect the youngest forms possible: *ik*/GÁL, URU, *li, šar* and of course *uk*.

33. See KUB 25, Vorwort regarding nos. 18 to 24.

34. See Güterbock, NHF 63 and 67 and Carter, Diss. 38 n. 10, 50 n. 1 as well as Košak, Linguistica 16 (1976) 58 (the latter in respect of the *nuntarriyašḫaš* Festival): KUB 20.63 + KUB 11.18 (CTH 611.1), KUB 20.42 (CTH 611.2), 14th–15th or rather 13th–14th days of AN.TAḪ.ŠUMˢᴬᴿ; KUB 25.18 (CTH 618.1) and KUB 25.20 (CTH 618.5), 33rd–34th days of AN.TAḪ.ŠUMˢᴬᴿ; KBo 11.43 (CTH 626 III A), KUB 2.9 (+?) KUB 20.50 + KUB 25.19 (CTH 626 III B [+?] B′), IBoT 3.39 (CTH 626 VI), 5th day of *nuntarriyašḫaš*. As far as can be ascertained—the beginning of KUB 25.20 is not preserved, but it mentions Tudḫaliya IV in iv 11′ and v 8′—the king is mentioned with a full genealogy at the beginning of each copy. Tudḫaliyaš IV is also mentioned in KUB 2.9 (+?) KUB 20.50 + KUB 25.29 iv 31′. See, too, sub 2 note 4.

35. Professor Güterbock, JNES 20 (1961) 91–92, adduced two important arguments in favour of a date during the reign of Muršili II: a) KUB 9.16 (= CTH 626 I A) iv 5′–6′ refers to Muršili

for these matters confined itself to only one of the two great festivals, the more so since CTH 568 deals with both festivals and the conception of both is in some respects strikingly similar (see above notes 16 and 28), I believe that one should seriously reckon with the possibility of a kind of modernization or renewal of the cult calendar at some point during the reign of Muršili II. In the case of Muršili II one should think in terms of a renewal or modernization, since this comes closest to what the king himself may intimate in the introduction to his 'Ten Years Annals.' These types of activities also seem to be indicated by the terminology used in the colophon (above sub 4). Moreover, the oracle inquiry, which may also stem from the time of Muršili II, twice mentions an older tablet, while in a fragment of the Deeds of Šuppiluliuma, Muršili II refers to the fact that his father performed the festival: "A[nd it happen]ed that my father placed the AN.TAḪ.ŠUM^{SAR} on behalf of the Gods of Ḫatti and on behalf of the Sungoddess of Arinna."[36] This passage possibly indicates that already during the reign of Šuppiluliuma I the highlight of the AN.TAḪ.ŠUM^{SAR} Festival consisted of the celebrations of the 8th day, although it may cause surprise that no role is reserved for the queen. Finally, there can be no doubt that all the foreign gods and goddesses mentioned in A had long since entered the Hittite pantheon.[37]

8. Two passages may be adduced to support this tentative historical re-

---

II in a broken context (line 5′); b) Nerik is not likely to have been mentioned in the Outline Tablets of the *nuntarriyašḫaš* Festival as a destination of the Hittite king. Presumably because the town itself could not be reached, a substitute offering to the Stormgod of Nerik takes place in Katapa on the 14th day, while the "Festival of the Nerik Road" is performed immediately upon the return to Ḫattuša on the 16th day. See now, too, the earlier celebration in honour of the Stormgod of Nerik on the 8th day of the Festival, after the king has returned to Ḫattuša from Arinna (KBo 14.76 i 3′–4′ which may be compared with KBo 22.228: 2′–6′).

36. Cf. JNES 25 (1966) 27–28 (KUB 19.22: 2′ = KBo 14.42: 9′), as corrected by Hoffner, AlHeth 49 n. 237 (see, too, note 28).

37. See in respect to the Stormgod of Aleppo the data collected by Klengel, JCS 19 (1965) 91 together with note 43 and see, too, Souček and Siegelová, ArOr 42 (1974) 39–52. See with respect to Aškašipa Kammenhuber, HW² 421–424, if really of foreign origin, as assumed by Kammenhuber. Also Ištar of Ḫattarina is at least attested from the time of Šuppiluliuma I onwards. In all three cases there are likely earlier attestations for those who are willing to rely on 'disputed' texts: KUB 26.41 (+) KUB 23.68 + ABoT 58 obv. 8, 10 (the Stormgod of Aleppo: Arnuwanda I); KUB 26.11 i 13 (Askašipa: a Tudḫaliya); KBo 16.97 rev. 26 (Ištar of Ḫattarina: too rashly dated to the time of Muwattalli by Lebrun, Samuha 29 together with note 73 and dated as late as the time of Ḫattušili III by Kammenhuber, OrNS 39 [1970] 564 and THeth 9: 226, but more likely stemming from the period between Arnuwanda I and Šuppiluliuma I, cf. Otten, StBoT 11: 35²). Particularly in view of the prominent role of ᵈU *Piḫaššaššiš* in A iii 1–18 (17th?–20th days) a case could be made for the origin of this form of the Spring Festival during this general period, see the data collected by del Monte, RGTC 6:340–341 on the "palace of the grandfather (of His Majesty)" in Samuḫa, i.e., presumably Tudḫaliya III.

construction. In the prologue to the 'Ten Years Annals' Muršili II first remarks: "Since my father had sojourned in garrison in the country of Mitanni and had lingered in garrison (i.e., had been delayed through his garrison duties), the festivals of the Sungoddess of Arinna, my lady, had been left undone." He then goes on to say: "After I had ascended (lit.: had seated myself on) the throne of my father, before I set out against any enemy country of those surrounding enemy countries, which made war upon me, I first addressed myself to the regular festivals of in particular the Sungoddess of Arinna, my lady, and celebrated them."[38] With respect to a revision during the reign of Tudḫaliya IV a curious passage from a prayer of Tudḫaliya IV to the Sungoddess of Arinna may be quoted, KBo 12.58 + KBo 13.162, which would seem to indicate that Tudḫaliya IV realized that it was high time for a thorough revision. The repentant king remarks:

> (obv. 2–10) "(2) I sinned [towards the Sungoddess of Arinn]a, my lady, and I [o]ffended the Sungoddess of Arinna, my lady, (3) [and whe]n I began to ask [you] for oracular guidance, (it turned out that) I omitted f[estival]s (due) to you. (4) [If] you, O Sungoddess of Arinna, my lady, became angry with [me] in any respect on account of the festivals, (5) [then], O Sungoddess of Arinna, my lady, reckon again with [me]. I want to defeat the enemy. (6) [If you, O Sungoddess] of Arinna, my lady, will step down to [me], I shall [de]feat the enemy and I shall [confess] (7) my sin [before you] and never again shall [I] omit the festivals, not again (8) shall I interchange [the festivals] of the spring and of [the autumn] and [the festivals of the sprin]g I shall perform (9) punctually in the spring, [the festivals of the a]utumn I shall perform punctually in the autumn [and to you] in the temple (10) I shall [n]ever leave out [the festivals]!"[39]

38. See KBo 3.4 i 16–22 = KBo 16.1 i 25–33 (Götze, AM 20–21).

39. See the provisional treatment of this text by Lebrun, Hymnes 357–361. I should like to suggest the following adjustments: line 2 [*A-NA* ^{d}UTU ^{URU}TÚL-*n*]*a*; line 3 [*nu-ut-ta ma*]-⸤*a*⸥-*an* and E[ZEN.ME]Š; line 4 [*nu-mu ma-a-an zi*]-⸤*ig*⸥; line 5 [*nu-mu-za* ^{d}UTU ^{UR}]^{U}TÚL-*na* and ^{LÚ}KÚR [*t*]*ar-aḫ-ḫa-al-lu*; line 6 [*ma-a-an-mu zi-ig*] and ^{LÚ}KÚR-*za* [*tar*]-*aḫ-mi*; line 7 [*tu-ug pí-ra-an tar-na-aḫ*]-*ḫi* and ⸤*kar*⸥-⸤*ša*⸥[-*nu-mi*]; line 8 [EZEN.MEŠ *zé-e-na-an-d*]*a-aš-ša* and [EZEN.MEŠ *ḫa-me-iš-ḫa-an*]-⸤*da-aš*⸥; line 9 [*e-eš-ša-aḫ-ḫi* EZEN.MEŠ *z*]*é-e-na-an-da-aš-ma* and *e-eš-ša-a*[*ḫ-ḫi nu-ut-ta* Š]À É.DINGIR-*LIM*; line 10 [EZEN.MEŠ *Ú-UL ku*]-*u̯a-pí-ik-ki*. The wording of the lines 5–6 resembles KBo 3.4 i 22–23 = KBo 16.1 i 34–35 and KBo 3.4 i 25–27 = KBo 16.1 i 39–41 (Götze, AM 20–23).

DIE HETHITISCHEN FRAGMENTE FHL 68 UND 106

ANNELIES KAMMENHUBER

München

Unter den von Durand edierten und von Laroche schon teilweise eingeordneten 191 kleinen und kleinsten hethitischen Tafelbruchstücken aus dem Louvre (= FHL)[1] gehören zwei zu den "hethitische(n) Opfertexte(n) mit *anaḫi, aḫrušḫi, ḫuprušḫi* und hurrischen Sprüchen"[2]. Ihre Bearbeitung sei unserem Altmeister H. G. Güterbock als bescheidene Gabe zum 75. Geburtstag gewidmet.

FHL 68 läuft par. zum SISKUR *šarraš* A. KBo XXIII 42 + KBo XXVII 119 (+ KBo XIV 130) i 24–30, mit Dupl. B. KBo XXIV 57 + KBo XXI 28 (+ FHG 12 + KBo XXI 29 + KBo XXIII 46 + KBo XX 128 + KBo XXVII 175 + 71/c i *23/1′ff. und nochmals in FHG 12 iii + KBo XX 128 [iii] y + 14′/11′ff.; weitere Par. sind KBo XXII 165: 11′ff.; KUB XXV 47 i 4′ff. und KUB XXXII 44 Rs. 5′ff. In FHL 68 [1] könnte auch eine andere Opfergabe als MUŠEN.GAL gestanden haben, jedoch nicht *tamain* MUŠEN.GAL "anderer (= zweiter) grosser Vogel", weil dann nur der zweite Tešub-Spruch folgen würde (l.c. §13).

1′ [. . . *n*]*a-at-ša-a*[*n* x *da-a-i nu-za* ^{LÚ}AZU MUŠEN.GAL$^{?}$]
2′ [GÙB-*la*-]*az da*$^{!}$-*a*$^{!}$-*i*$^{!}$[3]*k*[*u-un-na-az-ma-kán* (oder Z[AG-*az-ma-kán* ŠU-*az*/*kiš*(*ša*)*raz*) ^{DUG}*a-aḫ-ru-uš-ḫi-*(*i̯a-*)*-az*]
3′ [^{GIŠ}ERI]N *ša-ra-a da-a̧*[*-i na-aš-ta* Ì.GIŠ *A-NA* ^{DUG}GAL A (oder *ME-E*) *an-da za-ap-nu-zi*]
4′ [*nu-za ŠA*] ^{d}IŠKUR *ka-at-*[*ki-ša*]

5′ [*a-aš-še-eš*]^{d}IŠKUR-*up* ^{URU}*A*$^{!}$*-ra-a*[*p-ḫi-ni* ^{URU}*Kum-me-ni ir-ḫa-a-iz-zi*]

---

1. J.-M. Durand et E. Laroche, "Fragments hittites du Louvre," in: Mémorial Atatürk (1982), 73–107.

2. Vf., demnächst OrNS im Anschluss an die Arbeiten zu den hurrischen Sprüchen von E. Laroche, M. Salvini und I. Wegner (cf. Anm. 4).

3. Cf. ibid. §§12[–15], 26 mit Nachtrag.

6′ [*nu-uš-ša-a*]*n* ^{GIŠ}ERIN *kat-t*[*a A-NA* ^{DUG}GAL A (oder *ME-E*) *da-a-i nu(-za)* ^{DUG}GAL (oder *ME-E*) *ša-ra-a da-a-i*]

7′ [*nu u̯a-*]*ạ-tar A-NA*[DINGIR^{LIM} *me-na-aḫ-ḫa-an-da la-a-ḫu-i ḫur-li-li-ma me-ma-i*]

8′ [*a-aš-še-eš* ^{d}IŠKUR-*u*]*p šu-u-n*[*i-ip ši-i̯a-a-i a-ḫar-ra-a-i ú-na-am-ma* . . . (Bruch)

"Das/es [legt er auf x. Dann] nimmt[!] [sich der AZU[4] einen grossen Vogel[?]] (2′) mit der [Linken. Mit der] R[echten (bzw. rechten Hand) aber nimm[t er aus dem Weihrauchgefäss] (3′) [Zedernh]olz hoch. [Zedernöl tröpfelt er in den Becher[5] Wasser hinein.] (4′) [Des] Tešub *kat*[*kiša*] (§-Str., 5′) '*aššeš* Tešub von Arrapḫa . . .' opfert er reihum. (§-Str., 6′) Dann [legt er] das Zedernholz hin[ab in den Becher Wasser. Er nimmt (sich) den Becher Wasser hoch.] (7′) [Wa]sser [giesst er] dem [Gott entgegen, und (wörtl. aber) er sagt auf hurrisch . . .".

Arrapḫa, östlich des Tigris unter der heutigen Stadt Kerkuk, erwähnen die Hethiter nur in diesem hurrischen Spruch.[6]

Die Ortspartikel *-ašta,* die in den monotonen Opfertexten (vermutlich 13. Jh.) ebenso wie *-šan* unter anderem dazu benötigt wird, um dauernd nebeneinander auftretendes *dai* "er nimmt" und "er legt" zu unterscheiden, wird in allen Positionen ausser nach *nu* (*n-ašta*) durch das deutlichere *-kan* ersetzt gemäss den Regeln *-ašta* III. 3–6 aus HW[2].

FHL 106. 2′ scheint den hurr. Spruch *kalleš kammaḫineš* KI.MIN zu enthalten, der durch heth. NINDA.SIG *paršii̯a* (*paršii̯ari, paršii̯azzi*) "Dünnbrot (das charakteristischste Brot der hurrisch-jheth. Schicht) bricht er" bedingt ist (l.c.[2] §§6, 18).

Nach dort genannten Par. wie KBo XXIII 45 iv 1ff.; KBo XXVII 142. 7′ff.; KUB XXXII 44 Vs. 4ff. ergäbe sich ungefähr: (1′) [x ^{G}]^{IŠ}ER[IN[?] x] (§-Str., 2′) [^{LÚ}AZU-*ma-za* 1 NINDA.SIG *da-a-i na-an pár-ši-i̯a ḫur-li-li-ma me-ma*]*ị*[?] *ka-a-li-eš* [*kammaḫineš* KI.MIN] (3′) [*na-aš-ta A-NA* NINDA.SIG *a-na-a-ḫi pí-ra-an ar-ḫa da-a-i na-at-kán* ^{D}]^{UG}*a-aḫ-ru*[!]*-uš-ḫi-*[*i̯a A-NA* Ì.GIŠ *an-da da-a-i*] (§-Str., 4′) [x]x-*az* NINDA.SIG *A-N*[*A* (oder *a-n*[*a-a-ḫi*) x] (5′) [x -*š*]*a-an* ^{DUG}*ḫu-u*[*p-ru-uš-ḫi(-i̯a) ḫa-aš-ši-i* (x)] (6′) [x *šu-un-n*]*a-i*[?]

4. Zum ^{LÚ}AZU zuletzt Vf., THeth 7 (1976), 130–133; zu dessen hurrisch-jheth. Texten zuletzt M. Salvini, I. Wegner, SMEA 22 (1980 [1981]), 87–95.

5. Da auch die Pferde ihren purgierenden Trank aus dem ^{DUG}GAL saufen, lässt sich die z. Zt. bevorzugte Übersetzung "Trinkschale" nicht vertreten: Hipp.heth (1961) s.v. = J. Friedrich†, A. Kammenhuber, HW[2] 420 (*aška-* III. 4ab).

6. [Ed.: For a different view, cf. RGTC 6:29 which considers KUR ^{URU}*A-ra-ap-hi* KUB 15.34 i 56 as also referring to Kirkuk.]

(oder evtl. *la-a-ḫ*]*u-i*?) UD x[, Bruch; (2′) "[Der AZU aber nimmt sich 1 Dünnbrot. Er bricht es, und (wörtl. aber) hurrisch spricht er . . . (3′) [Von dem Dünnbrot nimmt er vorweg eine Kostprobe. Die/sie legt er] in das Weihrauchge[fäss in Zedernöl hinein.]"

Das *ḫupruš̮ḫi,* ein grösserer Behälter als das zur vorübergehenden Konservierung von Brot, Fleischteilen u.a.m. dienende "Weihrauchgefäss", findet sich in der hier diskutierten Gruppe von Opfertexten meistens auf dem Herd (l.c.[2] §2). [Ed.: On *ḫubrušḫi-* cf. also Güterbock, JNES 34:276 n. 17.]

THE TELEPINU MYTH RECONSIDERED

Galina Kellerman

Jerusalem

To Professor Hans Gustav Güterbock,
my teacher, colleague and friend

The Telepinu myth (henceforth: TM) is probably the most literary, the most frequently translated and the best known of the Anatolian myths.[1] Yet, in spite of H. Otten's claim that an edition of the text is urgently needed,[2] such an edition is still sadly lacking. Therefore, many questions concerning the linguistic peculiarities of the myth, its structure, its meaning and usage and its relationship with similar myths describing the anger and disappearance of other gods remain unanswered. This article will attempt to throw light on some of these questions.

1. THE DATING OF KUB 17.10

According to Ph. Houwink ten Cate, the tablet KUB 17.10 (the main text of the best-preserved first version) "constitutes a copy of a ritual from the beginning of the Empire period, in which an Old Hittite myth had been incorporated" (Records, 31). Houwink ten Cate also provides the reader with a list of mythological sections: i 1–39; ii 33–36; iii 1–12 and 28–34; iv 1–7 and 14–26. Some Old Hittite features of these sections are presented by him in a chart (Records, 32).

This chart may be supplemented by other typical Old Hittite spellings occurring in KUB 17.10, such as: *ú-e-ez-zi* (i 17), *pé-e-ta-aš* (i 22), *e-eš-tu* (ii 13, 16, 31), *mi-li-te-e-eš-t*[*u*] (ii 18), *pár-ku-e-eš-tu* (ii 25), *mi-i-e-eš-tu* (ii

1. The most important publications are: Th. Gaster, *Thespis,* 1961, 295–315; H. G. Güterbock, FsFriedrich, 207–211; O. R. Gurney, The Hittites, 1954, 184–186; V. V. Ivanov, Luna, upavshaja s neba, 1977, 55–61, 263–266 (henceforth: Luna); C. Kühne, in RTAT, 181–186; E. Laroche, Myth., RHA XXIII/77: 89–110; H. Otten, Tel.

2. "dringend erwünscht," see H. Otten, Tel., 7 n. 1.

27).[3] Several typical Old Hittite grammatical features also appear: directives *a-aš-ka* (ii 6), *gi-im-ra* (iii 17) and *pappa(ra)ššanta* KASKAL-*ša* (ii 29–30);[4] forms of verbs with the suffix *-ye-*, for instance *ka-ri*!*-i-e-et* (i 34) and *ar-ši*!*-e-ez-zi* (iii 26);[5] mediopassive with the particle *-ti*—*wišuriyantati* (i 6, 7, 8), *ešati* (i 34), *ḫandantati* (iv 22);[6] the correct and current usage of enclitic possessive pronouns with archaic spellings, such as *partawa(r)=še-et* "its wings" (nom.-acc. pl. neut. of 3rd pers. sg. pron., i 38); *tuggaz=še-e-et* "from his body" (abl. sg., iii 10); *ištappulli=š-me-et* "their lid" (nom. pl. neut., iv 15), etc.;[7] archaic constructions of nouns in the genitive with a following postposition, as GIŠ*ḫatalkišnaš=a kattan* "under the hawthorn" (iii 29), d*Telepinuwaš piran* "in front of Telepinu" (iv 27).[8]

It is evident that various Old Hittite features are attested not only in the parts designated as Old Hittite by Houwink ten Cate, but also in the rest of the tablet. Thus, one may assume that the whole of tablet KUB 17.10 derives from an Old Hittite original, though the script is Middle Hittite.[9]

Naturally, some of the Old Hittite features noted both by Houwink ten Cate and in the present article were still in use in the Middle Hittite period.[10] The question is whether one can posit a *terminus post quem* for this religious text. Houwink ten Cate points to some indications which favor the dating of the composition as a whole to the Middle Hittite period (Records, 55–56). However, these indications also permit a different interpretation.

Houwink ten Cate rightly remarks that several misspellings by the scribe "clearly show that he experienced considerable difficulties in the reading of his (hyp)archetype and that he felt obliged to copy only what he could make out" (*ibid.*). However, his theory of late ritual additions is not supported by

3. See N. Oettinger, Stammbildung, 131–134 (*uwē-* "to come"); H. Otten and V. Souček, StBoT 8: 121 (s.v. *peda-*), 52 and n. 15 (imp. 3 sg. *-tu*).

4. The directive KASKAL-*ša* is also attested in HG I §56 (OH). See F. Starke, StBoT 23: 37 (N 41), 58 (N 88); A. Kammenhuber, Heth.u.Idg., 125; CHD sub *luzzi-;* but cf. Melchert, JCS 31: 57–59. For this case in general, see E. Laroche, RHA XXVIII (1970), 22–49; H. Otten and V. Souček, StBoT 8:62–63; F. Starke, StBoT 23:25–45; A. Kammenhuber, Heth.u.Idg., 115–142; Hoffner, JNES 31 (1972), 32 and in CHD 3, p. xvi.

5. See O. Carruba, Kratylos 7 (1962), 157–159; O. Carruba, V. Souček, R. Sternemann, ArOr 33 (1965), 13–14; C. Watkins, Idg. Gr. III/1, 70–71; N. Oettinger, Stammbildung, 25–30, 343–356.

6. See J. Friedrich, HE I §153; C. Watkins, Idg. Gr. III/1, 78.

7. See J. Friedrich, HE I §107; H. Otten and V. Souček, StBoT 8:70–73.

8. See E. Neu, StBoT 18:68–69; cf. F. Starke, StBoT 23:173–177 and NN 287–296.

9. See N. Oettinger's list of tablets in Middle Script (Stammbildung, 576–579). CHD designates this tablet as OH/MS, see vol. 3: 49 (s.v. *lazzai-*) and 58 (s.v. *lelaniya-*).

10. Cf. lists of Middle Hittite characteristics given by S. Košak, AnSt 30 (1980), 32–33; O. Carruba, XVII Deutscher Orientalistentag (= ZDMG Suppl. 1 [1969]), part 1, tables I–II between pp. 260–261; Ph. Houwink ten Cate, Records, 10–25, col. B, C.

the fact that three out of six such misspellings occur precisely in these "ritual parts" (ii 14, 29; iii 26). The misspellings rather show that the scribe, probably a Luwian, copied the Old Hittite text mechanically and sometimes without real understanding, since most of his misspellings do not make sense in Hittite.

The unusual form *wa-ar-ku-uš-ša-an* (iii 12), marked by a gloss sign, can serve as another example of the scribe's inadequate knowledge of Old Hittite. Since in KUB 33.28 iii 6 the same word occurs as *wa-ar-ku-iš-ša-an* (< **warkuin=šan,* acc. sg. com. of the noun and of the enclitic poss. pron. 3 sg.), Houwink ten Cate characterized the spelling of KUB 17.10 iii 12 as a mistake (UŠ instead of IŠ, Records, 55). However, the spelling *wa-ar-ku-uš-ša-an* may be an archaism, since texts in Old Script sometimes use the spelling *-u-* instead of *-ui-*.[11] If this is the case, the scribe simply did not understand the archaic form and thus provided it with the gloss sign as an exclamation point.

The proposed Luwian origin of the scribe is further confirmed by the use of the Luwian words [*n*]*ūš tumantiya-* (iv 33) without a gloss sign (Records, 55–56), probably inserted by the scribe. However, in the absence of other Luwian words or Luwian grammatical forms in such a lengthy text and in view of the numerous Old Hittite features distributed throughout the tablet, these words alone cannot be regarded as sufficient evidence for dating the composition to the Middle Hittite period.

2. THE STRUCTURE OF THE TELEPINU MYTH

At least three versions of TM are extant,[12] each represented by several duplicates, written either in Middle or in New Script. This situation allows the assumption that the text was continuously in use from the Old Hittite to the Empire periods. Unfortunately, all the tablets inscribed with this text are damaged, and no version is complete. In order to complete missing or mutilated paragraphs of the first version, the translators of the text (A. Goetze,

11. See E. Neu, StBoT 18:43. Cf. also the spelling *tu-ug-ga-az(-)* in KUB 17.10 iii 10.

12. To the texts listed in CTH 324 should now be added the broken fragment KBo 26.127, which tells about Telepinu's anger (see H. G. Güterbock and Ch. Carter, "Inhaltsübersicht" to KBo 26). This fragment markedly differs from the preserved versions. Another fragment, KBo 24.84, which was defined by its editor, H. Otten, as a duplicate of KUB 17.10 i 1ff., may belong to any *mugawar* similar to TM. Finally, KUB 43.34, written in an archaic script (see n. 2 to the "Inhaltsübersicht"), is a fragment of a ritual performed in 1st sg. (cf. lines 4, 7, 18). This fragment contains several lines, 8–13, which are similar to KUB 17.10 iii 6–12 (as noted by the editor, K. Riemschneider), but the rest of it is totally different. The tablet could belong to CTH 322 (cf. the mention of the sea, line 21, and of an implement ^{GIŠ}*išḫawar,* line 5).

K. Kühne and V. V. Ivanov) used the other two versions together with similar texts about the disappearance of other gods. My purpose here is to investigate the plot of the myth as it was restored by Goetze (Kühne generally follows Goetze's translation) and by Ivanov.

Goetze, who made the first partial translation of TM as early as 1933 (Kl., 1st ed., 134ff.), published a complete English translation in ANET (127–128). He restored in the break after KUB 17.10 i 39 the following lines: KUB 33.5 ii 15–16 (second version); KUB 33.9 ii 3–6 and KUB 33.10 ii 1–16 (third version); KUB 33.8 ii 13–17 (second version). Then, after marking a gap, he translated KUB 17.10 ii–iv.

The result is confusing. The restored text tells how Telepinu, infuriated by the bee's sting, starts a general destruction. The frightened gods then decide to ask a mortal to pacify Telepinu. At this point the second version becomes fragmentary and the third one breaks off. One may presume, however, that the mortal carries out the divine commission, as is the case, for instance, in the myth of Illuyanka (first version). The text following the gap, i.e., KUB 17.10 ii 1ff., should thus consist of a magical ritual performed by the mortal in order to pacify Telepinu. Indeed, the lines ii 1–8, though fragmented and difficult to understand, do represent an address to Telepinu and are followed by several magic formulae intended to restore Telepinu's good qualities and his beneficence towards humanity (ii 9–32). Yet, after these formulae the text suddenly describes once again Telepinu's fury (ii 33–34). This time he is quieted by the goddess of magic, Kamrušepa, who performs a magical ritual for Telepinu in the presence of other gods. It is important to note here that the mortal is expected to bring back the angry god with the help of an eagle's wing (KUB 33.8 ii 15–17; cf. KUB 33.10 ii 19–20), whereas Kamrušepa actually does so by using the same magic device (KUB 17.10 ii 35–36).

According to this scheme, Telepinu was pacified twice, first by a mortal and second by Kamrušepa, each time by the same means. Moreover, no reason is given by the text for the renewed anger of Telepinu after the magical ritual has been performed by the mortal.

Can such a scheme possibly be correct? In his exposé of TM, H. G. Güterbock gives a clear answer: "The help to the helpless gods comes through magic: in one version it is the goddess Kamrušepa, in the other one it is the man who performs rites and pacifies the god."[13] Unfortunately, Güterbock did not develop this idea.

13. See H. G. Güterbock, Hethitische Literatur (in: W. Röllig, ed. Altorientalische Literaturen, 1978), 246 (henceforth: Heth. Lit.). Cf. also the remark of C. Kühne, RTAT, 184.

A similar idea apparently underlies Ivanov's Russian translation of TM. Ivanov not only restores, but also rearranges the text. In the break after KUB 17.10 i 39 he inserts first KUB 33.5 ii 15–16, then KUB 33.9 ii 3–6 and KUB 33.10 ii 1–16. These lines are followed directly by KUB 17.10 ii 33–iv 19. Afterwards, Ivanov inserts the magic formulae of KUB 17.10 ii 9–32, followed by KUB 17.10 iv 20–35. Since Ivanov does not give his reasons for such a rearrangement, noting only that he makes "a rearrangement of ritual additions which could have originally occupied a different place in the text in order to clarify it" (Luna, 263–264), I shall give my reasons for accepting his translation.

In fact, there are two basic differences between Ivanov's and Goetze's translations: 1) Ivanov does not include the episode of the divine appeal to a mortal to pacify Telepinu (KUB 33.8 ii 13–17 and the parallel KUB 33.10 ii 17–20) in his restoration of the first version; 2) he moves one sequence of magic formulae, KUB 17.10 ii 9–32, to the fourth column.[14]

These changes are interconnected. If one accepts that there was only one pacification of Telepinu, either by Kamrušepa or by the mortal, one cannot insert the episode with the mortal into the first version. In the third version (the only one where the scene with the bee's sting is preserved) the episode with the mortal follows the description of destruction wrought by the infuriated Telepinu. Since in the first version the mortal is replaced by Kamrušepa, one must, in restoring the first version, place the pacification ritual of Kamrušepa (whose beginning is parallel to the episode with the mortal in the second and third versions) immediately after the description of the destruction. In this case, either the lines KUB 17.10 ii 1–32 should be considered as later additions (made already in the Old Hittite period) or one should presume that these lines "originally occupied a different place in the text," as postulated by Ivanov.[15]

14. The lines KUB 17.10 ii 1–8 are left out, apparently in view of their bad preservation.

15. From a comparison of the order of the paragraphs in different versions of TM and in similar texts about the anger and disappearance of other gods, one can see that magic formulae and even mythologemes can move inside the text (cf. H. G. Güterbock in MAW, 144). Two examples of this will be given here. In KUB 17.10 the formula of plants *šaḫi-* and *ḫappuriyaša-* is placed in ii 28–32, long *before* the description of the Underworld (iv 14–19), yet in the second version a slightly different variant of the same formula (KUB 33.8 iii 16–22) is placed *after* the description of the Underworld. In KUB 17.10 the formula of ^{GIŠ}PISÀN (iii 24–27) is followed by the description of the divine assembly meeting under ^{GIŠ}*ḫatalkešna-* (iii 28–34 continued by dupl. KUB 33.1:9–12) and, after a gap, by a formula of ^{GIŠ}*ḫatalkešna-* (KUB 33.54 ii 13–15 + KUB 33.47:1–3 continued by par. KUB 17.10 iv 1–3); after two more paragraphs there follows a description of the Underworld. In CTH 334 (the disappearance of ^{d}MAḪ) the order is completely different: the Underworld (KUB 33.54 ii 5–9); formula of ^{GIŠ}PISÀN (ii 10–12); formula of ^{GIŠ}*ḫatalkešna-* (ii 13–19).

Both solutions are possible, though the second one seems more plausible to me, because the structure of the first version, as rearranged by Ivanov, acquires internal logic. It can be summarized as follows:

1) The angry Telepinu disappears, taking with him the fertility of the country (KUB 17.10 i 1–22);
2) The gods search for him in vain (i 23–34);
3) The bee, sent by Ḫannaḫanna, finds Telepinu and awakens him, arousing his fury (i 34–39 + {KUB 33.5 ii 15–16; KUB 33.9 ii 3–6; KUB 33.10 ii 1–16} + ii 33–34);
4) Kamrušepa pacifies Telepinu, destroys his bad qualities by magic actions and charms and purifies him before the divine assembly (ii 33–iv 19);
5) By magic actions and charms Telepinu's good qualities and beneficence towards humanity are restored (ii 9–32);
6) Telepinu returns home, restores fertility to the country and gives the whole wealth of the earth to the Hittite king (iv 20–35).

Surprisingly, the text as presented above does not contain any part of an actual magical ritual, performed by a ^{SAL}ŠU.GI or some other magician. It is merely a myth telling how Telepinu became angry and how Kamrušepa (or the mortal) succeeded in pacifying him. What is then the meaning and the usage of the myth?

3. THE MEANING AND USAGE OF THE TELEPINU MYTH

The type of sacred myth which tells how a certain ritual or practice was performed for the first time, *in illo tempore,* is known to most archaic societies. Such myths constitute paradigms of behavior of a given society or of a specific group inside this society (magicians, priests, etc.).[16]

In Mesopotamia, the mythical teachers of humanity in the field of exorcism were Ea and his son Marduk/Asalluḫi. This role of Ea and Marduk is especially prominent in a collection of Sumerian and Akkadian incantations called *Šurpu.*[17] In Anatolia, a similar role has been attributed to the goddess Kamrušepa who acts as a divine magician in the mythological parts of several rituals, namely CTH 727; 457.1; 441.1; 390.

Since not only TM but also CTH 457.1 (col. iv) go back to the Old Hittite period[18] and at least the bilingual mythological part of CTH 727 derives from

16. See M. Eliade, Aspects du mythe, 1963, chap. I, II.

17. The text has been published by E. Reiner, *Šurpu* (AfO Beih. 11). See V–VI 1–39; VII 1–87; IX 76–87.

18. The text is defined as OH/MS in CHD, vol. 3:44 (s.v. *lappiya-*).

an ancient prototype, one may safely maintain that Kamrušepa is a *Hittite* goddess of magic, known from the Old Hittite period. Kamrušepa belongs to the group of gods sung to by the so-called "singers of Kanish."[19] She may thus originally stem from the pantheon of Kanish, the oldest cultural center of the Nesites. On the other hand, the proximity of Kanish to the Luwian ethnic zone may explain why this goddess was adopted into the Luwian pantheon.[20]

As for the Telepinu myth, it apparently represents a sacred myth conveying to exorcists, namely to "Old Women" who are the almost exclusive performers of *mugawars*,[21] the means of pacifying an angry god, which were used for the first time by the divine magician Kamrušepa.[22] This text teaches exorcists how to act if a disaster occurs which may be ascribed to a god's

19. See A. Goetze, Kl. 134 and n. 13; cf. O. R. Gurney, Schweich, 16 n. 5.

20. For Kamrušepa in a Luwian milieu, see V. Haas, OrNS 40 (1971), 419–424; V. Haas and G. Wilhelm, AOATS 3 (1974), 23–26.

21. The *mugawar* for the Sun-deity and Telepinu is performed by the woman Annanna (VBoT 58 iv 3). ^{f}*Annan(n)a* ^{SAL}ŠU.GI from Zigazḫur(a) is named in catalogue tablets as an author of *mugawar*s for the Storm-god and for ^{d}KAL (KUB 30.42 i 3; KUB 30.51 i 22–23) and as a performer of a *mugawar* for Miyatanzipa (KUB 30.42 iv 6–7). The "Old Woman" Tunnawi(ya) is the author of a *mugawar* for the dead (KUB 30.57 + KUB 30.59 left, 5–6). According to the catalogue tablet KUB 30.51 i 15–16 + KUB 30.45 i! 8–9, the woman Mallidunna is the author of a *mukeššar* for the Sun-deity and ^{d}MAḪ; fragments of *mugawars* for the Sun-deity and for Ḫannaḫanna, whose author is the "Old Woman" Mallidunna from Durmitta, have actually been found (see KUB 9.12 i 1; KBo 7.58 rev. 2); cf. also KUB 33.70 iii 6. For further examples, see KUB 30.51 i 20, 24–26, 27; KUB 30.61 ii 6, 9, 10.

There are two notable exceptions in which a *mugawar* or a *mukeššar* is performed not by a ^{SAL}ŠU.GI, but by a male practitioner. In the first case, a *mugawar* for the Storm-god is included in a ritual of purification of a murderer (KUB 30.51 i 17–19 + KUB 30.45 i! 10–12). In the second case, a *mukeššar,* which is originally a magical ritual performed in an hour of need, is transformed into a yearly festival for the Storm-god of Kuliwišna (*mukišnaš* EZEN—KBo 15.34 ii 15), though no season was fixed for its celebration (see KBo 15.32 i 1–5). It is clear that both cases represent innovations to the old tradition. That is why the colophon to the second tablet of the *mukeššar* for the Storm-god of Kuliwišna states: ^{m}*Šippa*-LÚ-*iš newaḫḫaš,* "Šippa-ziti renewed (it)" (KBo 14.86 iv 14). Another exception is a *mugawar* for Anzili and Zukki which forms part of a birth ritual. This ritual is performed by a midwife, ^{SAL}ŠÀ.ZU (KUB 33.67 and duplicates; published by G. Beckman, Diss., 90–103 = StBoT 29:72–83).

The above-mentioned catalogue tablets have been published by E. Laroche, CTH ch. XIV; for the names mentioned, see E. Laroche, NH; part of the *mukeššar* for the Storm-god of Kuliwišna has been transcribed by E. Laroche, Myth. (RHA XXIII/77) 131–134; see also G. F. del Monte and J. Tischler, RGTC 6: 218–219; H. G. Güterbock, Heth. Lit. 244–245. For the notions of *mugawar* and *mukeššar,* see O. R. Gurney, AAA 27: 45–51, 60–61; E. Laroche, Prière hittite 20–24.

22. Cf. A. Goetze, Kl. 143 n. 2, 144.

disappearance. That is why Kamrušepa's ritual is performed in the "language of men" (*ŠA* DUMU.LÚ.ULÙ.LU.MEŠ *uddananteš*—iv 6).[23]

Indeed, several preserved *mugawar*s, undoubtedly composed for specific occasions, are constructed according to the TM model (though the narrative part is shortened). These are *mugawar*s for Storm-gods who "became angry" with certain persons (the queens Ḫarapšili and Ašmunikal, the scribe Pirwa);[24] there is also a *mugawar* for the goddesses Anzili and Zukki included in a birth ritual and a *mukeššar* to the Storm-god of Kuliwišna which was transformed into a yearly festival.[25]

It is unclear for which occasions two other texts were composed which resemble TM in their narrative and many magic formulae, namely a *mugawar* for the Storm-god (CTH 325) and a *mukeššar* for [d]MAḪ (CTH 334).[26] One can see, however, that both ceremonies included actual rituals.[27] It is not surprising that the text which shows the closest resemblance to TM, though there are considerable deviations both in the narrative and in magic, is CTH 325, going back to the Old Hittite period.[28]

Could then the TM model be applied to any god by means of a simple replacement of Telepinu's name by another divine name?[29]

23. See V. V. Ivanov, Luna, 58–59.

24. Ḫarapšili is apparently a queen of the Old Hittite Kingdom, the wife of either Ḫantili or Alluwamna (see E. Laroche, NH No. 297). If E. Laroche is right in his attribution of KBo 21.27 to CTH 327 (see CTH, 1st suppl. in RHA XXX), the name is written once as [f]*Ḫa-ra-ap-ši-ti* (KBo 21.27 obv. 1). The name Ḫarapšiti is also mentioned in DŠ Frag. 2 i 4, see H. G. Güterbock, DŠ p. 59 and note a. Ašmunikal was a well-known queen of the Middle Kingdom (see E. Laroche, NH No. 174). The scribe Pirwa is not attested elsewhere. One should note, however, that this name is rare in the Hittite period, but is the most frequent indigenous name attested at Kanish during the period of Assyrian colonies (see E. Laroche, NH No. 1017).

25. See note 21.

26. For CTH 325, see H. G. Güterbock in MAW, 144–148; Heth. Lit., 245–246. As for CTH 334, though many paragraphs are almost identical with TM, the arrangement of the text, as far as one can judge from the preserved fragments, markedly differs from TM (see note 15). Some parts of CTH 334 do not have parallels in TM.

27. The beginning of CTH 325 (KUB 33.22 + 23 i) resembles VBoT 58 iv 1–3 (noted by E. Laroche, Myth., RHA XXIII/77, 112, n. 2). In both ceremonies "old men" and "old women" (age or title?) participate. In CTH 325, the Storm-god, stung by the bee, is returned with the help of a magic "turning water" (see KUB 33.24 ii 2–11). His return is followed by the magical ritual of Kamrušepa, apparently recited by the practitioner. As for CTH 334, not only are the magical formulae recited, but the actions which are described are actually performed (see KUB 33.49 ii, iii; KUB 33.75). Cf. E. Laroche, Prière hittite 22.

28. See H. G. Güterbock, Heth. Lit. 246; CHD, vol. 3: 13 (s.v. *laḫ(ḫ)uwai-*).

29. Cf. H. G. Güterbock in MAW 143–144, 148; E. Laroche, CTH p. 159.

4. THE RELATIONSHIP OF THE TELEPINU MYTH WITH SIMILAR TEXTS

Among the preserved *mugawar*s there are different models: the *mugawar* for the Sun-deity and Telepinu (CTH 323); the *mugawar* for Telepinu (= TM) and similar texts for other gods (CTH 325–330, 332–335); CTH 331 and 336, which are only partly preserved, could be different types of *mugawar*. It is impossible to predict to which model the numerous *mugawar*s mentioned in different catalogue tablets would have belonged.[30] The discussion must therefore be limited to the texts which are actually preserved.

In order to define Telepinu's functions in TM, one should turn to the disasters described there as the result of his disappearance. These disasters fall into three groups: 1) drought and famine; 2) sterility of males (cattle and men); 3) incapacity of pregnant females to give birth. Telepinu appears here as a most powerful fertility god, responsible for the fertility of the soil, the animal world and humans.

There are, however, gods who are responsible for specific aspects of fertility: the Storm-god gives rain and ensures the growth of any product of the soil;[31] the goddesses ᵈMAḪ.MEŠ are celebrated during a special festival performed when a woman becomes pregnant (CTH 489); in general, both the goddess ᵈMAḪ (= Ḫannaḫanna) and the group of ᵈMAḪ.MEŠ are intimately involved with human fertility and birth;[32] finally, the very inclusion of a *mugawar* for Anzili and Zukki into a ritual for a difficult birth shows their connection with parturition. It is certainly not fortuitous that the TM model was applied precisely to these deities.

30. See the list in E. Laroche, Prière hittite 20–21; R. Lebrun, Hymnes et prières hittites (1980) 432–438.

31. For the functions of the Storm-god, see G. Kellerman, *Recherche sur les rituels de fondation hittites* (Ph.D., 1980) 114–116.

32. See G. Beckman, Diss., 295–306 = StBoT 29:238–248.

"THE GOSPEL OF IRON"*

SILVIN KOŠAK

Mainz

Say, are those plumed shadows
Flying Horsemen of the First Air Cavalry Division,
or Hittites bringing the gospel of iron
to confound Egyptians?

Bruce Dawe, *Phantasms of Evening*

Forty years ago, Professor Güterbock stated the need for collecting the evidence for iron in Hittite texts.[1] The pioneering work on this topic was undertaken by Laroche,[2] who discussed the various terms for iron and also presented a brief survey of iron artefacts. Since in recent years interest in the origin of ironworking has been growing[3] and there have been frequent references to a Hittite iron technology, a new look at the Hittite textual evidence is appropriate.

1. *ḫapalki-* n.; iron; wr. syll. and AN.BAR; from OS. AN.BAR is usually understood as "(smelted) iron," opposed to AN.BAR GE_6 "meteoric iron (lit. 'black iron')" based on the passage AN.BAR GE_6 *nepišaš nepišaz uter* "they brought black iron of the sky from the sky" KBo 4.1 i 39 w. dupl. KUB 9.33 obv. 15. In view of the parallel passage AN.BAR *nepišaz uter* "they brought iron from the sky" KUB 2.2 i 48, and AN.BAR AN-*E* "iron of the sky" KBo 12.56 i 14, AN.BAR can also sometimes be translated as "meteoric iron." Since the unmarked, generic term for the metal is AN.

*I would like to thank Prof. H. A. Hoffner for allowing me to use the lexical files of the Chicago Hittite Dictionary Project. The Project is supported in part by a grant from the National Endowment for the Humanities.

1. Güterbock, OrNS 12 (1943) 151.
2. Laroche, RHA XV/60 (1957) 9–15.
3. *The Coming of the Age of Iron,* ed. T. A. Wertime and J. D. Muhly, New Haven and London 1980; *Expedition* 25/1, 1982; *Biblical Archaeology Review* VIII/6, 1982; *Early Pyrotechnology: the Evolution of the First Fire-Using Industries,* ed. T. A. Wertime and S. F. Wertime, Smithsonian Institution Press, Washington, D.C. 1982.

BAR, it is likely that AN.BAR originally meant "meteoric iron" and that the term was later transferred to smelted iron, unless we assume that the Hittites were familiar with iron technology before they used iron in its native form. Also, while AN.BAR is attested from OS on, AN.BAR GE_6 occurs much later, probably only in NH.

(Hattic) *ḫa-pal-ki-ia-an* 412/b++ i 13, 15, 23 = (Hitt.) *ŠA* AN.BAR, AN.BAR-*aš* ibid. ii 12, 15, 23 (bil. foundation rit., OH), translit. Laroche, RHA XV/60:9.

a. personnel: LÚ.MEŠ AN.BAR 20 [*pur*]*puruš* AN.BAR x[. . .] "The blacksmiths [. . .] twenty [l]umps of iron" KBo 17.46 rev. 26 (KI.LAM fest., OS), translit. StBoT 25:56; preceded by LÚ.MEŠ KÙ.GI DÍM.DÍM ibid. rev. 23, 25, followed by LÚ.MEŠ KÙ.BABBAR and LÚ.MEŠ URUDU DÍM.DÍM ibid. rev. 27–28. Note that the guild of the smiths was divided into specialists from the Old Kingdom on; [*MELQ*]*ĪT* LÚ.MEŠ AN.BAR DÍM.DÍM "ration of the blacksmiths" KBo 16.68 iii 8 (KI.LAM fest., OH/MS), translit. StBoT 28:110 ii 15″; the smiths are listed in the same order as in the previous ex.: goldsmiths, blacksmiths, silversmiths, coppersmiths;

b. ingots: 20 [*pur-*]*pu-ru-uš* AN.BAR KBo 17.46 rev. 26 (see above, 1.a); *purpura-* "ball, lump" refers elsewhere in Hitt. texts to lumps of dough, bread, cheese, clay, or soap; 3 PAD AN.BAR KI[.LAL . . .] "three ingots of iron, their weight [is . . .]" KUB 42.76 obv. 1 (inv., NH), ed. THeth 10:190; 22 AN.BAR *ŠA* GUNNI "22 iron (ingots) from the brazier" KUB 42.21 obv. 6 (inv., NH), perhaps referring to a bowl furnace (see R. F. Tylecote, *Metallurgy in Archaeology,* 1962, p. 210);

c. tools and weapons—**1′** knives, daggers: ⌈EME⌉.GÍR AN.BAR (letter, Ḫatt. III), see below, 3.a; AN.BAR-*aš* GÍR-*an* KUB 33.23 i 12 (myth., OH/NS), translit. Laroche, Myth. [52]; 6 GÍR.TUR AN.BAR "six small daggers of iron" KUB 42.11 v 4; 56 EME.GÍR AN.BAR "56 dagger blades of iron" KBo 18.158:3 10 EME.GÍR AN.BAR KUB 42.11 v 5 (all inv., NH); 6 EME AN.BAR 6 EME ZABAR KÙ.GI AN.BAR "six blades of iron, six blades of bronze, gold and iron" KBo 18.172 obv. 14 (cult inv., NH);

2′ spears: 1 DUMU.É.GAL AN.BAR-*aš tū*[*ri* 1 DUMU.É.GAL AN. BAR-*aš*] *mārin ḫarzi* "one palace attendant holds a *tūri*-spear of iron, the other palace attendant holds a *māri*-spear of iron" KBo 25.28 rev. iii? 4–5 (fest.frag., OS), translit. StBoT 25:75; cf. KBo 25.9 i 3 (fest.frag., OS?), KUB 34.72 obv. 4 (fest.frag.), KBo 9.136 i 6 (monthly fest.), Bo 2839 iii 32 (KN 262), KUB 2.3 i 51–52 (KI.LAM fest., OH/NS), ibid. ii 5–8, KUB 20.4 i 25 (KI.LAM fest., OH/NS); 2 DUMU.MEŠ É.GAL 1 LÚ*MEŠEDI* GIŠŠUKUR A[N].BAR-*aš* (dupl. AN.BAR GIŠŠUKUR) *ḫarzi* 1 DUMU. É.GAL AN.BAR-*aš mārin ḫ*[*ar*]*zi* LUGAL-*i piran ḫūiyanzi* LUGAL-*uš* AN.BAR-*aš mārin ḫarzi* "There are two palace attendants. One bodyguard holds an iron *tūri*-spear, one palace attendant holds an iron *māri*-spear and they precede the king. The king holds an iron *māri*-spear" KUB 44.16 obv. ii 12–15 + IBoT 3.69 left col. 6–10 w. dupl. KBo 22.189 obv. ii 4–8 (fest.); the dupl. is corrupt and was written by a pupil of the scribe Anuwanza; dupl. ed. Lebrun, Hethitica 2:8, 11; 1 *IMIDDU* AN.BAR KUB 26.69 vii 12 (depos., NH), ed. StBoT 4:46f.; AN.BAR-*aš* (dupl. AN.BAR) *šakuwannaš* ^{GIŠ}ŠUKUR "a ceremonial spear of iron" KBo 10.51:9 w. dupl. KBo 10.23 i 23 (KI.LAM fest., OH/NS), cf. Goetze, JCS 16:29 who suggested an equation of *šakuwannaš* with IGI.DU$_8$.A and tr. "ceremonial"; 81 NÍG.GÍD.DA AN.BAR GE$_6$ "81 *ARIKTU*-spears of black iron" KUB 42.11 v 8 (inv., NH), cf. ibid. v 3 (five *ARIKTU*-spears), 15 (sixteen *A*.-spears), ed. but misunderstood THeth 10:33f., 38; cf. KUB 42:14 i 2 (inv., NH);

3′ hammers: (for a foundation deposit they take) 1 MA.NA URUDU *dannauwanza* 4 ^{GIŠ}KAK ZABAR 1 ^{GIŠ}NÍG.GUL AN.BAR TUR *nu ištarna pidi* ^{GIŠ}*kurakkiyaš pidi daganzip*[*a*]*n paddai nukan* URUDU *anda dāi nam=man IŠTU* ^{GIŠ}KAK.ḪI.A *araḫzanda tarmaizzi nu* EGIR-*anda IŠTU* ^{GIŠ}NÍG. GUL AN.BAR *walḫzi* "one mina of refined(?) copper, four bronze pegs, and one small iron hammer. In the center, at the place of the pole, he digs up the ground. He deposits the copper, secures it around with pegs, and drives them in with the iron hammer" KBo 4.1 obv. 3–6 w. dupl. KUB 2.2 i 1–5 (foundation rit., OH/NS), ed. Kellerman, Diss. 126, 134, tr. ANET 356; NÍG.GUL AN.BAR-*makan ŠA* ^{GIŠ}ŠUKUR *ANA* DUMU.É.GAL *appezzi ḫantezziš* DUMU.É.GAL *arḫa dāi* "the first palace attendant takes the iron hammer from the last palace attendant of the spear" KBo 10.24 obv. iii 27–30 (KI.LAM fest., OH/NS), translit. StBoT 28:19; *ŠA* ŠUKUR describes the palace attendant (see ibid. iii. 23), not the "iron head of the spear" (Goetze, JCS 16:29); the hammer was decorated with an image of the Stormgod (ibid. iv 1–3); cf. also ibid. ii 21; ⌜2⌝ NÍG.GUL AN.BAR KUB 42.77 obv. 7 (rit.frag.); AN.BAR NÍG.GUL KUB 53.24 rev.? 3 (rit.frag.);

4′ pegs, bolts: 30 ^{GIŠ}KAK.ḪI.A AN.BAR 1 GÍN TA.ÀM "thirty iron pegs of one shekel each" KUB 2.2 iv 7 (OH/NS) w. dupl. KBo 19.162 rev. 6 (OH/MS?), ed. HHB 76f.; 12 KAK AN.BAR 1 GÍN TA.À[M] "twelve iron pegs of one shekel each" KBo 17.78 ii 10 (rit., NS), a copy of an earlier text: "the name (of the author) is missing" ibid. ii 5; 10 KAK.ḪI.A AN.BAR KBo 15.24 ii 21 (foundation rit., MH/NS); 7 KAK.ḪI[.A AN.B]AR Bo 6342:4 (2 Mašt.), ed. Rost, MIO 1:362f. w.n. 156a; 7 ^{GIŠ}KAK *ŠA* AN.BAR KUB 17.28 i 9 (incant., NS); 6 ^{GIŠ}KAK AN.BA[R] KUB 41.7 ii 11 (rit., pre-NH/NS); 5 ^{GIŠ}KAK AN.BAR KUB 7.9:3 (fest.frag., OH); 2 KAK AN.BAR KUB 29.4 i 19 (rit., NH); *ŠA* AN.BAR ^{GIŠ}KAK.ḪI.A 412/b++ ii 12 (Hattic bil., OH), translit. Laroche, RHA XV/60:9; [(*kāša* DINGIR.MEŠ-*aš*)] *uddār* AN. BAR-*aš* ^{GIŠ}KAK-*an* [. . .] "The gods' words [. . .] a peg (acc. sg.) of iron"

KUB 43.68 rev. 12 w. dupls. Bo 2477 and 871/z (Otten, ZA 64:244) (prayer), ed. Lebrun, Hymnes 394, 396; *nan* ZAG.MEŠ-*ša IŠTU* ^{GIŠ}KAK AN.BAR *tarm*[*aši?*] "you (sc. the Sea) stake the limit for him and his borders with iron peg(s)" KBo 15.19 ii 7 (rit.); AN.BAR-*aššan tarmuš walḫandu* "may they drive in pegs of iron!" IBoT 3.98:10 (rit.); 9 *wallaš* AN.BAR "nine bolts of iron" KBo 4.1 i 48 w. dupl. KUB 2.2 i 58, cf. ibid. rev. 20 and KBo 15.24 obv. ii 20 (ten bolts), ii 36 (two bolts; for the mng. *walla-* "cheville (i.e. peg, bolt, pin)" see Kellerman, Diss. 71;

5′ axes: 1 *ḪAZINU* AN.BAR KUB 26.69 vi 16 (depos., NH), ed. StBoT 4:46f.; [x ^{UR}]^{UDU}*ḪAZZ*[*INNU* . . .]x AN.BAR GIŠ-*ru*=*ya* "[x] copper axe(s) (with) [. . .], iron and wood" KUB 32.86:6 + KBo 20.103:7 (list of offerings, NS?);

6′ staffs, poles: 1 PA.GAM (dupl. PA.ḪAL or PA.DIDLI) AN.BAR "scepter(?) of iron (as a present from the king of Purušḫanda)" KBo 3.22 rev. 75 (OS) w. dupls. KUB 26.71 i (17) and KUB 36.98b rev. 4 (both OH/NS) (Anitta), ed. StBoT 18:14f. (tr. "Krummstab"); [Ed. Cf. ^{GIŠ}*kalmuš* AN.BAR 44/u 3, ed. Alp, TTKY VI/23 320f.]; *tan* AN.BAR-*aš* ^{GIŠ}PA-*it walḫzi* "he strikes him with a staff of iron" KUB 20.87 i 12 (fest.frag.); 1 *kurakkin* AN.BAR "one pole of iron" KBo 4.1 i 26 w. dupl. KUB 2.2 i 30 (foundation rit., NH), for the mng. *kurakki-* "poteau (i.e. post, stake, pole)" see Kellerman, Diss. 138ff.;

d. vessels: GAL LÚ.⌈MEŠ⌉ SAGI [*iškariḫ*] ⌈AN.BAR⌉-*aš* LUGAL-*i pāi* "the chief cup-bearer offers an iron amphora to the king" KBo 17.74 i 14 (thunder fest., OH/MS), ed. StBoT 12:12f.; 1 BAL-*uwaš* (= *išpanduwaš*) AN.BAR "one libation vessel of iron" KUB 38.1 i 31 (inv., NH); ^{DUG}*KU*=*KUB* AN.BAR "*K.*-vessel of iron" KUB 2.13 ii 22 (monthly fest., OH?/NS), cf. KBo 12.86:5 (prayer); [. . .] AN.BAR 1 URUDU NÍG.ŠU.LUḪ.ḪA AN.BAR [. . .Š]À.BA 1 AN.BAR 1 URUDU DUG.SAGI.A AN.BAR "[a vessel?] of iron, one iron wash-basin. [x vessels], among them one of iron, one spouted pitcher of iron" KBo 18.181 rev. 31–32 (inv., NH), ed. THeth 10:121, 124; 2 *malitallenzi* ŠÀ.BA . . . 1 *ḫa-pal*⟨*-ki*⟩*-ia-aš* "two honey-pots, among them . . . one of iron" KUB 12.1 iv 31–32 (inv., NH), ed. Laroche, RHA XV/60:10; 1 TÚL AN.BAR KI.LAL.BI 90 MA.NA "one tub, ninety minas in weight" KUB 38.1 obv. ii 21 (cult inv., NH), ed. Rost, MIO 8:180 w.n. 81; (description of a fountain for the Stormgod) "it is built from copper, it is plated with *arzil(a)-*" AN.BAR=*at iškiyan* "it is coated with iron" KBo 21.22:41–43 (benedictions for Labarna, OH/MS), ed. Archi, FsMeriggi 2:46f.; GAM-*ŠU* 2 *wattatra* AN.BAR 1 *šekan* DÙ-*anzi* "underneath (the figurine of iron) they make two basins of iron, (measuring) one span (each)" KUB 38.32 obv. 2, cf. ibid. rev. 20 (cult inv., NH), ed. Jakob-Rost, MIO 9:194; *dankuwai taknī* AN.BAR-*aš* ^{DUG}*palḫiš kianda* "in the dark earth there lie pails of iron (their lids are of lead)" KUB 33.8 iii 7–8 w. dupl. IBoT 3.141 iv 11 (Tel. myth), translit. Laroche, Myth. [43f.]; cf. IBoT 3.98:8 w. dupl. KBo 13.106 i 22 (rit.); (pails of bronze with a lid of lead) *zakkišmeš* AN.BAR-*aš* "their clasps are made of iron" KUB 17.10 iv 16 (OH?/MS?) w. dupl. KUB 33.3:7 (MS) (Tel. myth), translit. Laroche, Myth. [37]; (pails of bronze) [*ištappulišmet*] AN.BAR-*aš* "their lids are of iron, (their clasps are of lead)" KUB 33.24 iv 7 (myth., OH/NS), translit. Laroche, Myth. [58];

e. braziers: AN.BAR-*aš* GUNNI 412/b++ ii 23, translit. Laroche, RHA XV/60:9; "the gods have installed the hearth. They ornamented(?) it with precious stones" *nan* AN.BAR-*it šan*[*n*(?)]*īr* "and they covered(?) it with iron" KUB 29.1 iii 39–40 (foundation rit., OH/NS), ed. Kellerman, Diss. 17, 30; 1 GUNNI AN.BAR KBo 4.1 rev. 19 (foundation rit., NH);

f. seats: (royal gift from the man of Purušḫanda) 1 ^{GIŠ}ŠÚ.A AN.BAR "one iron dais" KBo 3.22 rev. 75 (OS) w. dupl. KUB 36.98b rev. 4 (OH/NS) (Anitta), ed. StBoT 18:14f.; AN.BAR-*aš* ^{GIŠ}DAG-*ti* KBo 17.88 rev. iii 25 w. dupls. KBo 20.67 iv 11, KBo 22.201 iv 11 (monthly fest., pre-NH/NS); cf. KBo 23.101 v? (7), translit. StBoT 15:34; *ŠA* AN.BAR ^{GIŠ}GU.ZA "throne of iron" KUB 12.26 ii 3 (inv., NH);

g. statuettes—**1′** male: "Mt. Malimaliya: formerly there were no divine images" ^{d}UTU-*ŠI-an* ^{m}*Tudḫaliyaš* ALAM LÚ AN.BAR 1 *šekan* ½ *šekanna* IGI.ḪI.A KÙ.GI *ANA* UR.MAḪ AN.BAR-*aškan artari* "My Majesty Tud=ḫaliya (made) it (as) a statue of a man of iron, one and a half spans (in size), its eyes of gold. He stands on a lion of iron" KUB 7.24 obv. 1–3 (cult inv., NH), ed. Carter, Diss. 116, 119; cf. KBo 2.1 i 8, 36, ii 14, iii 15, 21, 31, KBo 2.16 obv. 13, KUB 17.35 obv. ii 36, iii 40, KUB 38.7 iii 9, KUB 38.13 rev.? (7), KUB 38.26 rev. 15, KUB 38.32 obv. 1, KUB 38.27 obv. 10, KUB 46.21 obv. 5 (all cult inv., NH); [ALAM ^{m}]*Uḫḫamuwa* AN.BAR KUB 7.55 obv. 1 (rit.frag.); "the statue is new, its chest is new, its manhood (*pišnatar*) is new" SAG.DU-*ZU* AN.BAR [(-*aš*)] "its head is of iron" KUB 20.54+ KBo 13.122:7 (benedictions for Labarna, OH/NS), w. dupl. Bo 2226 rev. 4, ed. Otten-Neu, IF 77:182; "they made for him (sc. the king) an image of tin" SAG.DU-*ZU* AN.BAR-*aš iēr* "its head they made of iron" KUB 29.1 ii 52–53 (foundation rit., OH/NS), ed. Kellerman, Diss. 15, 29;

2′ female (ALAM SAL): KBo 2.1 ii 15, 34, KUB 17.35 rev. iii 23, KUB 38.7 rev. 4, 8, KUB 38.14 obv. 1, KUB 38.17 rev. iv 4, KUB 38.23 obv. 9, KUB 38.26 obv. 31, KUB 38.33:5, VBoT 83 rev. 3, 9;

3′ girls (ALAM TUR.SAL): KBo 2.13 obv. 23–24 (representing rivers and springs), KBo 26.196 obv. 6;

4′ unspecified (ALAM): KBo 2.13 obv. 1, 21, 22, KUB 38.18 obv. 1, KUB 38.26 obv. (40), rev. 8, KUB 38.32 rev. 19 (all cult inv., NH); [ALAM?]

AN.BAR SAG.DU [. . .] "[statuette?] of iron, its head [of . . .]" KUB 15.5 rev. iii 43 (dream, NH);

5′ bulls: 1 GUD.MAḪ AN.BAR 1 *šekan* "one bull, (measuring) one span" KBo 2.1 ii 12, ii 24, 34, 41, iii 2, 8 (measuring two spans); cf. KBo 2.13 obv. (1), 21, KBo 2.16 obv. 11, KUB 38.13 rev.? 6, KUB 38.23:8, KUB 38.31 obv. 6, KUB 38.23 obv. 8, VBoT 26:6 (all cult inv., NH);

6′ oxen: 2 *TAPAL* GUD.ḪI.A AN.BAR *IŠTU* GIŠŠUDUN KÙ.BABBAR *turiyanteš nu kuišša* 1 GUD 1 GÍN KI.LAL.BI "two pairs of iron oxen, joined with a silver yoke. Each ox weighs one shekel" KBo 4.1 rev. 7–8 (foundation rit., NH), ed. Kellerman, Diss. 130, 136; cf. KUB 38.7 iii 22, VBoT 83:(8) (both cult inv., NH);

7′ lions: [SA]G!.DU UR.MAḪ *ḫa-pal-k*[*i*(-) . . .] "lion's head of iron" KUB 31.24:6 (cult inv., NH), cf. ibid. 4; KUB 7.24 i 3 (cf. above g 1′); UR.MAḪ AN.BAR AN-*E* "a lion of meteoric iron (lit. iron of the sky)" KBo 12.56 i 14 (cult inv., NH);

8′ pedestals: 1 GIŠ*tuppaš ŠUŠI* AN.BAR *palzaḫaš* ŠÀ-*ŠU* "one chest: contains 60 iron pedestals" KUB 42.21 obv. 7 (inv., NH), ed. THeth 10:46f.; KUB 42.11 v 7 (inv., NH) (seven pedestals); KBo 2.1 iv 5 (cult inv., NH);

h. miscellaneous and fragmentary items—**1′** in inv. and cult inv.: GÌR AN.BAR "a foot of iron" KBo 26.151 i 17; KUR(-*tar*) AN.BAR "mountain of iron" KUB 38.7 iii 6, KUB 38.18 obv. 3, 6; ḪUR.SAG AN.BAR "mountain of iron" KUB 38.13 rev.? 11, KUB 38.17 iv 5 (two mountains); 3 *puriaš* ŠÀ.BA 1 AN[.BAR] "three side-tables, among them one of ir[on]" KUB 42.11 v 8; 1 *ḪINZU* AN.BAR "one lightning bundle(?) of iron" KUB 42.30 i 6 (inv., NH), ed. THeth 10:175f.; for *ḪINZU,* cf. KBo 2.1 ii 23, as an attribute of the Stormgod; NA4ZI.KIN AN[.BAR] KUB 17.35 ii 35 (Rost, MIO 8:207) read *an*[*nallan*] (Carter, Diss. 128); cf. also KUB 38.11:14, KUB 38.36 obv. 10, KUB 42.14 i 2, KUB 42.21:1, 2, 8, 10, KUB 42.74 obv. 3–6, KUB 42.76 obv. 1, KBo 20.103:7;

2′ in other texts: 10 *ēnzi* AN.BAR KBo 15.24 ii 21; [2] *ēnzi* AN.BAR ibid. ii 37 (foundation rit., MH/NS); 1 *šamanaš* AN.BAR "one foundation deposit of iron" KBo 4.1 obv. 21 w. dupl. KUB 2.2 i 24; 1 ZAG.GAR.RA AN.BAR "one iron altar" KBo 4.1 rev. 15 w. dupls. KUB 2.2 ii 17 and KBo 18.169:3; 1-*NUTUM* GIŠIG AN.BAR [*ŠA* 1 GÍN] "one set of doors, [one shekel (in weight)]" KBo 4.1 rev. 25; [AN.B]AR-*aš nēpiš* "sky of iron" KBo 17.1 i 8 w. dupl. KBo 17.3 i 3 (rit., OS); *lālan* AN.BAR-*aš* KBo 17.1 i 18, KBo 17.4 ii 6, KBo 17.2 i 4, KBo 17.3 i 13 (all OS); *nepiš tēkan* AN.BAR *d*[*a*-. . .] KUB 17.20 ii 24 (rit., NS); cf. also KBo 13.256 i 4, KBo 17.74 i 14, KBo 26.150:5, KUB 44.60 rev. iii 15; *ḫa-pal-ki* KBo 24.51 obv.? (5) w. dupl. KBo 24.52:6; *ḫa-pal-ki-it* KUB 51.56:2, HT 38 iii 12;

i. jewelry and ornaments: *TUTITTUM* GAL AN.BAR "large iron pectoral" KUB 42.21:5 (inv., NH); 2 *TŪTITTUM* AN.BAR KÙ.GI GAR.RA "two pectorals of iron, inlaid with gold" KUB 29.4 i 19 w. dupl. KUB 29.5 obv. (3) (rit., NH), ed. Schw.Gotth. 8f.; 1 *KAMKAMMATUM* AN.BAR *ŠA* A.BÁR-*ia* "one ring of iron and lead" KUB 9.32 i 9 w. dupl. KUB 41.18 ii 10 (rit., NH); 1 *šit*[*tar* A]N.BAR "one sun-disc of iron" KBo 2.1 iv 1 (cult inv., NH); ḪAR.GÌR AN.B[AR . . .] "anklet of iron" KUB 39.61 i 12 (rit.frag.); GAB *lupanneš* AN.BAR "fronts of headbands of iron" KUB 12.1 iii 12 (inv., NH), cf. CHD 3:86 (differently); 4 ^{GIŠ}ḪAŠḪUR *ŠA* AN.BAR "four apples of iron" KBo 4.1 ii 30 (foundation rit., NH); 15 *ŠUPPAT* KÙ.[GI] ŠÀ 1 *ŠA* AN.BAR 7 *iššanāpiš* AN.BAR *unuwašḫeš ŠA* $^{\text{LÚ.MEŠ}}$*ḫāpeš* ^{URU}*Ḫatti* "fifteen *Š.* of gold, among them one of iron, seven *i.* of iron: adornments of the *ḫ.*-men of Ḫattuša" 1620/c + 253/c + KBo 16.80 rev. iii 8–10 (KI.LAM fest.), translit. StBoT 28:116, cf. StBoT 27:165; cf. also frag. refs. KUB 16.83 obv. 52 (oracle, NH), KBo 18.165 i (1), 4, KBo 18.165a: (2) (inv., NH);

j. quantities: The largest item is the iron tub of 90 minas, see above, 1.d (KUB 38.1 obv. ii 21); 3 MA.NA AN.BAR HT 98:5 (rit.frag.); [. . .]x MA.NA 30 GÍN AN.BAR KUB 26.66 iv 3 (inv., NH); 1 MA.NA AN.BAR KUB 24.5 i 4 (rit., NH); [x] MA.NA AN.BAR KBo 22.142 iv 4 (rit.); 10 GÍN AN.BAR IBoT 1.6 rev. 14 (fest.frag.);

k. lists of metals and minerals (see Laroche, RHA XXIV/79:171ff.): "silver, gold, blue stone, rock crystal, *iron,* bronze, alabaster, basalt" KBo 4.1 rev. 23–26; "silver, gold, blue stone, copper, tin, *iron,* [. . .]" KUB 24.12 ii 17–18 (rit., NH); "silver, gold, blue stone, carnelian, tin, *iron,* copper" ibid. ii 26–27, iii 2; "silver, gold, blue stone, red stone, Babylonian stone, antimony, life stone, marcasite, *iron,* tin, copper, bronze" KUB 27.67 ii 59–61, iii 61–63, iv 34–35 (rit., MH/NS); "silver, gold, blue stone, [. . .], Babylonian stone, rock crystal, *iron,* copper, [. . .], tin" KBo 12.42:10–12 (epic, OH); "silver, gold, tin, *iron,* copper, lead, antimony" KUB 43.60 iv 13 (incant., OH/NS); "silver, gold, *iron,* tin, blue stone, carnelian" KUB 41.8 iii 19–20 (rit., MH/NS); "silver, black iron, tin, *iron,* copper, blue stone, life stone, red stone, lead" KUB 12.24 i 7–12 (rit.); "silver, gold, *iron,* black iron, tin" KUB 15.9 iii 3 (dream, NH); "gold, copper, tin, *iron,* lead" KUB 24.5 obv. 24–25 + KUB 9.13:12 (rit., NH); "all stones, *iron,* black iron, tin" KUB 32.129 i 13 (rit., NH); "gla[ss, . . .], blue stone, [. . .], [. . .]-stone, tin, *iron,* [. . .]" KBo 17.91 i 1–3 (rit.frag.); "*iron,* tin" KUB 35.162 rev.$^{?}$ 3 (rit.frag.);

l. symbolic references: "O Stormgod of Nerik, my lord!" AN.BAR-*aš tarr*[*iyašḫaš* NU.GÁL] "there is no fatigue in iron!" KUB 31.136 obv. ii 2 (prayer, NS), ed. KN 196f. and Laroche RHA XV/60:14; ^{d}UTU-*wa*⟨*š*⟩

AN.BAR *kišar*[*u*] "May he (sc. Labarna) become the iron of the Sungod!" KBo 21.22:40 (benedictions for Labarna, OH/MS), ed. Archi, FsMeriggi 2:46f.; *labarnašma* LUGAL-*uš* AN.BAR-*aš* GIŠ*šušiyazzakel ēšdu* "May Labarna, the king, be a *š.* of iron!" KUB 11.23 vi 4–5 w. dupl. KUB 25.20 + KUB 46.23 iv? 24 (AN.TAḪ.ŠUM fest.); the reading GIŠ*šušiyazzakel* as one word based on KUB 11.23 vi 7 and KBo 17.90 ii 8′, by courtesy of H. A. Hoffner; for a different analysis, see Jasink-Ticchioni, SCO 27:160; *nušmaš=kan uizzi* LUGAL-*uš Labarnaš kardišmi* AN.NA AN.BAR-*ia* x x "it will come that the king Labarna [will put] tin and iron into your heart!" KUB 29.1 i 48f. (foundation rit., OH/NS), ed. Kellerman, Diss. 12, 27, tr. ANET 357; AN.BAR-*aš* [*ḫ*]*ui*[*šwatar* . . .] / [. . .] *tarḫuilātar* DINGIR.MEŠ-*aš āšš*[*iyauwar*?] "the life of iron, the bravery [of . . .], the love of gods" KBo 9.137 iii 12–13 (rit., MH/MS), translit. HW² 403a; DINGIR.MEŠ *ḫ*[*a-p*]*al-ki-ia-aš* KUB 16.34 i 1 (oracle, NH); *natkan* AN.BAR-*aš tuppi ḫazziyanun* "I have inscribed it (sc. the drawing of the borders) on a tablet of iron" KBo 4.10 rev. 22 (tr., Tudḫ. IV); *AWAT Tabarna* LUGAL GAL *ŠA* AN.BA[R] "The words of Labarna, the Great King, are of iron (and must not be altered)!" İnandık rev. 19–20 (land grant, OS), ed. Balkan, İnandık 2f.; cf. KBo 5.7 rev. 49–50 (land grant, Arn. I, MS), ed. Riemschneider, MIO 6:354f., and passim in land grants;

m. cosmology: *nu* dU-*ni* GIM-*an nepiši* AN.BAR-*a*[*š* . . .] / *aranda nu nepiš karpan ḫark*[*anzi* . . .] "Just as the [pillars(?)] of iron (belonging) to the Stormgod stand in the sky and support the sky" KUB 34.77 obv. 9–10 (rit.frag., MH?/NS); *šerašši nēpiš* AN.BAR-*aš* "above him is the sky of iron" KUB 33.34 obv. 9 (myth., OH/NS), translit. Laroche, Myth. [67];

n. institutions: É*ḫa-pal-ki* KUB 39.76 obv. 3, 15, KUB 39.73:12 (rit.); belonging to the word for "iron" according to Laroche, RA 67:130 n.2, but questioned by Kammenhuber, HW² s.v. *apalki*.

2. AN.BAR GE$_6$ "black iron"; NH; The dating depends on KBo 20.103++ which is either early NS or MS. The frequent tr. "meteoric iron" is based on the passage AN.BAR GE$_6$ *nepišaš nepišaz uter* KBo 4.1 i 39 w. dupl. KUB 9.33 obv. 15, but note the dupl. AN.BAR *nepišaz uter* KUB 2.2 i 48, and see the discussion sub 1.

a. ornaments and jewelry—**1′** earrings: [x] *ašušaš* AN.BAR GE$_6$ KUB 38.4 i 6 (cult inv., NH), ed. Jakob-Rost, MIO 8:185; [. . .] *INZABTUM* AN.BAR GE$_6$ KUB 42.11 i 4;

2′ strips for diadems: EME ZABAR *luwanneš* GAB AN.BAR GE$_6$ KBo 18.170 rev. 2; [1]-*EN* EME AN.BAR GE$_6$ *lupanneš* KUB 42.42 iv 5; 2 EME AN.BAR GE$_6$ GAB *lupann*[*eš*] KUB 12.1 iii 8;

3′ sun-discs: 1-*EN* AŠ.ME NA$_4$.ZA.GÌN AN.BAR GE$_6$ KÙ.GI GAR.RA "one sun-disc, inlaid with blue stone, black iron and gold" KUB 42.78 obv. ii 13;

4′ lunulae: 1-*EN armanneš* AN.BAR GE_6 KUB 42.43 obv. 5;

5′ pins: 1 *GIRIZU* AN.BAR GE_6 KUB 42.75 obv. 10;

6′ other: 4 *aramniuš* KÙ.GI NA_4 AN.BAR GE_6 "four *a.*-ornaments of gold, stones and black iron" KUB 12.1 iii 22; 1-*EN šikkiš* AN.BAR GE_6 ibid. iii 13; [. . .]x AN.BAR GE_6 8 ḪAR.⌜GÌR⌝ AN.BAR GE_6 "[. . .] of black iron, 8 anklets of black iron" KUB 42.11 i 2; [. . .]x *UNQU* AN.BAR GE_6 "[x] stamp seals of black iron" ibid. i 11; cf. also KBo 18.170 obv. 3, KUB 42.43 obv. 6;

b. tools and weapons—**1′** daggers: 15[o]⌜AN⌝.[BAR] x ⌜GÍR⌝ AN.BAR GE_6 ŠÀ.BA 5 ⌜TUR⌝ [. . .] / ^{GIŠ}*tuppa* EME AN.BAR GE_6-*kan* "15 [. . .] of iron, [x] daggers of black iron. The chest (contains) blades of black iron" KUB 42.76 obv. 2–3 (inv., NH), ed. THeth 10:190; 5 EME GÍR TUR AN.BAR "five small daggers of black iron" KUB 42.11 v 4;

2′ maces: 16 ^{GIŠ}TUKUL AN.BAR G[E_6] KBo 18.158:5; 3 ^{GIŠ}TUKUL x[o] / [o o o o o o o] ŠÀ.BA 1 AN.BAR G[E_6] KUB 42.11 v 1–2;

3′ axes: [. . . *ḪAZZ*]*INNU* GAL KÙ.GI NA_4.ZA.GÌN NA_4.TI AN.BAR GE_6-*ia* KBo 20.103 obv. ii 2 + KBo 21.87 obv. ii 10 (list of offerings, early NS? or MS?);

c. vessels: 1 GÚ GUD AN.BAR GE_6 "one rhyton (in the shape of) an ox head" KUB 42.19 obv.? 4; 1 *pian pitummaš* AN.BAR GE_6 KÙ.GI "one tray (lit. 'of carrying forward') of black iron and gold" KUB 42.64 rev. 16, cf. KUB 42.11 i 3 (all inv., NH);

d. statuettes: [. . .] UDU (or: -]*LU*) AN.BAR GE_6 / [. . . ^{UR}]^{U}*Mizri* "one sheep(??) of black iron, [destination(?)] Egypt" KBo 14.72 obv. 1–2 (inv., NH); (a large statue of one hundred minas is made of) "silver, gold, iron and black iron" KUB 15.9 rev. iii 3 (dream, NH);

e. other: [x ^{GIŠ}*tuppaš*] SA_5 TUR AN.BAR GE_6 *kīnān* "[x] small red [chest(s)]: (containing) assorted black iron" KUB 42.14 i 11; NA_4.ḪI.A *ḫūmanda* AN.BAR AN.BAR GE_6 *ANNAKU* "all stones, iron, black iron and tin" (are put on scales) KUB 32.129 i 13 (rit., NH); cf. also KUB 12.24 i 8 (rit., NS).

3. AN.BAR SIG_5 "good iron"; from Ḫatt. III.

a. (Akk.) "As for the good iron (AN.BAR SIG_5) you wrote me about, good iron in my seal-house is not available. That it is a bad time for producing iron (A.BAR) I have written. (But) they will produce good iron; so far they will not have finished. When they will have finished, I shall send (it) to you. Today now I have an iron dagger blade brought on its way to you" KBo 1.14 obv. 20–24 (letter of Ḫatt. III to a king of Assyria), ed. Kizz. 28f.;

b. other: [x *pal*]*zaḫaš* AN.BAR SIG_5 KUB 42.14 obv. i 3 (inv., NH); x *palzaḫaš* AN.BAR SIG_5 *ŠA* KASKAL "x pedestals of good iron: by caravan" KUB 42.11 rev. v 9; [1 GI]Š*tuppaš* GAL ŠÀ-*ŠU ŠUŠI* 6 AN.BAR SIG_5 "one large chest: (containing) 66 (ingots?) of good iron" KUB 42.21 obv. 6 (inv., NH), ed. THeth 10:46f.

4. AN.BAR BABBAR "white iron"(?); NH.
ALAM SAL AN.BAR BABBAR GIŠ 1 *UPNI* DÙ-*anzi* "they fashion a statuette of a woman, of white iron (and) wood, (measuring) one *upnu*" VBoT 83:10 (inv., NH); it is conceivable that BABBAR defined GIŠ, but cf. the word order GIŠŠUKUR GIŠ-*ZI* BABBAR-*TIM* "spear of white wood" KBo 11.43 i 25, and GIŠ *ḫar-ki* "white wood" KUB 5.9 i 12 (Ertem, Flora 157).

* * *

The following development in iron technology can now be discerned:
1. from the Old Kingdom (ca. 1650 onwards): iron (AN.BAR);
2. from Šuppiluliuma I (ca. 1380 onwards): black iron (AN.BAR GE_6);
3. from Ḫattušili III (ca. 1275 onwards): good iron (AN.BAR SIG_5), and white iron (AN.BAR BABBAR).

By a cursory count, the items listed in Hittite texts add up to several hundred artefacts. Most of them, such as statuettes and jewelry, are small, while the production of, for instance, the notable iron tub weighing ninety minas (see above, 1.d) must have posed a considerable technical challenge.

Although most references come from the Empire period, it would be misleading to conclude that the production of iron was steadily increasing from the Old Kingdom to the end of the Hittite Empire. The bulk of the evidence comes from inventories which were compiled during the late Empire, while the earlier references stem from texts of a different nature, mainly from rituals and festivals where single items of iron are mentioned only sporadically.

Most artefacts, including weapons, served ornamental, prestigious and ceremonial purposes. Any notion of a Hittite supremacy based on their technological superiority, may therefore be relegated to the status of fiction: "There is a rumor that Hittites have discovered some new metal and that weapons made of this can chip the edges of the finest copper ax." (Mika Waltari, *The Egyptian*)

Addendum.
New textual ref.: "Afterwards, the cupbearer libates wine once with a depas" *parā=ma* NINDA.KUR_4.RA *ANA* 2 d*Tiyapentašš=a* DINGIR.MEŠ *ḫa-pal-ki-ia-aš paršiya* "next, he also breaks up a thick loaf for the two T., the deities of iron" KBo 30.71 obv. iii 16–18 (fest., NS).

New lit: Melchert, JCS 35 (1983) 141 w.n. 14 (proposing a new equation of words for iron, Anat. *kiklu-* = Akk. *parzillu* = Sum. AN.BAR); Siegelová, Annals of the Náprstek Museum 12 (1984) 71–168 (presenting full textual evidence with context, maintaining a tr. "meteoric iron" for AN.BAR GE_6, advocating utilitarian rather than ceremonial use of iron during the Late Empire).

HITTITE *nakkuš—nakkuššiš*

EMMANUEL LAROCHE

Paris

Le paragraphe 98 du Code Hittite contient un mot très rare qui a donné lieu à plusieurs interprétations, depuis l'édition de Hrozný (1922).

takku LÚ-*aš ELLUM* É-*ir lukkizzi* É-*ir* EGIR-*pa wetezzi andan-a* É-*ri kuit ḫar(a)kzi* LÚ.ULÙ.LU-*ku* GUD-*ku* UDU-*ku ešzi na-ak-ku-uš Ú-UL šarnikzi* (A: *na-at* [*šar-ni-ik-*]*za*) "Si un homme libre allume (i.e. incendie[1]) une maison, il rebâtit la maison, et ce qui périt dans la maison—que ce soit une personne ou un boeuf ou un mouton[2]—*nakkuš* il ne remplace pas."

nakkuš a été compris de deux façons[3]: 1) les uns en font l'acc. plur. animé de l'adjectif *nakki-* "grave, lourd, précieux," et le traduisent comme attribut adverbial de *šarnikzi*. Ainsi Friedrich, HG 49 n. 1: "ersetzt er nicht im(?) vollen(?) Werte(?)," "wörtlich 'die schweren (vollwichtigen) ersetzt er nicht' (?)"; F. Imparati, Leggi 95 n. 3: "come preziosi non risarcisca," "cioè . . . nel loro normale, giusto valore"[4]; 2) d'autres imaginent une négation *nakkuš*, non autrement connue (on n'a que *nikku*), que l'on combine avec *UL* (= *natta*) pour obtenir une affirmation forte, comme parfois en latin: ainsi Goetze, ANET 193: "he shall replace as a matter of course."

Ces deux explications me paraissent désespérées. La seule solution grammaticalement correcte est celle-ci: *nakkuš* est un nom neutre, thème en *-uš-* comme *kalmuš*, accordé avec *kuit* et objet de *šarnikzi*. On gagne aussitôt un

1. Cf. CHD 3, 1, 1980, p. 78 a, sous *lukki/a-*.

2. *-ku* est la particule enclitique de disjonction, équivalant au lat. *sive . . . sive . . . sive . . .*: elle détaille la notion générale contenue dans *kuit . . . nakkuš*. Il ne s'agit pas d'une conjonction de subordination, comme l'ont soutenu récemment plusieurs auteurs; celle-ci est *takku*, remplacée plus tard par *mān;* cf. Annuaire Coll. France 1980–81, p. 488. *sq*.

3. Résumé des analyses chez F. Imparati, Leggi p. 270 *sqq*.

4. Je ne connais pas l'acc. plur. régulier **nakkiuš* de *nakki-:* le *na-ak-ki-i-uš* de KUB 3.94 i 28 est un nom. sg., celui du thème *nakkiu-*, pl. *nakkiweš*, dont la relation à *nakki-* est obscure, peut-être illusoire; cf. KUB 35.40 i 1; 54 i 16, etc., avec les notes de H. Otten, LTU p. 41; Luv. p. 38. Le mot isolé *na-ak-ki-mu-uš-(ša)*, KBo 24.61:6, serait-il l'acc. pl. en *-imuš*, analogique des adj. en *-u/aw-*? Il n'y a pas trace de la flexion en *-a-* de *nakki-*, en dehors du prétendu *nakkuš*.

sens satisfaisant: "et ce qui périt dans la maison, que ce soit une personne ou du bétail, le *dommage* il ne remplace pas."[5]

nakkuš qualifie bien *kuit ḫarakzi* à la manière d'une apposition ou d'un attribut, d'où sa place immédiatement avant le verbe. Or le mot existe ailleurs, dans deux contextes malheureusement fragmentaires:

a. KBo 3.60 = BoTU 21 i 12: -]x-*wa-tar-ra na-ak-ku-uš*
b. KBo 8.74+ = CTH 752 = StBoT 25, No. 137 i 5: -*z*]*i na-ak-ku-uš*.

N. van Brock, à la suite de Friedrich, avait déjà noté les références, à propos de *nakkušši-* "substitut vivant," mais elle les avait trop vite rejetées comme non pertinentes.[6] Obsédée par l'idée que le hittite *nakkušši-* est un emprunt au hourrite,[7] elle est passée à côté de l'étymologie évidente: *nakkušši-* n'est pas autre chose que le doublet animé de *nakkuš*. Ainsi qu'elle-même l'a parfaitement établi, *nakkušši-* désigne un *être vivant porteur d'une faute et réputé coupable*. Le passage décisif est au rituel de Maštigga III 38 *sqq.*: "on amène un mouton et on le nomme *(ḫalziššai) nakkušši*."[8] Par quoi il est clair qu'une personne ou un animal n'est pas *nakkušši* de nature, mais qu'il/elle est réputé tel(le) sous l'effet d'une convention verbale, d'une qualification circonstancielle. L'opération a un caractère magique; elle consiste à conférer à l'être vivant l'état de *nakkuši/a-*, ce qui s'appelle normalement en hitt. *nakkuš-atar*, en louv. *nakkušaḫit*.[9]

Il faut donc reconnaître un couple de notions connexes opposées par le genre: d'un côté l'inanimé *nakkuš*, objet subissant ou ayant subi un dommage, à la limite "objet détruit"; de l'autre un animé (masc. fém.) *nakkušš-i/a-*, incarnation vivante d'une faute commise, personne ou animal désigné comme future victime, bouc émissaire. Un couple analogue existe en grec, *mutandis mutatis:* c'est le neutre *phármakon*, plante à vertu médicinale (et son con-

5. Le duplicat fragmentaire KUB 29.20 conserve devant *šarnikzi* une moitié de signe que l'on peut lire -*m*]*a* avec Friedrich, HG p. 48 n. 4, et F. Imparati, Leggi p. 94: "Il rebâtit . . . [mais] il ne remplace pas." [Ed.: Or [*na-a*]*t šarnik*[*zi*] following KBo 6.2 iv 55? There is insufficient space for [*Ú-UL-m*]*a*, and [*UL-m*]*a* would be a late 13th century writing.]

6. RHA XVII/65, 1959, p. 144 n. 33.

7. L'emprunt au hourrite a été proposé avec réserves par Friedrich, HW p. 148; à sa suite, sans réserves ni doute, N. van Brock, RHA XVII/65, p. 144 n. 33; H. Kümmel, StBoT 3, 1967, p. 142, 144, etc.; Friedrich, HW 2.Erg., 1961, p. 18; A. Goetze, JCS 13, 1959, p. 36 *sq.;* O. R. Gurney, Schweich, 1977, p. 51.

8. Van Brock, *ibid.*, p. 127. Pour l'emploi de *ḫalzai-*, *ḫalzeššai-* dans la magie, voir les textes cités par A. Goetze, Tunnawi, 1938, p. 40.

9. La variante *nakkuššan*, *ibid.* 128 (sous Bo 5585 = KUB 41.11 iii 12; Hoffner, FsGordon 86 *sq.* n. 31) suffit à justifier les dérivés en -*atar* et -*aḫit;* elle n'est pas une preuve d'emprunt à une langue étrangère, mais l'indice du caractère secondaire de l'animé à voyelle.

traire le poison), auquel s'oppose un masculin secondaire, aussi de valeur magique: *pharmakós,* victime expiatoire à rejeter loin de la société qu'elle souille.[10]

La doctrine de l'origine hourrite du hitt. *nakkušši* s'est tôt répandue chez les hittitologues, mais elle repose sur des bases extrêmement fragiles.

1) N. van Brock utilise un passage mutilé de KBo 1.22, restauré par Goetze sur la foi du *nakkuššu/e* nouzien.[11] Or, la restauration est erronée.

Au cours de ses recherches sur la correspondance égypto-hittite, E. Edel a réussi à identifier le fragment KBo 1.22, qui est un duplicat de KUB 3.31 Vo 2, et par suite aussi, de KBo 1.15+19 = CTH 156.[12] Au lieu de *na*]-*ak-ka-aš-šu* en KBo 1.22 Vo 3–8, il faut lire [*il-qa-*]*ak-ka-aš-šu ia-nu-ú* d'après KUB 3.31 Vo 2.

2) le mot *nakkuššu/e,* documenté plusieurs fois à Nuzi et à Alalah en contexte akkadien, est maintenant inséré comme "emprunt" hourrite dans les deux grands dictionnaires.

CAD N (1), 186 b: a group of persons. Définition exacte et prudente, car il n'y a rien dans les textes qui suggère un rapport sémantique ni avec le *nakkušši* hittite ni avec une notion de "substitut" ou "victime expiatoire."

L'anthroponyme *Nakkušše* à Alalah se concilie mal avec le sens du mot hittite.

W. von Soden, AHw 722 b, propose "Ersatzmann?" Mais qui ne voit que cet essai de traduction est simplement emprunté au hitt. *nakkušši,* cité à l'appui?[13]

3) reste le mot *nakkašše/a* de la lettre mitannienne, apparemment un adjectif (ou un participe du verbe *nakk-*??), qualifiant des objets de métal[14]; *nakkašše* n'est pas *nakkušše*: il faudrait justifier les vocalismes divergents par une analyse morphologique précise; le sens présumé, "serti, coulé" d'après l'akk. *uḫḫuzu,* éloigne le mot à la fois du hitt. *nakkušši* et du verbe *nakk-*. N. van Brock a dépensé en vain un trésor d'ingéniosité pour concilier les inconciliables.

L'homonymie trompeuse du hitt. *nakkuš(ši)* et du hourr. *nakkušu* doit être abandonnée. Le regrettera-t-on? Non, puisqu'en libérant le hittite de l'hypothèque hourrite, et en restituant à l'anatolien le groupe de *nakkuš* et ses dé-

10. Définition de ces termes chez Chantraine *et al.,* Dict. étymol. de la langue grecque, 1980, p. 1179.

11. A. Goetze, Kizz. 1940, p. 34.

12. E. Edel, ZA 49 NF 15, 1951, p. 206; Goetze, Kizz., p. 207 n. 2.

13. C'est le lieu de rappeler avec Gurney, Schweich, p. 51, que le terme pour "substitut, échange" est *puḫugari,* dérivé hourrite en *-ugar-* d'un *puḫu* emprunté à l'akk. *pūḫu.*

14. GLH, p. 177.

rivés, on récupère le représentant de la racine indo-européenne **nek-* "périr, faire périr."[15] A cette racine appartient le vieux terme juridique latin *noxa,* pratiquement synonyme du hitt. *nakkuš*: en grec, le dérivé *nekus* "cadavre" et en latin *-nocuus* "nuisible" ont le même thème d'adjectif en *-u-* que le hitt. *nakkuš(i)* < **nok-u-s-(i)*.[16]

15. Ernout-Meillet, Dict. étym. lat. sous *nex, noceo, noxa.*

16. Le verbe dénominatif *nakkušiya-,* étudié en dernier lieu par K. Riemschneider, StBoT 9, 1970, p. 55, demeure énigmatique.

EIN aA VERTRAG ÜBER GEMEINSAME HAUSHALTSFÜHRUNG AUS DER ZEIT DER KÜLTEPE-SCHICHT I^{b}*

LUBOR MATOUŠ†

Prague

Wenn ich hier meinem lieben Freund H. G. Güterbock als bescheidene Ehrengabe zu seinem 75. Geburtstag einen Keilschrifttext aus den Sammlungen der Prager Karls-Universität präsentiere, so bin ich mir bewusst, dass ich mich nicht unbedingt im unmittelbaren Kerngebiet der wissenschaftlichen Betätigungen des Jubilars bewege. Dennoch hoffe ich, dass mein bescheidener Beitrag sein Interesse finden wird, zumal es sich um ein von der äusseren Erscheinung wie auch vom Inhalt her ganz ungewöhnliches Textexemplar handelt. Leider ist die Tafel—sie trägt die Inventar-Nummer I 837—vor allem auf der Rückseite in einem sehr schlechten Erhaltungszustand, sodass zahlreiche Einzelheiten und damit auch das Gesamtverständnis einstweilen leider unsicher bleiben.

Beginnen wir mit der äusseren Beschreibung der Tafel, so ist auf Grund des Schriftduktus klar, dass wir es mit einem aA Text zu tun haben, ein Eindruck, der bei Überprüfung von Sprache und Orthographie alsbald Bestätigung findet. Es liegt somit nahe, als Herkunftsort den Kültepe anzunehmen[1], wenngleich entgültige Gewissheit darüber nicht zu gewinnen ist. Gegenüber sonstigen Kültepe-Tafeln fallen jedoch das Fehlen der Zeilenlinierung und die auf der Tafel angebrachten Siegelabdrücke auf. Die Tafel ist also so behandelt, wie bei den Texten der klassischen Kültepe-Schicht II die Tafelhülle. Siegelung der Tafel gilt aber als Merkmal der Texte aus der Kültepe-Schicht I^{b}[2]. In ihrer Stilisierung entspricht unsere Tafel ebenfalls

*The editors would like to express their thanks to Prof. K. Hecker for his considerable help with the manuscript of the late Prof. Matouš.

1. Hierfür spricht auch das rein anatolische Onomastikon des Textes. Zumindest stammte er nicht aus Assur.

2. Vgl. K. Balkan, Observations (TTKY VII/28) 65[8], wo auch andere publizierte Texte ähnlicher Art aufgezählt sind. Für eine zahlenmässige Zusammenstellung gesiegelter Tafeln aus den Ausgrabungen am Kültepe vgl. N. Özgüç, TTKY V/25, 62.

der der Hüllen der Schicht II, insofern als sie wie diese die Namen der Zeugen mit Hinweis auf den Siegelungsvorgang (KIŠIB *Pn*) dem zu beurkundenden Wortlaut voranstellt. Innentafeln der Schicht II lassen dagegen gewöhnlich die Zeugen (IGI *Pn*) dem beurkundeten Text nachfolgen.

Entsprechend der Zahl der Zeugen trägt die Tafel richtig drei Stempelabdrücke. Von diesen lässt allein Abdruck C Spuren der figurativen Ausgestaltung erkennen. Dargestellt ist ein ruhender Vierfüssler, der von einem Spiralband und 8 symmetrisch angeordneten Doppelkreisen umgeben ist[3]. Die Darstellungen der beiden anderen Abdrücke sind offenbar unmittelbar nach der Siegelung verwischt worden und nicht mehr zu erkennen. In der Grösse bestehen zwischen den Abdrücken nur minimale Unterschiede (A ca. 15×14 mm, B und C ca. 14×16 mm), die u. U. auch auf unterschiedliche Verdrückung der Tafel während der Stempelung und Beschriftung zurückgehen könnten. Es wäre also denkbar, dass zwei, wenn nicht gar alle drei Abdrücke von einunddemselben Siegel stammen; dies würde freilich bedeuten, dass einer oder gegebenenfalls zwei der Zeugen über kein persönliches Siegel verfügt hätte[4].

Der Wortlaut des Textes ist wegen des schlechten Zustandes vor allem der Rs. leider nur zum Teil verständlich. Der Sachverhalt ist offenbar der, dass vier Personen, von denen zwei als "die Eltern" (*abum ummum* Z. 5)—doch wohl der beiden anderen—bezeichnet werden, einen gemeinsamen Hausstand führen (*bētam puḫur ušbū* Z. 7). Für den Fall, dass einer der beiden Söhne[5] gegen die Eltern unrecht handelt oder dass eine der Parteien stirbt, werden verschiedene, im einzelnen zumeist unklare Regelungen vereinbart. Juristisch gesehen liegt wohl kein Testament auf Gegenseitigkeit, sondern ein Vertrag auf gemeinsame Haushaltsführung vor. Hierfür spricht nicht nur, dass das in aA Testamenten[6] zu erwartende *šimtum* "Bestimmung" in unserem Text fehlt, sondern auch, dass mit der Regelung für den Fall unrechten Tuns der Söhne gegenüber den Eltern (Z. 9–12) eine dem Erbfall zeitlich vorangehende Bestimmung vorgesehen ist.

Vs. KIŠIB *Ḫu-dar-lá-ni* GAL *ur-dí-e*?
KIŠIB *Pè-ru-wa* IḪ.ME *ša*⟨d⟩IM?!

3. Beschreibung des Siegels durch M. Matoušova.

4. Benutzung eines gemeinsamen Siegels lässt sich auch sonst gelegentlich beobachten, jedoch wohl nur bei interfamiliären Bindungen der Siegelnden. Vgl. M. T. Larsen, BiMes. 6, 99 m. A. 62 und L. Matouš, Kappadokische Keilschrifttafeln mit Siegeln (Prague, 1984), S. 19.

5. Dass es sich tatsächlich um die Söhne der beiden Z. 4–5 genannten Personen handelt, ist zwar nirgends ausdrücklich gesagt, in Anbetracht der juristischen Situation aber kaum anderes vorstellbar.

6. Zu den aA Testamenten vgl. zuletzt C. Wilcke, ZA 66, 1976, 196ff.

KIŠIB Ḫa-ar-šu-lá (Ras.) DUMU Šu-pì-a-n[a]
Ḫa-pu-a-šu / Ḫi-iš-ta-aḫ-šu-šar
a-bu-um um-mu-um Wa-li-a-ša-zu
Ku-nu-wa-an a-(Ras.)-ḫu-šu be-tám
pu-ḫu-ur uš-bu a-qá-tí
iš-tí-in ú-kà-⟨lu⟩-šu-ú
šu-ma ma-ma-an i-ba-ri-šu-nu
i-ṣé-er a-bi$_4$-im um-mì-im i-ša-lá
mì-ma ú-ba-x zi-tám i-ša-x
a-ší-mì-im i-dí-nu-š[um]?
i-nu-mì a-bu-um um-[mu-um]
ki-lá-lá-šu-nu i-[mu-tù-ni]
šu-ba-at be?!-t[im]?
K. pu-ḫu-ur uš-[bu šu-ma]
lá ṭá-bu be-[tám ú mì-ma]
Rs. i-ba-ší-ú 2$^{tu[m]}$
mì-it-ḫi-ri-i[š i-zu-zu]
šu-ma Wa-li-a-š[a-zu]
i-mu-a-at a[m-tám]?
Ga-aḫ-šu-šar x [x x (x)]
i-da-gu$_5$-lu [x? z]i? r[i? (x)]
lu ma-ma-[a]n lu e-d[um]
ša qá-tí-šu [x (x x)]
šé-lu-im?! [Ku-nu-wa]-an
be-el ṣé-eḫ-[ri-im x (x x)]
ú šu-ma Ku-nu-wa-an i-mu-a-at
zi-tù-šu / ma-li-a
x-šu-x-šu i-da-gu$_5$-lu
[š]í?-im x ru x ba x x x x
[š]a? ma-li-a
u.K. [x]? ki li-it-bi$_4$-i
⟨i⟩?-qá-tí-šu-nu i-nu-mì x [x]
i-zu-zu-ni / ur-dam
l.S. Ku-nu-wa-an ut-ra-am i-lá-qé i-qá-tí
[Z]u-zu ru-ba-im Ištar-ip-ra
GAL sí-mì-il$_5$-tim

Vs. Siegel des Ḫudarlani, des Obersten der Sklaven?,
Siegel des Peruwa, des Priesters des Adad?,
Siegel des Ḫaršula, des Sohnes von Šuppiana.
Ḫappuaššu, Ḫištaḫšušar

—Vater und Mutter—Waliašazu
und sein Bruder Kunuwan
bewohnen gemeinsam ein Haus. Als einen
einzigen Anteil halten sie es.
Wenn einer von ihnen (beiden)
gegen Vater und Mutter Unrecht tut,
wird man, was an *dem Gemeinbesitz* als Anteil *er hat,*
i[hm]$^{?}$ verkaufen.
Sobald Vater und Mu[tter]
beide s[terben],
werden die Wohnung des Hauses
K. sie (weiterhin) gemeinsam bew[ohnen. Wenn]
sie (daran) keinen Gefallen haben, [werden sie] das Ha[us und alles, was sonst]
Rs. da ist, zu zw[eit]
gleichmässig [teilen].
Wenn Waliašazu
stirbt, werden sie die Sk[lavin]
Gaḫšušar [und/auf . . .]
anschauen [. . .],
sei es irgendwer oder ein ei[nziger],
das seines Anteils [. . .]
hinaufzuführen, [wird . . . Kunuw]an,
den Herrn des Kle[inen . . .].
Und wenn Kunuwan stirbt,
werden sie seinen Anteil, den vollen
. . . , anschauen.
Der [Pr]eis von . . .
. . .
u.K. . . . soll aufstehen.
⟨Von⟩$^{?}$ ihrem Anteil wird, wenn . . .
sie teilen, einen weiteren Sklaven
Kunuwan nehmen. Aus der Hand von
[Z]uzu, dem Fürsten und Ištar-ipra,
dem Treppenoberst.

Kommentar

Z. 1) Der hier erstmals belegte Pn Ḫudarlani ist gewiss mit sonstigem Ḫudarla (dies zu luv. *ḫutarli* "Diener", vgl. P. Garelli, AC 140) zusammenzubringen. Der Titel eines *rabi urdī* "Sklavenoberst" war bislang nicht bekannt.

Z. 2) Zur Lesung der letzten beiden Zeichen: Gegen den Ansatz IḪ.ME *ša-dí,* wie der Text zu bieten scheint, sprechen folgende Erwägungen: Ein solcher "Priester des (vergöttlichten) Gebirges" ist in anatolischem Kontext vielleicht zwar nicht unvorstellbar, aber zumindest in aA Texten bislang unbelegt. Ferner wird der Name der Gottheit nach IḪ.ME/gudu$_4$ = *kumrum* immer durch dazwischen tretendes *ša* eingeführt[7], und schliesslich sind Priester des Adad häufiger bezeugt, darunter auch einmal ein Peruwa[8].

Z. 5) Die sich auf den ersten Blick anbietende Lesung *Wa-li a-ša-sú* "W. (und) seine Ehefrau" ist wegen Z. 20–21, wo diese Zeichenfolge Subjekt zu singularischem *i-mu-a-at* ist, unmöglich. Wegen des sonst ausschliesslich anatolischen Onomastikons des Textes wird man davon ausgehen können, dass auch *Wa-li-a-ša-zu* kein Assyrer war; es empfiehlt sich daher auch kaum, nach einer assyrischen Etymologie dieses Namens zu suchen.

Z. 7) *puḫrum* "Versammlung" ist im st. absol. mit der Bedeutung "gemeinsam, miteinander" aA bislang nicht belegt. *uš-bu* muss hier wie auch Z. 16 Stativ sein.

Z. 11) Nach *mimma* erwartet man entweder einen Subjtv. oder einen Gen. Mit *ú-ba* (oder *pá*[9])-x, wobei x wie *mu* oder auch *šeš* aussieht, kann ich nichts anfangen.

Z. 12) Ein Prt. passt nicht in den Kontext, der laute Bestimmungen für die Zeit nach der Urkundenabfassung enthält. Falls in *i-dí-nu* ein Fehler für *i-du-nu* vorläge, wäre damit der Nachsatz des *šumma*-Satzes Z. 9–10 gefunden. In der Sache ist eine Bestrafung für das unrechte Verhalten gegenüber den Eltern zu erwarten, wobei folgende Möglichkeiten vorstellbar sind: Verkauf des Anteils des 'Übeltäters' und dessen Ausbezahlung, d.h. er würde ohne sonstigen finanziellen Schaden aus der Hausgemeinschaft ausgestossen, oder aber Verkauf und anschliessende Aufteilung des Erlöses auf die anderen Mitglieder. In beiden Fällen wäre das Suf. *-š*[*um*][10] als Dat. (in)commodi, nicht aber als Objekts-Dat., der bei *tadānum* ja den Käufer bezeichnet, zu verstehen.

Z. 18) Es liegt nahe, *2^{tum}* sachlich auf die beiden Brüder bzw. auf deren Anteile an dem Haus zu beziehen. Die Auflösung dieser Schreibung ist mir unklar. Zu erwarten wäre eine Formulierung wie *mišla izuzzū,* vgl. dazu CAD M/2 126a.

Z. 19) Zu dem Wechsel von *ā*/*ī* in *mitḫīriš*/*mitḫāriš* (dies aA bislang nicht belegt) vgl. GKT §8a.

Z. 22ff. sind mir weitgehend unverständlich.

Z. 24) Am Zeilenende erscheint *we-d*[*um*]—darauf folgt offenbar kein weiteres Zeichen mehr—epigraphisch einigermassen sicher. Falls diese Lesung wirklich die richtige ist, wird man für *mamman* "irgendwer" eine pluralische Nebenbedeutung ("irgendwelche Leute") anzusetzen haben, da sonst *(w)ēdum* "ein einziger" wenig sinnvoll wäre.

7. Vgl. die Wörterbücher s.v. *kumru;* weitere Beispiele bei H. Hirsch, UAR (AfO Beih. 13/14) 56.

8. TC III 214 B, 1.

9. Der Zeichenform nach jedenfalls weder *ma* noch *ku.*

10. Eine Lesung -*š*[*u*], die zu einem Akk.-Suf. führen könnte ist ausgeschlossen.

Z. 26) Der Text scheint vor dem Siegelabdruck *šé/í-lu-tí* zu lesen. Da dieses unverständlich ist, ziehen wir *tí* mit dem auf den Abdruck folgenden, von zwei senkrechten Keilen gekreuzten wagerechten zu *im* zusammen.

Z. 32) Das erste Zeichen könnte statt [*š*]*a* auch [*t*]*a* sein; [*t*]*a-ma-li-a* "ihr werdet voll" passt aber kaum in den Kontext, der sonst nur 3. Personen enthält.

Z. 34) Auch andere Verbindungen erscheinen denkbar, z.B. [x]-*ki-li-it*[11] *pì-i,* von welchem dann *qá-tí-šu* Z. 35 als Gen. abhängig gemacht werden könnte. Sinn?

Z. 36) Zur *iqqāti*-Formel vgl. P. Garelli, AC 61 m. A. 2.

Z. 37) Ein anatolischer Fürst namens Zuzu ist sonst unbekannt, ebenso ein Kronprinz[12] Ištar-ipra. Der Name Zuzu erscheint zumeist in assyrischem Personalkontext, z.B. CCT III 36^{b}, 9 (Sohn von Šum-abīja). IV 1^{a}, 12; KTBl. 1, 11, und nur ausnahmsweise in anatolischem, so vor allem EL 5, 3. 21, 18. Zum Pn Ištar-ipra vgl. E. Bilgiç, AfO 15, 1950/51, 4. m. A. 21.

11. Am Zeilenanfang ist nur ein ganz kurzes Zeichen möglich; sogar eine Ergänzung des "*ki*" zu [*n*]*a,* die zu dem Pn Nakkilit führen würde, wäre denkbar.

12. Dass "Treppenoberst" der Titel des Thronfolgers Anitta war, demonstriert Garelli, l.c. 61f.

I 837

Vs

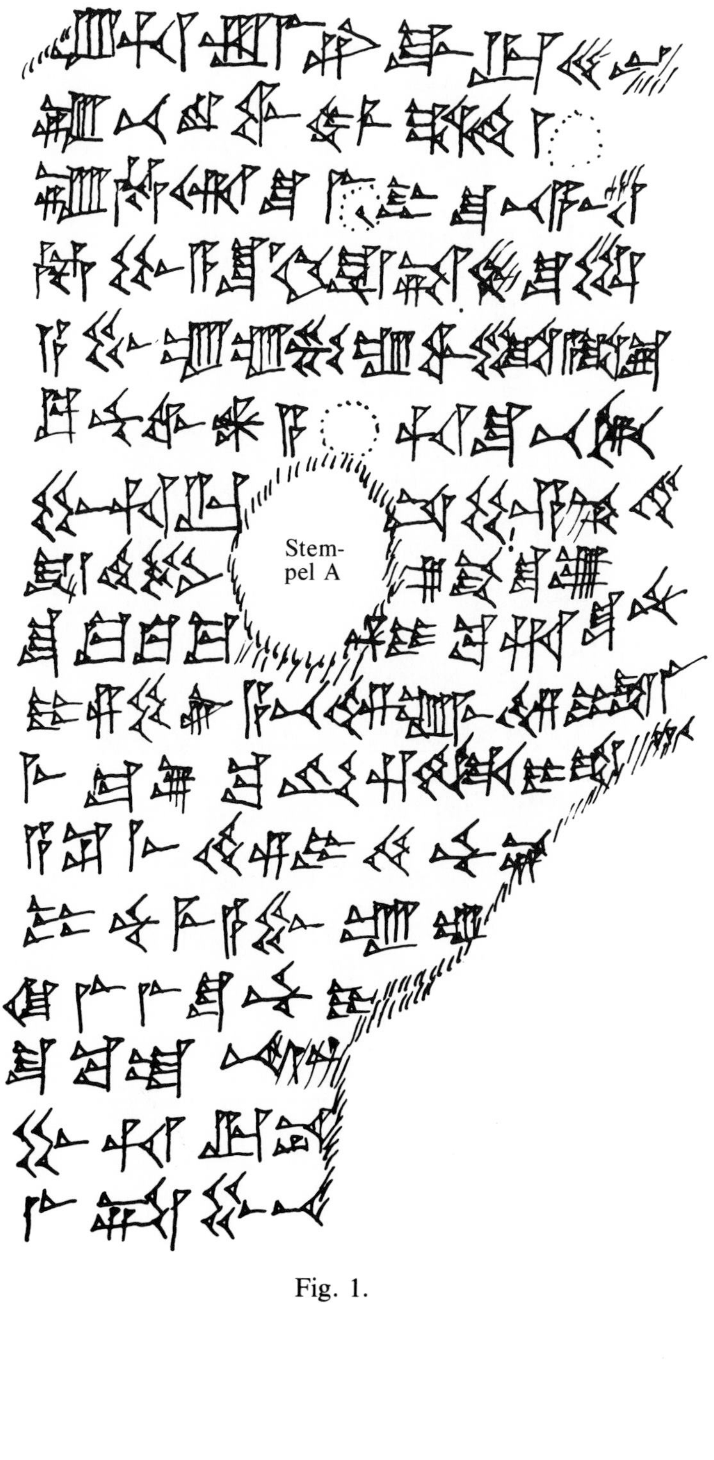

Fig. 1.

I 837

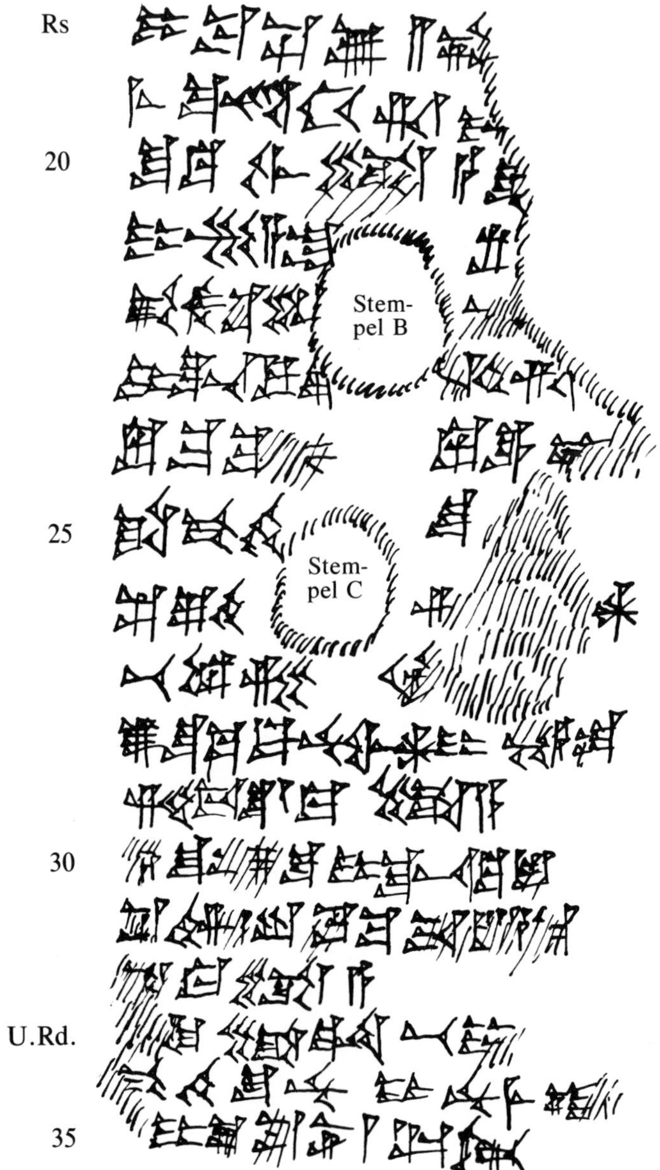

Fig. 2.

I 837

LS 

Fig. 3.

I 837

Fig. 4.

ZUR DATIERUNG DER HETHITISCHEN PFERDETEXTE

ERICH NEU

Bochum

0.1 Die hethitischen Pferdetexte (CTH 284–287) waren schon mehrfach Gegenstand intensiver Forschungstätigkeit; auch der Verehrte Jubilar, dem diese kleine Abhandlung ergebenst gewidmet sei, hat sich mit dieser Thematik befasst[1] und auch mehrere hippologische Fragmente in Autographie vorgelegt[2]. Die noch heute grundlegende Bearbeitung, in der die Pferdetexte auch im Rahmen der Geschichte Vorderasiens behandelt werden, verdanken wir A. Kammenhuber[3], die sich dort auch zur Datierung der im wesentlichen aus drei Trainingsanleitungen bestehenden Textgruppe geäussert hat. Entsprechend der von ihr vorgenommenen Gruppierung und Zählung meinen wir im folgenden mit der 1. Trainingsanleitung (= TrAn I) den sogenannten "Kikkuli-Text" (H 54–147; CTH 284), verstehen unter der 2. Trainingsanleitung (= TrAn II) die "rituell eingeleitete" (H 148–169; CTH 285) und sehen als 3. Trainingsanleitung (= TrAn III) die "rein hethitische" (H 170–225; CTH 286 bzw. 287.2) an.

0.2 Als Ergebnis ihrer Textanalysen der drei hethitischen Trainingsanleitungen glaubte A. Kammenhuber, "bereits bedenkenlos folgende Daten angeben" (H 317) zu dürfen:

TrAn I: "wohl erst in der 2. Hälfte des 14. Jh.s, z.Zt. Muršilis II. entstanden".

TrAn II: "keinesfalls vor Ḫattušili III. (2. Viertel des 13. Jh.s) verfasst".

1. Vgl. vor allem H. G. Güterbocks tiefschürfende, im Grundsätzlichen wie in vielen Einzelheiten weiterführende Rezension zu A. Kammenhubers Monographie Hippologia Hethitica (unten Anm. 3) in JAOS 84, 1964, 267–273; RHA XV/60, 1957, 3–6 (zu *palša-* und *šakruu̯ai-*); s. auch schon bei H. Ehelolf, KUB 29, 1938, vii.

2. KBo 14.62, 63, 63a; KBo 16.88–90.

3. Hippologia Hethitica, 1961. Aus Raumgründen benutzen wir dafür hier das Siglum "H". Textstellen werden, wenn nicht anders vermerkt, nach dieser Ausgabe zitiert. Zu wichtigen Vorarbeiten der Autorin s. die Literaturangaben bei H. G. Güterbock, JAOS 84, 1964, Anm. 6.

TrAn III: "ziemlich gegen Ende des Hethiterreiches (z.Zt. Tudḫaliias IV. oder Arnuuandas III.?) angefertigt".

Ausgelöst durch einen Vortrag bzw. Aufsatz O. Carrubas[4], der (ohne Einbeziehung der Pferdetexte) einen umfangreichen Katalog von Datierungskriterien für hethitische Texte vorgelegt hatte, meinte A. Kammenhuber[5], einige dieser Kriterien, vor allem bezüglich der Pronominalformen *-us, -as,* ad absurdum führen zu können, weil deren Anwendung auf die Pferdetexte das "unsinnige Ergebnis" (552) zur Folge habe, "dass die Hethiter die ältesten Pferdetrainingsanweisungen verfasst haben und die Mitanni-Hurriter mit ihrer arischen Oberschicht erst nach den Hethitern und beeinflusst von diesen den 'Kikkuli-Text' schreiben konnten, und zwar zu einem Zeitpunkt, als es gar kein Mitanni-Reich mehr gab!". Nach Auffassung der Autorin hätten sich die Hethiter erst nach ihrem Sieg über die Mitanni-Hurriter von diesen hurri(ti)schen Trainingsanweisungen für Wagenpferde erbeten, "wodurch sich für die Abfassung des 'Kikkuli-Textes' die Mitte des 14. Jh.s als terminus post quem ergibt" (H 34).

0.3 Demgegenüber hat O. Carruba[6] die Berechtigung der von ihm zusammengestellten Datierungskriterien verteidigt, in grösserem Rahmen ausführlicher erläutert und zugleich auch für die hethitischen Pferdetexte folgende chronologische Reihenfolge aufgestellt (219): (1) TrAn III; (2) TrAn II; (3) TrAn I, somit also die Reihenfolge in der relativen Chronologie gegenüber A. Kammenhuber gerade umgekehrt. Alle drei Trainingsanleitungen gehören nach O. Carruba (220) "in die Zeit vor Šuppiluliuma bis in die Jahre von Muršili II., als es noch das Mitanni-Reich gab oder nachwirken konnte".

0.4 Weder A. Kammenhuber noch O. Carruba haben für ihre Auffassungen paläographische Argumente vorgebracht, was sich wohl dadurch erklärt, dass erst 1972 mit dem Erscheinen von Chr. Rüsters Hethitischer Keilschrift-Paläographie (StBoT 20) dieser Forschungsbereich für die Hethitologie eröffnet wurde, auch wenn zuvor schon von H. Otten—Vl. Souček (StBoT 8, 1969, 43) im Zusammenhang mit dem sogenannten alten Duktus

4. "Die Chronologie der heth. Texte und die heth. Geschichte der Grossreichszeit", ZDMG Suppl. I, 1969, 226ff., Tabellen 260/261.

5. "Konsequenzen aus neueren Datierungen hethitischer Texte: Pferdetrainingsanweisungen eine Erfindung der Hethiter", OrNS 38, 1969, 548ff. (mit einem langen Zitat, S. 550–552, ihrer Datierungsangaben aus H 316f.); s. auch "Die Sprachstufen des Hethitischen", KZ 83, 1969, 256ff., dazu O. Carruba "Die Sprachstufen des Hethitischen. Eine Widerlegung", KZ 85, 1971, 226ff.

6. "Über historiographische und philologische Methoden in der Hethitologie", OrNS 40, 1971, 208ff. (zu *-us, -as* 216f.); s. auch S. Heinhold-Krahmers Forschungsbericht in THeth 9, 1979, 21ff.

alte und junge Zeichenformen in grösserem Umfang gegenübergestellt worden waren. An die Keilschrift-Paläographie aus StBoT 20, die alt-, mittel- und junghethitische Texte berücksichtigte, schloss sich 1975 mit StBoT 21 (E. Neu—Chr. Rüster) eine paläographische Untersuchung vornehmlich zum Junghethitischen (14./13. Jh. v. Chr.) an[7].

H. C. Melchert hat 1977 in seiner Dissertation[8] bei der Aufstellung alt-, mittel- und junghethitischer Textkorpora dem paläographischen Gesichtspunkt, soweit dies allein anhand der Editionsbände überhaupt möglich ist, Rechnung zu tragen versucht. Seine Analyse der Zeichenformen unter Einbeziehung auch sprachlicher Eigentümlichkeiten führte ihn zu der Auffassung, dass sämtliche Pferdetexte mh. Kompositionen darstellen. Während aber der TrAn III auch paläographisch mh. Alter zukomme, sei die TrAn I ("Kikkuli-Text") nur in späteren, bereits modernisierten Niederschriften (= Abschriften) überliefert. "The Kikkuli manuscripts are either late Middle Hittite or early Neo-Hittite" (109). Abweichend von O. Carruba könnte nach H. C. Melchert der "Kikkuli-Text" trotz seiner späten Bezeugung eine durchaus frühere Entstehungszeit haben als die TrAn II and III (106). Sieht man vom paläographischen Alter der Texte ab, bliebe also A. Kammenhubers relativ chronologischer Ansatz, wonach der "Kikkuli-Text" hinsichtlich seiner Entstehungszeit am Anfang der hethitischen Pferdetexte stünde, grundsätzlich möglich. Das paläographische Alter der TrAn II erscheint H. C. Melchert insgesamt weniger klar ("probably so" [Middle Hittite], 109).

0.5 In dem von A. Kammenhuber herausgegebenen und mitverfassten Buch Probleme der Textdatierung in der Hethitologie (THeth 9, 1979)[9] werden die Pferdetexte ebenfalls unter paläographischen Gesichtspunkten behandelt. Gemäss der tabellarischen Übersicht von I. Hoffmann (244ff.) erlaubt die Analyse der Keilschriftzeichen die Feststellung, dass die Tafeln I–III der TrAn I ("Kikkuli-Text") ab Šuppiluliuma I. geschrieben sein könnten, Tafel IV (KBo 3.2) jedoch erst ab Muršili II., was G. Mauer (253), auch unter Einbeziehung sprachlicher Gegebenheiten, zu der Aussage veranlasste, dass die Tafeln I–IV des "Kikkuli-Textes" nicht vor Muršili II.

7. S. auch E. Neu, Chr. Rüster, "Zur Datierung hethitischer Texte", FsOtten (1973), 221ff. Die Abkürzungen ah., mh., jh. meinen im folgenden: alt-, mittel-, junghethitisch.

8. "Ablative and Instrumental in Hittite", Diss. phil. Harvard University 1977 (maschinenschriftlich), 93, 105f. Im Forschungsbericht aus THeth 9 bleibt H. C. Melcherts Arbeit, wohl weil noch nicht bekannt, unerwähnt.

9. S. Heinhold-Krahmer, I. Hoffmann, A. Kammenhuber, G. Mauer, Probleme der Textdatierung in der Hethitologie (Beiträge zu umstrittenen Datierungskriterien für Texte des 15. bis 13. Jahrhunderts v. Chr.). THeth 9, 1979.

niedergeschrieben seien. Über das Alter der Tafel V wird wohl wegen des geringen Textumfanges keine eigene Aussage getroffen (246).

Von besonderer Wichtigkeit für die weitere Diskussion erscheint mir die Feststellung in THeth 9, dass die TrAn III, die von A. Kammenhuber "bereits bedenkenlos" (H 317) an das Ende des Hethiterreiches datiert worden war, nun aufgrund der Keilschriftzeichen immerhin schon ab Arnuu̯anda I., was auch mh. Alter bedeuten kann, niedergeschrieben sein könnte (I. Hoffmann, a.a.O. 244, 248, 249). Dies gilt auch für die TrAn II (KUB 29.44+; S. 249)[10].

0.6 Nach diesem Rückblick auf die bisher wesentlichsten Äusserungen zum Alter der hethitischen Pferdetexte (wobei die hier kurz referierten Auffassungen natürlich immer auf dem Hintergrund des jeweiligen Forschungsstandes zu sehen sind) soll im folgenden die heikle Problematik ihrer Datierung noch einmal aufgegriffen werden mit dem Ziel, anhand weitgehend objektiver Kriterien eine möglichst unanfechtbare Entscheidung zur Chronologie der Pferdetexte herbeizuführen. Die Argumentation wird in der für einen Festschriftbeitrag gebotenen Kürze zu geschehen haben. Daher muss auch eine ausführliche paläographische Beschreibung der einzelnen Tafeln unterbleiben.

1. Den Ausgangspunkt unserer Untersuchung bildete die Frage nach dem paläographischen Alter der drei Trainingsanleitungen[11]. Die Durchsicht sämtlicher Pferdetexte unter dem Gesichtspunkt von Duktus und Zeichenformen hat ergeben, dass die TrAn III unzweifelhaft in mittelhethitischen Niederschriften überliefert ist.

Von denjenigen Zeichenformen, für die sich eine ältere und eine jüngere Variante deutlich unterscheiden lassen, treten in der TrAn III fast nur die älteren Varianten auf (vgl. H. C. Melchert, a.a.O. 108). Von AZ und UK überwiegen zwar die (relativ) jüngeren Formen, doch begegnet auf der Tafel VI (KUB 29.50) auch die ältere Variante von AZ (i 21′), und Tafel V (KUB 29.51) kennt auch die ältere Zeichenform von UK (i 12). Für mh. Alter der gesamten TrAn III sind aber insbesondere zwei Umstände sehr aussagekräftig.

Als charakteristisch für die TrAn III haben nämlich die typisch mh. Zeichenformen von DA und IT mit dem etwas eingerückten obersten waage-

10. Das Fragment KUB 29.41 (CTH 285.2; A. Kammenhuber, H 168f.) bleibt wohl wegen seines geringen Textumfangs undatiert (THeth 9, 248).

11. Für die Benutzung von Textfotos des Boğazköy-Archivs (Mainz) danke ich sehr herzlich H. Otten. Eine Autopsie der Originale wäre noch nachzuholen.

rechten Keil zu gelten, worauf auch schon H. C. Melchert (a.a.O. 108) aufmerksam gemacht hat[12].

Beweiskraft für mh. Alter kommt schliesslich auch dem Auftreten des Zeichens UZ mit einem gebrochenen Waagerechten auf der Tafel VI (KUB 29.50 i 40′, iv 38′) zu[13]. Diese Zeichenform von UZ bleibt m.W. mit bisher nur einer einzigen Ausnahme auf mh. Texte beschränkt; so begegnet man ihr u.a. in dem mh. "Gebet" Arnuu̯andas/Ašmunikals (CTH 375.1 A: KUB 17.21+; StBoT 20, Nr. 271, Spalte VI)[14], in der grossen *MEŠEDI*-Instruktion IBoT 1.36 oder in mh. Exemplaren der Kaškäer-Verträge[15]. Ausserhalb des mh. Textkorpus ist mir diese besondere UZ-Form bisher nur noch ein einziges Mal begegnet, und zwar in einem Fragment mit altem Duktus (145/d Vs. 8 in ᴰ*Ku*-UZ-*za-ni-šu-ú-u*[*n;* s. StBoT 26, 1983, 369). [Ed.—Also in KBo 7.28: 15 (OH/MS).] Da Tafel VI der TrAn III keinen alten Duktus zeigt[16], die besondere Zeichenform von UZ aber in jh. Niederschriften bisher nicht nachweisbar ist, ergibt sich für Tafel VI konsequenterweise mh. Alter. Die fast durchweg älteren Zeichenformen, insbesondere aber die Zeichenformen von DA, IT und UZ lassen am paläographisch mh. Alter der TrAn III nicht zweifeln. Folglich muss auch deren Sprachform mittelhethitisch sein. Die sprachlichen Argumente A. Kammenhubers (H 316f.) zugunsten einer Spätdatierung von TrAn III sind damit hinfällig (s. auch schon H. C. Melchert, a.a.O. 105f.)[17]. Die Datierung von TrAn III in

12. S. auch die am Ende von CTH 286 aufgeführten Fragmente KBo 16.89, 90, 91 gegenüber dem Tafelbruchstück KBo 16.88, das deswegen auch nicht der mittelhethitischen TrAn III zuzuordnen sein dürfte. Zu mh. DA und IT s. auch H. Otten, FsNeumann 1982, 249.

13. In der Edition ist die besondere Zeichenform von UZ mit einem Ausrufezeichen versehen, das A. Kammenhuber (H 210) für i 40′ auch in ihrer Umschrift anbringt, für iv 38′ (H 214) jedoch weglässt.

14. Vgl. Verf., FsNeumann 1982, 209 Anm. 20.

15. Zur Überlieferung und zur Datierung der Kaskäer-Verträge s. jetzt Verf. in FsBittel 1983, 391–99.

16. Die akkad. Präposition *A-NA* findet sich, soweit ich dies am Foto der Vorderseite überprüfen konnte, auch mit der typisch mh. Graphie (KUB 29.50 Vs. 29′), die, wie ich vermute z.B. auch in dem mh. Maşat-Brief 75/15 lk. Rd. 2 vorliegen dürfte, wofür S. Alp (Belleten, Cilt XLIV, Sayı: 173, 1980, 43) jedoch II?-*na* transkribiert hat.

17. Damit sind auch Verbalformen wie *anšii̯anzi* "sie wischen ab", *u̯a-ar-pí-i̯a-an-zi* "sie waschen" oder *u̯aššii̯anzi* "sie bedecken" als mh. anzuerkennen. Mittelhethitisches Alter kommt dann auch Graphien zu wie *e-ez-za-zi*/*e-ez-za-az-zi* (Prs.Sg. 3. zu *ed-* "(fr)essen", *ḫa-a-az-za-aš-ta* (Prt.Sg. 3.) "es trocknete", *iš-ša-an*[*-zi*] "sie machen, wirken", *iš-pár-ra-an-zi* "sie breiten aus", *kar-aš-ša-an-zi* "sie schneiden (ab)", *pa-la-aḫ-ši-i̯a-an-zi* "sie beruhigen (trans.)", *pé-ḫu-da-an-zi* "sie schaffen hin", *pé-eš-ši-i̯a-az-zi* "er wirft" (vgl. ibid. *ḫu-it-ti-i̯a-a*[*z-zi*] "er zieht"), *tu-ug-ga-ri* "es ist wichtig" oder *tu-u-ri-i̯a-an-zi* "sie spannen an". Zu beachten ist auch das Nebeneinander von *i-en-zi*/*i-i̯a-an-zi* "sie machen", *ir-ḫa-an-zi*/*ir-ḫa-a-an-zi* "sie beendigen", [*t*]*i-i-e-ez-zi*/*ti-i̯a*(*-az*)*-zi* "er tritt hin", *ti-it-nu-an-zi*/*ti-it-ta-nu-an-zi* "sie stellen hin", *u̯a-aš-ša*[*-an-zi*]/*u̯a-aš-ši-i̯a-an-zi* (sogar auf demselben Tafelfragment: II. Taf. ii 14′ bzw. 6′; H 178)

die mh. Zeit widerspricht auch nicht dem Befund aus THeth 9, wo ja die Niederschrift ab Arnuu̯anda I. ausdrücklich für möglich gehalten wird (s. oben 0.5). Im CHD III/1, 1980, 75b sub 2′ wird die TrAn III mit MH/MS klassifiziert, was mh. Alter sowohl für den Archetypus von TrAn III als auch für die uns vorliegenden Tafeln von TrAn III bedeutet.

2. Auch das Schriftbild der TrAn II (CTH 285.1) ist durch ältere Zeichenformen geprägt (vgl. H. C. Melchert, a.a.O. 107f.; altes AZ begegnet z.B. in iii 18′), auch wenn daneben, wie z.B. für E, schon jüngere Varianten auftreten, die aber aufgrund ihrer sonstigen Bezeugung nicht gegen mh. Alter sprechen. Für DA (vgl. i 10, ii 27, 40), IT (vgl. ii 4, 41), EN und TAR finden sich, wie das Tafelfoto deutlich erkennen lässt, die typisch mh. Zeichenvarianten, wobei man für IT und DA neben 'Übergangsformen' auch 'Normalformen' (vgl. ii 41 für DA, i 37′ für IT) begegnet. Beachtenswert ist die ligaturartige Schreibung von *kat-ta* (vgl. ii 49, iii 42′), auch in *lu-uk-kat-ta* (i 1), doch insgesamt weniger ausgeprägt als auf ah. Tafeln. Auch ligaturartiges *A-NA* tritt mehrfach auf (vgl. i 10, ii 38, 58). Die Schrift wirkt elegant und fein (vgl. StBoT 25, 1980, XVI). Aufgrund der paläographischen Gegebenheiten habe ich keine Bedenken, auch die TrAn II für eine mh. Niederschrift zu halten (s. auch CHD III/1, 1980, 75b sub 1′), die jedoch etwas jünger sein dürfte als die TrAn III. Sprachlich kündigt sich darin schon Junghethitisches an, wie der Wechsel von *nu-uš* und *na-aš* (beides "et eos") zeigt (vgl. A. Kammenhuber, H 316f.; O. Carruba, OrNS 40, 1971, 218f.; H. C. Melchert, a.a.O. 106) oder auch das Nebeneinander von *u̯aššanzi* und *u̯eššanzi* "sie bedecken" (TrAn II Kol. iii 33′ bzw. 23′; A. Kammenhuber, H 162, 164 mit Anm. 88; 351a) erkennen lässt. Dass die TrAn II luwischen Wortlaut enthält, ist kein Hinderungsgrund für deren mh. Alter, ist doch luwisches Wortgut auch schon in Texten mit altem Duktus bezeugt (s. StBoT 25, 1980, 118f.; StBoT 26, 1983, 315f.). Auch dem Fragment KUB 29.41 (CTH 285.2) dürfte mh. Alter zukommen (vgl. vor allem die Zeichenformen von AḪ, E und TAR, ferner *nu-uš u̯a-ar-pa-an-zi* Z. 6).

3.1 Die umfangreiche TrAn I ("Kikkuli-Text") hat man trotz vielfach älterer Zeichenformen[18] insgesamt als eine jh. Niederschrift anzusehen. Diese auch von H. C. Melchert (s. oben 0.4) vertretene Auffassung deckt sich mit der Aussage in THeth 9 (s. oben 0.5), wonach der "Kikkuli-Text" aufgrund seiner Zeichenformen und sprachlicher Gegebenheiten nicht vor Mursili II.

"sie bedecken". Bemerkenswert für die mh. TrAn III ist die Zusammenschreibung von Adverbien (Präverbien): *au̯an(-)katta, kattan(-)arḫa, kattan(-)šara, peran(-)arḫa,* was in anderen mh. Texten Parallelen hat; vgl. A. Kammenhuber, FsGüterbock 1974, 157f. (*au̯an-katta, peran-šara, šer-arḫa,* mit Anm. 26 und 27).

18. Vgl. H. C. Melchert, Diss. 107 (hier auch zu jüngeren Formen).

niedergeschrieben sein kann. Nach A. Kammenhuber (H 317; s. oben 0.2) soll diese TrAn zur Zeit Muršilis II.[19] entstanden sein. Es gibt aber aus heutiger Sicht einen, wie ich meine, untrüglichen Beweis dafür, dass die TrAn I als eine Niederschrift erst des 13. Jh. v. Chr. zu gelten hat.

3.2 Mehrfach hat A. Kammenhuber darauf aufmerksam gemacht, dass bezüglich des Verbums *šakruu̯ai-* "tränken" (dazu H. G. Güterbock, oben Anm. 1) in der TrAn I die Graphie *ša-ak-ru-u̯a-,* in der TrAn III hingegen die Graphie *ša-ku-ru-* auftritt (H 345b). Inzwischen wissen wir (s. oben 1), dass es sich bei der TrAn III unzweifelhaft um eine mh. Niederschrift handelt. Nun hat H. Otten (FsNeumann 1982, 247ff.) die unterschiedlichen Graphien des Ortsnamens Karkiša, nämlich URU*Ka-ra-ki-ša* und URU*Kar-ki-ša,* überzeugend mit dem unterschiedlichen Alter der Texte, in denen diese Schreibungen auftreten, in Verbindung gebracht. Danach hat man URU*Ka-ra-ki-ša* als mh., URU*Kar-ki-ša* aber als jh. Graphie anzusehen. Wie H. Otten nachweisen konnte, hat der (Ab)schreiber des 13. Jh.v.Chr. die in der mh. Vorlage stehende Graphie URU*Ka-ra-ki-ša* zu URU*Kar-ki-ša* verändert.

Wenn wir unter diesem Gesichtspunkt die unterschiedlichen Graphien *ša-ku-ru-* (mh.) und *ša-ak-ru-* betrachten, so lässt sich die Schreibung *ša-ku-ru-* typologisch ohne weiteres mit mh. *Ka-ra-ki-* vergleichen, die Graphie *ša-ak-ru-* hingegen entspricht, abgesehen von dem im hethitischen Syllabar als phonetisches Silbenzeichen ungebräuchlichen KVK-Zeichen *šak/g* (**šak-ru-*)[20], der jungen Graphie *Kar-ki-*.

Nun hat aber ein hethitischer Kopist des 13. Jh. nicht nur die mh. Graphie "modernisiert", sondern hat damit zugleich auch die im 13. Jh. übliche Zeichenform von AK[21] in Anwendung gebracht, die sich im "Kikkuli-Text" fast ganz auf das Verbum *šakruu̯ai-* konzentriert. Diese Feststellung zur Verwendung des jungen AK-Zeichens betrifft allerdings nur die IV. Tafel des "Kikkuli-Textes", deren Schreiber von A. Kammenhuber (H 42) insgesamt für wenig sorgfältig gehalten wird. Ausser auf der IV. Tafel findet sich das Verbum *sakruu̯ai-* auch noch auf der I. Tafel des "Kikkuli-Textes". Der Schreiber dieser Tafel, von dem A. Kammenhuber meint (H 42), dass er besonders pedantisch gewesen sei, hat auch von ihm modernisiertes *ša-ak-ru-u̯a-* weiterhin mit dem alten AK-Zeichen geschrieben. Der Trainings-

19. Die Diskussion um die Dauer der Regierungszeit Šuppiluliumas I. und Muršilis II. (s. C. Kühne, BBVO 1, 1982, 226ff.) kann hier unberücksichtigt bleiben.

20. Das Syllabogramm wurde in Boğazköy-Texten nur vereinzelt als phonetisches Silbenzeichen verwendet; vgl. L. M. Mascheroni, StMed I/2, 1980, 357f. Anm. 24.

21. Zum Alter (13. Jh. v. Chr.) der jungen Zeichenform von AK s. F. Starke, OrNS 50, 1981, 468. Bezüglich StBoT 20, Nr. 14, Spalten VII, VIII, gilt es zu berücksichtigen, dass es sich sowohl bei dem Išmirika-Vertrag (CTH 133) als auch bei der Arnuu̯anda-Instruktion (CTH 257.1 A) um Abschriften aus jh. Zeit handelt.

bericht KUB 29.54 (CTH 287.1), in welchem die Verbalform *ša-ku-ru-u-e-ẹr* "sie tränkten" auftritt, stellt wieder eine mh. Niederschrift dar (vgl. vor allem die typisch mh. Zeichenformen DA und IT).

3.3 Auch wenn sich die TrAn I ("Kikkuli-Text") paläographisch insgesamt[22] als eine Niederschrift des 13. Jh. v. Chr. herausgestellt hat, so wird man diesen Text doch als in mh. Zeit entstanden ansehen dürfen, d.h. wir haben es bei dem auf uns gekommenen "Kikkuli-Text" mit einer Abschrift zu tun. Nicht nur ist die Diktion ähnlich der der gesichert mh. TrAn III, beredte Zeugen für höheres Alter der Entstehung sind auch Verbalformen wie *ḫu-it-ti-e-ez-zi* (neben modernisiertem *ḫuittii̯azi*), *iš-ša-i, ti-i-e(-ez)-zi* oder *tu-u-ri(-e)-zi*. Während in der mh. TrAn III *pé-ḫu-da-an-zi* "sie schaffen hin" geschrieben ist, zeigt der "Kikkuli-Text" durchweg die Graphie *pé-e-ḫu-da-an-zi* (vgl. zum Alter dieser Graphien Verf., StBoT 18, 1974, 39). Im Hinblick auf phonetisch geschriebene Possessivpronomina gehören hierher Wortformen wie *pár-ga-tar-še-et* Tafel IV (neben *pár-ku-u̯a-tar-še-et* Tafel III) oder *pal-ḫa-tar-še-et* Tafel IV (neben DAGAL-*SÚ* Tafel III)[23]. Auch temporales *mān* (I. Tafel i 3) wird man in diesen Zusammenhang stellen dürfen[24]. Im Gegensatz zur mh. TrAn III, die durchweg *nu-uš* "et eos" zeigt, und der (relativ) jüngeren, aber noch mh. TrAn II, in der *nu-uš* und *na-aš* (beide "et eos") schon nebeneinander auftreten, ist im "Kikkuli-Text" des 13. Jh. altes *nu-uš* der Vorlage konsequent zu *na-aš* modernisiert worden (vgl. A. Kammenhuber, Materialien 3, 1973, 50). Die Verwendung des Pronomens *-aš* (Akk. Pl. c.) hinter einem auf *-a* ausgehenden Wort oder Wortkomplex (also hinter *-ma, -i̯a namma*) entspricht dem mh. Usus wie in der TrAn III, ist aber auch schon im Althethitischen zu belegen[25]. Beachtung verdient auch der Allativ URU-*i̯a* (*uu̯anzi-;* IV. Taf. Vs. 24) neben Dat.-Lok. URU!-*ri* (*anda uu̯anzi-;* ibid. Rs. 34, vgl. unt. Rd. 3). Die Ortspartikel *-ašta* ist korrekt gebraucht mit der Bedeutung "darin" (mit Bezug auf den vorher genannten Fluss; IV. Taf. Vs. 29, Rs. 2).

3.4 Auf den einzelnen Tafeln der TrAn I gibt es vielfältige Hinweise für eine Abschrift. Rasuren[26], Zeichenauslassungen[27] und sonstige Verschrei-

22. Man beachte auch das in mehreren Tafeln der TrAn I auftretende Zeichen Ú mit nur zwei Senkrechten. Auch bei dem kleinen Duplikat KUB 29.47 (CTH 284, 3e tabl., B) handelt es sich um eine junge Niederschrift (wohl 2. Hälfte des 13. Jh. v. Chr.), wie vor allem ḪA, aber auch EN ausweist; s. auch DAGAL-*SÚ* (statt *palḫatar-šet*) iii 4′.

23. S. dazu auch H. C. Melchert, Diss. 107. Hat man *parkuu̯atar* (gegenüber *pargatar*, das sich auch ausserhalb der Pferdetexte mehrfach findet) als 'Neologismus' zu werten?

24. Doch s. auch A. Kammenhuber, KZ 83, 1969, 268.

25. Vgl. Verf. StBoT 26, 1983, 5 mit Anm. 16.

26. Vgl. I. Taf. iii 66, iv 11, 17–20, 67, II. Taf. ii 5, iii 24, III. Taf. iv 13.

27. Vgl. *tu-u*⟨*-ri*⟩*-i̯a-an-zi* I. Taf. i 26, *ú-e-ta*⟨*-ni*⟩*-it* iii 51; *ú-zu-uḫ-ri*⟨*-in*⟩ II. Taf. iii 15, *la-a-an*⟨*-zi*⟩ iv 31; *ša-at*⟨*-ta*⟩- III. Taf. ii 43; *ḫu-u-ma-an-da*⟨*-an*⟩ IV. Taf. Vs. 46.

bungen[28] sind nicht gerade selten. Die Graphie *iš-eš-ša-i* (Prs.Sg. 3.; II. Taf. iv 46, vgl. iii 70) kann Hinweis dafür sein, dass der Kopist des 13. Jh. zunächst *iš-ša-i* der Vorlage (wie auf III. Taf. i 42) übernehmen wollte, dann aber bezüglich der Anlautschreibung den modernen Graphien seiner eigenen Zeit gefolgt ist; die "Norm" wäre jedoch wohl *e-eš-ša-i* gewesen[29].

3.5 Da die auf uns gekommene TrAn I ohne Zweifel eine Abschrift des 13. Jh. darstellt, wird man genauer zu unterscheiden haben zwischen denjenigen sprachlichen "Unebenheiten" des Textes, die durch die hurri(ti)schen Verfasser[30] verursacht sind, und denjenigen, die zu Lasten des Abschreibers gehen. Als "Norm" hätte die mh. Sprachform zu gelten, da mit einer mh. Vorlage zu rechnen ist. Aus vornehmlich paläographischen Gründen ordnen wir heute zwar sehr viele Tafeln bzw. Tafelfragmente dem mh. Textkorpus zu, es würde aber beim gegenwärtigen Forschungsstand, sieht man einmal von einigen besonders auffälligen Eigentümlichkeiten ab, gewiss nicht leicht fallen, die oder eine mh. Sprachnorm deutlich gegen die oder eine jh. Sprachnorm abzugrenzen. Dennoch liesse sich schon jetzt anhand der recht gründlichen Beobachtungen A. Kammenhubers eine grössere Liste von Spracherscheinungen zusammenstellen, die eigentlich nur dann überzeugend erklärt werden können, wenn die Verfasser mit der hethitischen Sprache nicht richtig vertraut gewesen sind. Das betrifft z.B. die Verwendung des Infinitivs *arrumanzi* als 3. Pl. (= *arranzi* "sie waschen"; H 80 Anm. 21), die Unform *aruizzi* "er wäscht" (H 96 Anm. 102), die Verwendung von *išpii̯a-* "sich (mit Speise) sättigen" auch in Verbindung mit *u̯etenit* "mit Wasser" (H 82 Anm. 24; 331 s.v.), den Gebrauch des Pronomens *-ši* (Sg.) statt *-šmaš* "ihnen" (Pl.; H 90 Anm. 70), auch von *-aš* für *-šmaš* "ihnen" (H 321b), die Vernachlässigung der Aktionsart (II. Taf. iv 59; H 102 Anm. 141) und auch von Satzanschlüssen (vgl. H 115 Anm. 43; 106f. Anm. 8) oder inkonsequente oder auch fälschliche Setzung der Ortspartikel *-kan* (H 332), überflüssiges *-a* "und, auch" in Verbindung mit der Akkusativ-form *uzuḫrin* (vgl. II. Taf. i 2, iii 21; III. Taf. iii 15, 17; IV. Taf. Rs. 42; s. H 322a; vgl. A. Goetze, JCS 16, 1962, 31), holprige Syntax (vgl. die Wortstellung auf der II. Taf. i 11, ii 26; s. auch H 88 Anm. 59), uneinheitliche Verwendung von

28. Vgl. "1" statt "½" I. Taf. iv 66, s. auch H 75 Anm. 116; *ši* statt *u̯a* II. Taf. i 47, *ni* statt *nu* i 50, *nam* statt *zi* i 33, *pí* statt *mu* iii 4, *an* statt *ḫu* iii 72, *pé-en*[!]*-i̯a* iv 67, unvollständiges *u̯a* in *akuu̯anzi* i 18, EGIR-*pa* ausgelassen iv 18, KASKAL.GÍD.DA (ii 62) für übliches DANNA "Meile", *u̯a-aḫ-ḫu-zi* iii 4 (das A. Kammenhuber, H 92 Anm. 87, dem Schreiber anlastet); Korrekturen auf III. Taf. ii 42, iii 1; *ḫu* statt *ri* IV. Taf. Vs. 31.

29. Vgl. H. C. Melchert, Diss. 107. Zu *išša-/ešša-* s. auch O. Carruba, ZDMG Suppl. I, 1969, 235, 246; Verf., KZ 93, 1979, 70f.

30. Zur Verfasserschaft der TrAn I s. A. Kammenhuber, H 42.

ANA und *INA* (vgl. H 70 Anm. 82), etwas schwerfällig wirkende Konstruktionen (z.B. von *parḫ-* in Verbindung mit IKU: s. H 110 Anm. 25, zu IKU s. H. C. Melchert, JCS 32, 1980, 53f.), Ausdrucksschwierigkeiten bei der Beschreibung und Erklärung von Fachtermini (s. zu *u̯ašanna* H 121 Anm. 79) u.a.m.

3.6 Dass sich die hurri(ti)schen Verfasser mit der Verwendung hethitischer enklitischer Pronomina schwer taten, davon war schon die Rede. So fungiert z.B. *-at* gelegentlich auch als Akkus. Pl. c. (vgl. I. Taf. iv 46; II. Taf. i 41: s. H 320f.). Ob jedoch der Gebrauch von *-aš* als Nom. Pl. c. an allen Stellen fehlerhaft ist, wie A. Kammenhuber (H 321b) meint, scheint mir noch nicht sicher erwiesen. Immerhin lässt sich *-aš* als Nom. Pl. c. auch ausserhalb der Pferdetexte nachweisen (vgl. Verf., IBS V 23, 1980, 17 mit Anm. 36; A. Kammenhuber, Materialien 3, 1973, 99), und schon das Althethitische kennt hinter *-ma* "aber" diesen Gebrauch (s. StBoT 26, 1983, 5 mit Anm. 12).

Die Verwendung der Akkusativform *parḫanduš* (H 342b) in der Funktion eines Nominativs Pluralis könnte auf die unvollkommenen Sprachkenntnisse der hurri(ti)schen Verfasser zurückgehen, könnte aber auch, zumal da die betreffende Konstruktion nicht ganz üblich ist, durch den Kopisten des 13. Jh., wo pluralische Akkusativformen in Nominativfunktion bekanntlich nicht ganz ungewöhnlich waren, bewirkt sein. Ähnlich unentschieden wird bleiben müssen, ob einmaliges *pé-en-ni-i̯a-u-an-zi* (II. Taf. i 58; H 84 Anm. 42) für *pennumanzi* so schon in der Vorlage gestanden hat (II. Taf. ii 4 auch *pennuanzi*) oder ob der Kopist daran Schuld trägt[31].

3.7 Die Erkenntnis, dass es sich bei der TrAn I ("Kikkuli-Text") um eine junge Abschrift einer mh. Vorlage handelt, lässt auch den Bereich des Lexikons, auf den A. Kammenhuber in ihrer Textbearbeitung mehrfach aufmerksam gemacht hat, in einem neuen Licht erscheinen. Allerdings können auch für diesen Bereich hier nur einige Gesichtspunkte kurz gestreift werden.

Es fällt auf, dass die mh. TrAn III das Verbum *irḫai-* "beendigen" (mit und ohne *adanna*) gebraucht, die später überlieferten TrAn II (mh.) und I (jh.

31. Mehrfaches fehlerhaftes (GE_6-*an*) *ḫu-u-ma-an* (statt Akk.Sg.c.; s. A. Kammenhuber, H 330a, J. Friedrich, HE I^2 §191b) der jungen Abschrift des "Kikkuli-Textes" findet jetzt vielleicht eine Parallele in einer jungen Abschrift (13. Jh. v. Chr.) der mh. *ḪAZANNU*-Instruktion. So heisst es in KUB 26.9+ i 9f.: DUMU-*KA na-aš-ma* ÌR-*KA*[ ] / *ḫa-ad-da-an u-i-i̯a* "Sende deinen Sohn oder deinen vertrauten Diener!" (Umschrift und Übersetzung nach H. Otten, FsKammenhuber 135, der ibid. haplographisches *ḫa-ad-da-an-*⟨*-da-an*⟩ erwägt, zugleich aber auch auf die wohl parallele Wendung *tuel-u̯a ḫa-a-an-da-an* UN-*an u̯i̯a* [KBo 18.24 iv 11f.] hinweist, was ihn eher an eine Verbindung mit *ḫant-*"Vorderseite" [*ḫanda-* "erster"] denken liesse).

Abschrift) dafür aber *(adanna) zinna-* verwenden (A. Kammenhuber, H 331a, 353a), wie übrigens auch der (mh.) Bericht KUB 29.54 (H 229 Anm. 28)[32]. Hat dies seine Ursache in einem veränderten Sprachgebrauch? Dass in der TrAn I statt *šakruu̯anzi-i̯a-aš* "man tränkt sie" mehrfach die Phrase "man gibt ihnen Wasser" begegnet (vgl. H 69 Anm. b), ist möglicherweise dem Kopisten anzulasten, der vielleicht auch den ihm wenig geläufigen terminus technicus *zallaz uu̯a-* "traben" (H 352b; zu *zallaz* s. F. Starke, KZ 95, 1981, 155 Anm. 58) durch schlichtes *penna-* (eigentlich "hintreiben", dann "traben lassen"; H 344a) ersetzt hat (doch s. auch H. G. Güterbock, JAOS 84, 1964, 270f.). Solche Eingriffe in die fachsprachliche Textvorlage könnten dem Wunsch nach besserer Verständlichkeit entsprungen sein, beim Ersatz fremdsprachlich anmutender Ausdrücke aber auch eine Art von interpretatio hethitica zur Ursache haben, die vielleicht auch schon in den hethitischen Trainingsanleitungen II und III wie auch im Bericht (CTH 287.1) den Ausdruck *u̯elku ḫātan* "getrocknetes Gras; Heu" für hurri(ti)sches *uzuḫri*-ḪÁD.DU.A (H 189 Anm. b) des "Kikkuli-Textes" gebrauchen liess.

Solche und ähnliche Beobachtungen sind für eine hethitische Wortgeschichte, die auch Stilschichten und Fachsprachliches miteinzubeziehen versucht, wohl ebenso bedeutsam wie für den gesamten Bereich der hethitischen Übersetzungsliteratur. Wir sehen also, wie als Folge des hier für die hippologischen Texte vorgetragenen Datierungsbefundes gegenüber früher nun modifizierte oder auch neue Fragestellungen an diese Textgruppe mit ihrer nur schwer erschliessbaren Fachterminologie herangetragen werden können.

4.1 Fassen wir abschliessend die vornehmlich durch paläographische Kriterien gewonnenen Datierungsergebnisse dieser kleinen Untersuchung zusammen:

TrAn III: mittelhethitische Niederschrift (wohl gegen Ende des 15. Jh.v. Chr.), also zeitgenössischer Text[33].

TrAn II: mittelhethitische Niederschrift (wohl Anfang des 14. Jh.v.Chr.), also zeitgenössischer Text.

TrAn I ("Kikkuli-Text"): Niederschrift des 13. Jh.v.Chr., Abschrift einer mittelhethitischen Vorlage.

32. In diesem Zusammenhang wäre auch dem Wechsel von *irḫaitta* und *zinnattari* (mit *-ri*!) in Omina der Übersetzungsliteratur Aufmerksamkeit zu schenken; vgl. Verf., StBoT 5, 1968, 72f. mit Anm. 12; 207 mit Anm. 5.

33. Wie weit die TrAn III und II zeitlich auseinanderliegen, lässt sich schwerlich genau ausmachen. Zum Begriff "zeitgenössisch" s. I. Hoffmann, THeth 9, 1979, 97. Zum mh. Alter des Trainingsberichts (CTH 287.1) s. oben am Ende von 3.2.

Auch wenn die TrAn I ("Kikkuli-Text") von den drei Trainingsanleitungen am spätesten überliefert ist, kann das Original sehr wohl am Anfang dieser hethitischen Textgattung gestanden haben[34], was man auch aus sachlichen Gründen erwarten würde. Der zeitliche Unterschied zwischen dem Original der TrAn I und der TrAn III wäre aber dann gewiss nicht sehr gross.

4.2 Bekanntlich stand die hethitische Dynastie, die das für uns zusehends heller werdende Geschichtsbild der mh. Sprachperiode geprägt hat, unter starkem hurri(ti)schen Einfluss[35]; das Land Mitanni war damals noch eine selbständige, politisch und militärisch feste Grösse. Hinsichtlich des immer stärkeren Einsatzes von Streitwagen[36] wird man am hethitischen Königshof das Bedürfnis empfunden haben, das Training der Streitwagenpferde auf eine solide fachmännische Grundlage zu stellen, was die Berufung eines Pferdetrainers (^{LÚ}*aššuššanni*) und seines Stabes aus dem Lande Mitanni nach Ḫattuša zur Folge gehabt haben könnte. Abgesehen von dem gewiss sehr wichtigen militärischen Gesichtspunkt wird dieser Wunsch nach einer schriftlichen Fixierung von Behandlungsmethoden für Pferde auch dem damals am Königshof und in der Tempelverwaltung von Ḫattuša herrschenden Zeitgeist entsprochen haben, der für die verschiedensten Bereiche Instruktionen verfassen liess. Aus keiner anderen hethitischen Sprachperiode ist uns ein so reichhaltiges und differenziertes Textkorpus an Instruktionen und Dienstanweisungen überliefert wie gerade aus der mh. Epoche. Dass im 13. Jh. v. Chr. in Ḫattuša noch einmal der gesamte "Kikkuli-Text" hergestellt, d.h. abgeschrieben worden war, wird man vielleicht auf ähnliche Interessen zurückführen wollen wie die, die während des 13. Jh. v. Chr. in Assyrien Trainingsanleitungen für Wagenpferde[37] hatten aufschreiben lassen. Dabei darf nicht übersehen werden, dass, wie aus dem Vorhandensein

34. O. Carruba (s. oben 0.3; OrNS 40, 1971, 219) ist aufgrund sprachlicher Kriterien zu derselben (relativ) chronologischen Reihenfolge gelangt, liess jedoch die TrAn I (mit A. Kammenhuber) in der Zeit Muršilis II. entstanden sein und hat sie somit auch nicht als Abschrift einer mh. Vorlage verstanden (s. dazu auch H. C. Melchert, Diss. 106f.).

35. Vgl. O. R. Gurney, CAH II, 1, 1973³, 675f.; A. Kammenhuber, THeth 7, 1976, 61f., 176f.; O. Carruba, KZ 85, 1971, 229; OrNS 40, 1971, 212f.

36. Zu Pferd und (Streit)wagen bei den Hethitern seit den frühesten Quellen s. A. Kammenhuber, H 27ff., die übrigens für die Zeit zwischen den Königen Telipinu und Šuppiluliuma I. einen "Umschwung in der Kampfpraxis" zu erkennen glaubt, für die eine wesentliche Erhöhung der Anzahl von Streitwagen charakteristisch gewesen sei. Diese Aussage wäre jedoch jetzt noch hinsichtlich der vielen vom 13. Jh. v. Chr. in mh. Zeit rückdatierten historischen Texte zu überprüfen.

37. Zur Datierung dieser Textgruppe s. E. Ebeling, Bruchstücke einer mittelassyrischen Vorschriftensammlung zur Akklimatisierung und Trainierung von Wagenpferden (VIO 7), 1951, 6; vgl. A. Kammenhuber, H 35.

zahlreicher im 13. Jh. v. Chr. angefertigter Abschriften ah., mh. und sogar jh. (des 14. Jh. v. Chr.) Texte zu schliessen ist, gerade im letzten Jahrhundert des hethitischen Grossreichs in den Archiven von Ḫattuša eine überaus rege Kopiertätigkeit im Gange gewesen sein muss, in deren Zusammenhang möglicherweise auch die Anfertigung einer Abschrift des seinerzeit sehr bedeutsamen mh. "Kikkuli-Textes" zu stellen wäre.

Trotz der insgesamt recht spröde anmutenden Sprachform der hethitischen Pferdetexte wird man sich wegen ihrer schon mh. Entstehungszeit gerade unter philologischen und sprachwissenschaftlich-grammatisch-lexikalischen Gesichtspunkten wieder verstärkt mit dieser Textgruppe zu befassen haben.

EIN RITUAL VON AŠDU, DER HURRITERIN

HEINRICH OTTEN

Mainz

Mit der Aufarbeitung und Neuordnung der Tafelkataloge[1] aus Boğazköy wird eine bisher unbekannte, zumindest nicht identifizierte Ritualgruppe greifbar[2], deren Darstellung hiermit dem Jubilar im Gedenken an langjährige gemeinsame Bemühungen um die Wiedergewinnung des hethitischen Schrifttums in seiner Festschrift zum fünfundsiebenzigsten Geburtstage gewidmet sei.

In Catalogue des textes hittites (1971) hatte E. Laroche den Katalogeintrag KUB XXX 65 + KBo XIV 69 iii 5f. auf S. 170f. in Umschrift und Übersetzung vorgelegt:

VII *ṬUP-PU* [INIM ^{f}x-]*du-ú ma-a-an al-u̯a-an-za-aḫ-ḫa-an-da-an* UKÙ-*an pár-ku-nu-um-m*[*i*] *QA-TI*

"7 tablettes; [paroles de] . . . du.—Quand je purifie une personne ensorcelée.—Fin."

Diese Wendung: "Den/einen verzauberten Menschen reinige ich" begegnet wieder im Kolophon von IBoT II 116:

Rs. iv 4′]x ^{SAL}ŠU.GI ^{URU}*Ḫur-la-aš* [
-*a*]*n-da-an* UKÙ-*an pár-ku-nu-um-m*[*i*]
6′ *ták-n*]*a-az da-aḫ-ḫi Ú-UL QA-TI*
a-pé-]*e-da-ni*
8′ U]D$^{?}$ II^{KAM} *túḫ-ḫu-uš-ta*

Das Zitat findet sich—wohl wegen seiner Bruchstückhaftigkeit—nicht bei A. Kammenhuber, HW^{2} 63b, aber eine Ergänzung [*alu̯anzaḫḫa*]*ndan* bzw.

1. Vgl. Jahrbuch der Akademie der Wissenschaften und der Literatur, Mainz, 1981, 184; 1982, 209.

2. Vgl. die Zusammenstellung der bisher bekannten Beschwörungsrituale hurritischer Herkunft nach den Namen ihrer Verfasserinnen: V. Haas, H. J. Thiele, Die Beschwörungsrituale der Allaituraḫ(ḫ)i (= AOAT 31, 1978) 23 Anm. 56.

[U+KAK-*a*]*ndan* UKÙ-*an* steht wohl ausser Zweifel, gerade auch im Rückblick auf den Katalogeintrag KUB XXX 65 + iii 5.

Der oben zitierte Text wird von E. Laroche, CTH 490.2 als *Rituel de contre-magie* aufgeführt, wobei CTH 490.1 = KUB VII 33 als Paralleltext angegeben wird[3]. Von der Tafel ist nur die Vorderseite mit dem oberen Teil der Kolumne i, und damit der Textanfang, in wesentlichen Teilen erhalten. Drei unveröffentlichte Duplikate gestatten es, den Text in seinen ersten 25 Zeilen fast vollständig wiederzugewinnen, so dass eine Vorlage hier in Umschrift sinnvoll scheint.

Der Name der hurritischen Verfasserin ist aber auch hier abgebrochen: [. . .]x = senkrechter Keil an der Bruchkante, und so gewinnt Bo 2495 besondere Bedeutung, dessen Kolumne i Duplikat ist zu KUB VII 33+ i 17ff., während die Rs. iv 4 im Kolophon den Namen [^{f}]*A̤-aš-du*[bietet. Diese Lesung findet im Kolophon zur "zweiten Tafel" (1419/u) ihre Bestätigung:

1419/u iv
x+1 DUB II^{KAM} *Ú-UL QA*[*-TI*]
2′ INIM ^{f}*A-aš-du* SAL ^{URU}[*Ḫur-la-aš*]
ma-a-an al-u̯a-an[*-za-aḫ-ḫa-an-da-an*]
4′ UKÙ-*an* EGIR-*pa* S[IG$_5$*-aḫ-mi*]
na-an-kán ták-n[*a-az/za da-aḫ-ḫi*]
(Es folgen die Spuren von zwei getilgten Schreibernamen)

Damit erweisen sich die Texte von CTH 490 als ein Beschwörungsritual von Ašdu, der Hurriterin, und nach dem gegenwärtigen Stand der Textaufarbeitung kann nunmehr die folgende Zusammenstellung (in Ergänzung zu CTH 490) gegeben werden:

1. A KUB VII 33 + 703/v
B 698/v
C Bo 6968 (+) Bo 3509
D Bo 2495 + 2000/g
(evtl. o. A. zu Expl. B gehörig)
2. IBoT II 116
3. 1419/u: zweite Tafel
4. KUB XLI 5 + XLIV 54 + IBoT II 46: dritte Tafel[4]
5. KBo XIX 144: vierte Tafel[5]

3. Das Ende der Zeilen 13ff. wird nunmehr durch 703/v vervollständigt.

4. Join von E. Laroche, OLZ 1977 Sp. 33, bestätigt von H. Klengel ibid. Anm. 1—jedoch nicht Ritual der Allaituraḫi, wie seinerzeit vermutet.

5. So in Anlehnung an E. Laroche, RHA XXX, 1972, der unter CTH 790, 4. A. und B. KBo XIX 144 und KUB XLI 5 zusammenstellt.—Fundort des Fragmentes KBo XIX 144 = 1305/z im Südareal von Tempel I im Schutt, vgl. Edition S. xii, xvi.

Bei den folgenden Textwiedergaben stand mir für Bo 2495 sowohl eine alte Umschrift von H. Ehelolf wie eine Photographie von Frau Luise Ehelolf zur Verfügung. Die vier Textfragmente 2000/g, 1419/u, 698/v und 703/v aus den Grabungen von K. Bittel stammen alle aus den Ostmagazinen des Tempels I; hier war demnach einmal die ganze Textgruppe—darunter die Anfangstafel in drei Exemplaren—aufbewahrt.

KUB VII 33 + 703/v (1.A)

Vs. i

[*UM-MA* ^{f}*A-aš-d*]*u* ^{SAL}ŠU.GI ^{URU}*Ḫ̣ur-l*[*a-aš*]
2 [*ma*^{a}*-a-an al-u̯*]*a-an-za-aḫ-ḫa*$^{!}$*-da-an* UKÙ-*an* EGIR-*pa* [ ]
[SIG$_5$-*aḫ-mi*] *ṇa-an-kán ták-na-za da-aḫ-ḫi*
4 [*nu ki-*]*i̥*[b] *da-aḫ- ḫi*

I DARÀ.MAŠ I GUD I UDU I TI$_8$^{MUŠEN} I SÚR.DÙ.A^{MUŠEN}[ ][c]
6 I *AR-NA-BU* I MUŠ V MUŠEN$^{ḪI.A}$ I *mu-ú-ta-mu-t*[*i-iš*$^{?}$]
V KU$_6$$^{ḪI.A}$ I LÚ^{LUM} I ANŠE.KUR.RA I ANŠE.GÌR.NUN.N[A][d]
8 I ANŠE-*i̯a da-a-i ki-i-ma ku-e ḫu-u-i̥*[*-tar*
nu ḫu-u-ma-an-pát[e] *ḫu-u-iš-u̯a-* [*an*[f]]

---

10 III GUD$^{ḪI.A}$ IV UDU$^{ḪI.A}$ ½ PẠ BULÙG ½ PẠ BAPP[IR ½ PA ZÍD.DA ZÍZ][g]
½ PA ZÍD.DA *še-ep-pí-it-ta-aš* I PA[
12 I$^{?}$ PA ZÍD.DA *kar-aš* I DUG KA.DÙ[h] III DUG[
I MA.NA GAB.LÀL *ŠA* UD III^{KAM} NINDA$^{ḪI.A}$ x[ ] x x x [
14 *Ù* XXXIV MUŠEN$^{ḪI.A}$ *da-a-i* III *ME* NINDA.SIG^{MEŠ} III NINDA. KAxUD
Ú-NU-UT GIR$_4$ I DUG KA.DÙ Ì.UDU *kụ-uk-ku-ul-la-aš*
16 I *u̯a-ak-šur* Ì.DÙG.GA I *u̯a-ak-šur* LÀL

VII$^{?}$ GA.KIN.AG VII *EM-ṢÚ*[i] I BÁN ^{GIŠ}*IN-BU*[k] ^{GIŠ}MA
18 [(^{GIŠ}*S*)]*E*$_{20}$*-ER-TUM* ^{GIŠ}GEŠTIN.ḪÁD.DU(.A) *an-da im-mi-i̯a-an*
[(IV TÚG^{TUM})] IV ^{TÚG}*ku-re-eš-šar*$^{ḪI.A}$ I TÚG ZA.GÌN I TÚG SA$_5$
20 [(I TÚG *Ḫ̣A-Ṣ̣A*)]*R-TUM* I TỤ́G BABBAR$^{!}$ IV *TA-PAL* ^{KUŠ}E.SIR$^{ḪI.A}$
[(IV *TA-PA*)]*L* $^{TỤ́G}$*KẠ-BAL-LI*$^{ḪI.A}$ [ ]

---

22 [(I KUŠ GUD SA$_5$ I KUŠ GU)]D GE$_6$ I KUŠ GUD BABBAR I KUŠ ÙZ SA$_5$
[(I KUŠ ÙZ GE$_6$ I K)UŠ ÙZ BABBAR] IX$^{?}$ *ga-an-g*[(*a*-LIŠ SÍG ZA.GÌN
24 [(IX *ga-an-ga*-LIŠ SÍ)G (IX *tar-pa-l*)]*a-aš* SÍG BABBAR
[(IX *tar-pa-la-aš* SÍG ZA.GÌN IX *tar-pa-la-aš* SÍG) S]IG$_7$.SIG$_7$

a. Dupl. 698/v Vs. 1′ *ma*[-.
b. Bo 6968 Vs. 2 -*n*]*a-za da-aḫ-ḫi nu ki*[-.
c. Keine Lücke nach Bo 6968 Vs. 3.
d. Dupl. 698/v Vs. 5′ I ANŠE.GÌR.NUN.[NA; Bo 6968 Vs. 4]I ANŠE.KUR.RA I ANŠE.GÌR.NUN[.NA.
e. 698/v Vs. 6′ *nu da-pí-an*[*-pát*.
f. Bo 6968 Vs. 5 TI-*an*[(-).
g. So nach Bo 6968 Vs. 6.
h. Bo 6968 Vs. 7 DUG KA.DÙ.A.
i. Hier beginnt Dupl. Bo 2495 Vs. 3′]VII$^{?}$ DỤG *Ẹ̣M-ṢÚ* [.
k. Dupl. Bo 3509 (evtl. o. A. zu Bo 6968) Z. 3 om. GIŠ.
l. Dupl. Bo 2495+ Vs. 5′ und Bo 3509 Z. 5 om. I TÚG BABBAR.

Bo 2495 + 2000/g (1.D)

Vs. i

---

x+ 3′ [VII$^{?}$ GA.KIN.AG] VII$^{?}$ DỤG *Ẹ̣M-ṢỤ́* [I BÁN $^{(GIŠ)}$*IN-BU*[a] ^{GIŠ}M]A ^{GIŠ}*SE*$_{20}$*-ER-TUM* ^{GIŠ}GEŠ[TIN.ḪÁD.DU.A]

4′ [*an-d*]*a im-mi-ị̯a-an* IV TỤ́G^{TUM} [IV ^{TÚG}*ku-re-eš-ša*]*r*$^{ḪI.A}$ I TÚG ZA.GÌN I TÚG SA$_5$ [ ]

I TÚG *ḪA-ṢAR-TUM IV TA-PAL* ^{KUŠ}E.S[IR$^{ḪI.A}$] IV$^{?}$ *TA-PAL* ^{TÚG}*KA-BAL-LI*$^{ḪI.A}$[ ]

6′ I KUŠ GUD SA$_5$ I KUŠ GUD GE$_6$ I KUŠ [GUD BABBAR I] KỤŠ ÙZ SA$_5$ I KUŠ ÙZ GE$_6$ I K[UŠ ÙZ BABBAR]

IX *ga-an-ga-*LIŠ SÍG ZA.GÌN IX *ga*[(*-an-ga-*LIŠ SÍ)G[b] *ḪA-ṢAR-TU*]*M* IX *tar-pa-la-aš* SÍG BABBAR [ ]

8′ IX *tar-pa-la-aš* SÍG ZA.GÌN IX *tar-pa*[(*-la-aš* SÍG S)A$_5$ IX *tar-pa-*]*la-aš* SÍG *Ḫ*[*A-ṢAR-TUM*

I *ku-ut-ta-na-al-li* KUBABBAR GUŠ[(KIN ZAB)AR[c]

10′ *nạ-ạt an-da ú-e-šu-ri-ị̯*[(*a-an-zi*)[d]

]x IV *ku-un-ga-li-ị̯a-ti*[*-i*(*n an-d*)*a*[e]

12′] KUBABBAR I SI.GAR KUBABBAR I[

[*ne-pé-e*]*š*$^{?}$ URUDU *ER-ṢE-TUM* URUDU x[

14′ [(^{GIŠ})*ḫa-aḫ-*]*ḫar* URUDU[f] III *mu-i-la-aš* [URUDU[f]

[I$^{?}$]*kạ-lạ-am-ma*[f] URUDU I ŠU.x[

16′ [I ^{URU}]$^{DU?}$ BAL I ^{NA_4}*kar-pu-zi-*x[

V$^{?}$ TI$_8$$^{MUŠEN\ ḪI.A}$ *ka-ru-ú-i*[-

18′ I^{NU-TUM} GIŠ.NUNUZ (= GIŠ.RIN$_x$) *ZI-PA-NA* ^{NA_4}[*za-ap-za-ga-ị̯a*[g] II-*ŠU*[h] IX ^{GIŠ}*zu-up-pa-r*[*i*$^{ḪI.A}$

20′ *nu ma-aḫ-ḫa-an ŠU-TUM*[i] *ḫa-an-da*[-
i-i̯a-an-za ŠÀ^{BI} ^{GIŠ}*ta-ḫa*[*-ra-am-ma(-)*
22′ *nu-kán* ^{GIŠ}KUN$_5$ URUDU *an-da* [
DINGIR^{MEŠ}*-aš ŠA* IM *an-d*[*a*

24′ *nu-uš-ma-aš a-da-an-na a*[*-ku-u̯a-an-na*
A-NA ^{GIŠ}*ta-ḫa-ra-am-ma̩*[(-)

a. KUB VII 33 i 17 mit Determinativ, Bo 3509 Z. 3′ om.
b. Erg. nach Bo 3509 Z. 7′.
c. Erg. nach Bo 3509 Z. 8′.
d. Erg. nach Bo 3509 Z. 9′.
e. Erg. nach Bo 3509 Z. 10′.
f. Zur Erg. vgl. KUB XII 51 i 11′f. und IBoT III 96 i! 9′f.
g. Zur Erg. vgl. KUB VII 37 Z. 11′(f.).
h. Rasur, etwa GIŠ?
i. Als akkadische Pronominalform interpretiert in Entsprechung zu KUB VII 37 Z. 13′ [*nu ma-aḫ-ḫa-*]*an ki-i ḫa-an-da-a-an-zi*.

Bo 2495 (1.D)

Rs. iv
x+1] *an-da A̩-N*[*A*
2′]x-*ša-an* EGIR-*p*[*a*

[DUB I^{KAM}] *Ú-UL* [*QA-TI*]
4′ [*A-U̯A-AT* ^{f}]*A̩-aš-du* [SAL ^{URU}*Ḫur-la-aš*]
[*ma-a-an*] U+KAK-*a̩ḫ-ḫa-a*[*n-da-an* UKÙ-*an*]
6′ [EGIR-*pa*] SIG$_5$-*aḫ-mi* [
[*na-an-*]*kán ták-na-a*[*z da-aḫ-ḫi*]

Das Beschwörungsritual zeigt in der ersten Tafel eine überreiche Aufzählung von benötigten Opfergaben und Zubehör: Tiere (Hirsch, Rind, Schaf, Vögel, Haase, Schlange, Fische usw.: dieses "alles lebendig" Z. 9) sowie Speisen: Mehl, Brot und Geschirr—aber auch "1 Mine Wachs", Stoffe und Häute ("Haut eines roten Rindes, eines schwarzen Rindes, eines weissen Rindes, Fell einer roten Ziege" Z. 22). Gerade diese Aufzählungen geben die Möglichkeit an die Hand, aufgrund der lexikalischen Belegsammlungen Zugehöriges an Duplikaten und Anschlüssen einzuordnen.

Demgegenüber ist das weitere Ritual nur in wenigen Tafel-Kolophonen bezeugt, und es wird noch einiger Mühe bedürfen, den damit gegebenen Rahmen auszufüllen.[6]

6. Es kämen in erster Linie die unter CTH 781 und 790 aufgezählten *Fragments* infrage. Erste Vorarbeiten zu entsprechenden Textzusammenstellungen von Chr. Rüster und Verf. in ZA 68,

Textreste eines "zweiten Tages" sind IBoT II 116 erhalten[7], den Nachweis einer "zweiten Tafel" bietet der Kolophon von 1419/u (weiteres nicht erhalten); zur Umschrift s. S. 166.—Der "dritte Tag" ist in KUB XLI 5 + XLIV 54 + IBoT II 46 überliefert, und zwar mit dem Textanfang von Kol. i und ii sowie 15 Zeilen vom Ende der Kol. iii. Ausgeschrieben sei hier Kol. iv.

x+2 [*pa/ša-*]*ra-a da-an-z*[*i*

DUB III^{KAM} *QA-TI* INIM ^{f}*Ạ*[*-aš-du*]
4′ ^{SAL}ŠU.GI ^{URU}*Ḫur-la-aš*
ma-a-an UḪ$_{\mathrm{X}}$*-aḫ-ḫa-an-da-an* [UKÙ*-an*]
6′ EGIR*-pa* SIG$_5$*-a*[*ḫ-mi*] x x x [
ši-ip-pa-an-ta[*-aḫ-ḫi*]

Der Kolophon entspricht der Angabe von Tafel I "Anweisung der A[šdu], der hurritischen 'Alten': Wenn ich einen verzauberten Menschen wieder in Ordnung bringe."—Das Objekt der Ritualhandlung (*šippantaḫḫi*) ist im Augenblick nicht zu ergänzen.

KBo XIX 144 + KBo XXVII 154 bietet Vs. i und Rs. iv einen Ritualtext mit umfangreichen hurritischen Rezitationen der ^{SAL}ŠU.GI; gegen Ende des Textes tritt auch der ^{LÚ}AZU, der Beschwörungspriester, auf. Den Kolophon möchte ich heute lesen:

23′ [DUB] IV/V$^{?\mathrm{KAM}}$ *A-ṶA-AT* ^{f}*A-ạš-d*[*u*(*-*)
24′ [*ma-a-a*]*n al-ṷa-an-za-ạḫ-ḫ*[*a-an-da-an*
25′] x [

Fassen wir zusammen: Es gibt ein umfangreiches hethitisch-hurritisches Beschwörungsritual, das der Behandlung (Reinigung, "Heilung") eines verzauberten Menschen dient. Als Verfasserin wird ^{f}*A-aš-du* SAL ^{URU}[*Ḫur-la-aš*] genannt—so 1419/u und Bo 2495 Kolophon aus Raumgründen ergänzt—bzw. vollständiger ^{f}*A-aš-du* ^{SAL}ŠU.GI ^{URU}*Ḫur-la-aš;* lediglich der Katalogeintrag bietet die Graphie [^{f}*A-aš-*]*du-ú*.

Derartig wechselnde Auslautschreibungen sind bei Eigennamen häufiger zu registrieren, vgl. ^{m}*A-pal-li(-i),* ^{m}*A-pal-lu(-ú),* ^{m}*Ḫi-eš-ni(-i),* ^{m}*Ma-a-ti(-i)* und ^{m}*Ja-ar-ri* (KUB VII 29 i 1) gegenüber Kolophon KBo XXIX 203 [. . . ^{m}*Ja-ar-*]*ri-i* (Hinweis F. Starke).—Die Korrektheit der Ergänzung des Namens in KUB XXX 65+ iii 5 wird demnach durch die Plene-Schreibung nicht infrage gestellt.

1978, S. 276f. unter Nr. 69 und ZA 71, 1981, S. 132f. unter Nr. 80: KBo XXIII 43 + KBo XXIV 63; KBo XXVII 159 + KUB XLV 26 usw.

7. Vor dem Kolophon noch die Reste von Z. 1′ ^{LÚ}]SIMÚG.A[(-) "Schmied", Z. 2′]Ì.UDU GẠB[.LÀL$^{?}$ "Fett, Wachs$^{?}$" und Z. 3′ ^{SAL}ŠU.GI.

Hinsichtlich der Angabe im Katalog, dass das Werk "sieben Tafeln" umfasst, während KUB XLI 5+ im Kolophon vermerkt: "Dritte Tafel, beendet", ist eine gewisse Diskrepanz festzustellen, was aber erklärt werden könnte mit zwei (etwa in der Schriftgrösse) unterschiedlichen Exemplaren, oder der Interpretation des Kolophons, dass damit lediglich die abgeschlossene Abschrift der dritten Tafel vermerkt ist, nicht des ganzen Werkes[8].

8. Vgl. den Vermerk von KUB XXX 39 Rs. 4′ [DUB] I^{KAM} *QA-TI* EZEN$^{\text{ḪI.A}}$ AN.TAḪ.ŠUM.SAR . . . , während das Gesamtwerk für eine Festdauer von 38 Tagen wesentlich umfangreicher war.

SOME RARE OBJECTS FROM THE KARUM OF KANISH

TAHSIN ÖZGÜÇ

Ankara

A great variety of remains has been unearthed at Kanish—an important trade center of the ancient world. Private houses, archives, workshops, business offices, depots, streets and open courtyards have been found preserved in successive levels. The construction techniques and style of the monuments of this period are representative of central Anatolian city planning of the twentieth to the seventeenth centuries B.C. In addition to such interior architectural features as the ovens, fireplaces, rooms with built-in divans and corner cabinets and burials below the floors, there have also been revealed many other types of archaeological and philological remains which have escaped the ravages of fire and of time.

In many respects Kanish is an archaeological counterpart to Pompeii. If the textual and archaeological evidence were combined, we would be able to form an even more complete and detailed image of life at Kanish than has been possible at Pompeii. There is no other site in the Middle East where the potential for obtaining information is so great and where it should be possible to draw a detailed picture of the affairs of individuals and families from their letters and kitchenware, storeroom contents and intramural burials.

In the settlements of level Ia–b and II, native Anatolian objects have been found side-by-side with objects brought by the traders from their own countries and from the regions through which they passed. This is to be expected at an international trade center such as Kanish.

My esteemed teacher, Professor H. G. Güterbock, has visited Kanish many times as an honored guest, and I recall with fondness the excited discussions we had during those long days and cool evenings of the central Anatolian summers. It is with great pride that I am able to publish in this Festschrift several of the rare objects from the Kārum of Kanish.

RELIEF OF THE NUDE GODDESS
(*Figs. 1a–b–c–d*)

Found in a private house of level Ib in the Kārum (Kt. 82/k 110), this moulded bronze object portrays the nude goddess in high relief on a flat plaque measuring 1.3 cm. in width and 4.7 cm. in height. The presence of the plaque with flat back parallels that of a nude goddess in faience also found in level Ib (Kt. z/k 41). The figure of the goddess is represented standing on a high and massive base, 1.4 cm. in height. The upper edge of the plaque is more regular than its sides.

The headdress of the goddess bears a row of superimposed horns on either side which converge at the center. The top of this headdress can be reconstructed from that in the *Burney* relief.[1] No hair is depicted but a small trace of the left ear is preserved. The headdress has greatly shortened the forehead. The eyes and nose are small, the cheeks full, the chin rounded and the small mouth has been damaged. Most details have been destroyed by oxidation. The face has a full and fleshy character and the neck is short and thick.

The figure of the goddess is rounded and fleshy. The hips and shoulders are of the same width and the thick waist sets this representation apart from others of the nude goddess where she is rendered more shapely and with a thin waist. Her hands are clasping her small breasts and, in contrast to the majority of nude woman statuettes or representations on seals, there is no opening or hollow between the arms and the body. The irregular knees are portrayed by a pair of indentations, and the thighs and abdomen are fleshy. The figure is poorly preserved below the knees, and details of the feet are not shown.

This style of portraying a goddess is encountered here for the first time in a central Anatolian work from this period. A nude female statuette in ivory from level Ib, with headdress, face and body preserved above the waist, entirely differs from our example.[2] In addition, the nude, winged-goddess figurine from Karahöyük also betrays a different style of work.[3] The style of the Kanish goddess is also distinct from that often found on cylinder seals of the Old Syrian style, where the nude goddess is represented with or without

1. André Parrot, Sumer, Die mesopotamische Kunst von den Anfängen bis zum XII. vorchristlichen Jahrhundert, München 1960 (Universum der Kunst), p. 300, fig. 367 A.

2. Tahsin Özgüç, Kültepe-Kanish, New Researches at the Center of the Assyrian Trade Colonies (TTKY V/19), Ankara 1959, p. 107, pl. 34,2. A similar faience figurine imported from Mesopotamia was discovered at Alishar—H. H. von der Osten, The Alishar Hüyük Seasons of 1930–32, Part II (OIP 29), Chicago 1937, p. 193, fig. 230, d2971.

3. Sedat Alp, "Ištar auf dem Karahöyük," Mélanges Mansel (TTKY VII/60), Ankara 1974, pp. 704ff., pl. 225–226.

wings, armed, with head in profile and body in a frontal position, and holding her breasts or separating her skirt.[4] The headdress of the Kanish figure is modeled in the Old Babylonian style,[5] and is one of our rare examples in that style. In cylinder seal impressions from level Ib at Kanish, there are various distinct styles of representations of the nude goddess with different horned headdress.[6] In addition, one such impression from level II portrays the nude goddess in a very interesting and different manner (Fig. 2).

This seal, of native style, depicts the nude goddess frontally, standing on a lion and clasping her breasts. Her wide shoulders are rounded, her legs are spread apart, and her hips are narrow. She is wearing a double-stranded necklace and a headdress, also seen from the front, with lines on both sides representing horns. Two scenes are depicted on this seal:

(a) A representation in Anatolian style with a deity seated opposite the god Adad who is standing on a lion/monster.

(b) A god standing on an antelope opposite a bull. Behind him there is another deity holding an antelope and behind this figure is a nude goddess. Below the bull are two animals in juxtaposition, and to their right there is a monkey. The back of the bull being worshipped bears a cone, while in front of the bull there is an altar in the form of a table. Between the deities and the bull there is a star.

The horned headdress of the Kanish goddess is in the same style as the Old Babylonian examples. However, Old Babylonian portrayals of the nude goddess on cylinder seals are generally more schematically rendered.[7] For these reasons, the Kanish goddess betrays a very strong Old Babylonian influence in its style, with ties to the Syrian style—no doubt borrowed from northeastern Syrian cities. As we know, Assyrian traders brought cylinder seals, weapons, pottery, jewelry and faience objects in great number to Kanish from north Syrian cities. This nude goddess is a new find which substantiates the ties between Kanish and these two regions.

4. Marie-Thérèse Barrelet, "Les déesses armées et aillées Inanna-Ištar," Syria 32, 1955, p. 237 H.

5. A. Parrot, Sumer, p. 300, fig. 367 A; and Henri Frankfort, The Art and Architecture of the Ancient Orient, London 1954, p. 56, pl. 56.

6. Nimet Özgüç, Seals and Seal Impressions of Level Ib from Kārum Kanish (TTKY V/25), Ankara 1968, p. 65, pl. 9, A, p. 68, pl. 22,2; Nimet Özgüç, "New Light on the dating of the levels of the Karum of Kanish and of Acemhöyük near Aksaray," AJA 72, 1968, p. 319, pl. 103,2; and Nimet Özgüç, "Gods and Goddesses with Identical Attributes during the Period of Old Assyrian Trade Colonies," FsLaroche pp. 279, 289, i.

7. Edith Porada, The Collection of the Pierpont Morgan Library, Washington 1948, I, p. 55 H, pl. 67–69.

DOUBLE-HEADED BULL RHYTON
(*Fig. 3a–b*)

I know of no other example of this unique type of drinking vessel dating to this period at Kanish (Kt. p/k 135; 94-12-64). It was found, together with various other vessels, in a private house of level Ib. The height is 28 cm. and the width 18.5 cm. The coarse clay has fine sand inclusions and is covered in a reddish-brown slip. The body is in the form of a cylinder and the legs are rendered as simple, short protuberances. The contents were poured into the body through a circular, slightly raised hole at the center of the back, and dispensed through a straight tubular spout, situated between the two heads and attached to the rim by a double handle. The bull heads have prominent eyes, nose holes, roughly worked mouths, short horns and are wearing halters.

Detailed studies have been made of the *BIBRU*'s which hold an important place in the Hittite texts.[8] While the Kanish rhyton has two bull's heads, the texts reveal the existence of three types of bull-rhyta.[9] Although our example does have two heads, it only has four feet and must represent a single bull.[10] The greatest variety and quantity of animal-form rhyta, portraying a large variety of animals and described in Hittite texts, were found in levels II and Ia–b at Kanish.[11]

EAGLE RHYTA
(*Figs. 4 and 5*)

One of the most beautiful examples of the highly developed representa-

8. H. Ehelolf, ZA 45 (N.F. 11), 1939, p. 71; C. G. von Brandenstein, Hethitische Götter nach Bildbeschreibungen in Keilschrifttexten, MVAeG 46, 2, 1943, p. 23; H. G. Güterbock, "Hethitische Götterdarstellungen und Götternamen," Belleten VII/26, 1943, pp. 295ff.; L. Rost, "Zu den hethitischen Bildbeschreibungen," MIO 8, 1961, pp. 161–217; MIO 9, 1963, pp. 175–239; O. Carruba, "Rhyta in den hethitischen Texten," Kadmos 6, 1967, pp. 88–97; and Yaşar Coşkun, Boğazköy metinlerinde geçen başlıca Libasyon Kapları, AnDergi 27/3–4, 1969, pp. 39ff.

9. Tahsin Özgüç, "A Bull-Shaped Drinking-Cup discovered in the vicinity of Kırşehir," Mélanges Mansel II (TTKY VII/60^a), 1974, p. 964.

10. *Ibid.*, p. 965.

11. For examples published to date, see: Nimet Özgüç, Ausgrabungen in Kültepe . . . 1949 (TTKY V/12), Ankara 1953, pp. 218ff.; Nimet Özgüç, "Assyrian Trade Colonies in Anatolia," Archaeology 22, 1969, pp. 250ff.; Tahsin Özgüç, "Die Grabungen von 1953 in Kültepe," Belleten XVIII/71, 1954, p. 383, fig. 16; "Excavations at Kültepe 1954, Finds on Level Ib," Belleten XIX/73, 1955, p. 67, fig. 14; "Excavations at Kültepe, Level II Finds," Belleten XIX/76, 1955, pp. 455ff., figs. 15–21; Kültepe-Kanish (TTKY V/19), pp. 112ff., pls. 44–47; and Tahsin Özgüç, Les Hittites (Ankara Turizmi, Eski Eserleri ve Müzeleri Sevenler Derneği Yayınları 7 Ankara), pp. 10–11, 14–15, 17, 19b, 22b and 24b.

tions of eagles which have been found in the Kārum areas as well as on the city mound are the drinking cups in the form of eagles and eagle-heads.

Our first example of this type is an eagle in a perched position with a camel-colored slip and decoration in black paint (Fig. 4: Kt. e/t 200; 125-2-64). This piece measures 15.8 cm. high, 8.2 cm. wide and 8.8 cm. thick. It was filled through a hole on the back of the body and emptied through the curved beak. The thick eyelids and oval pupils are nicely formed and painted in black. The tail, legs and tip of the beak are restored. Examples of this type of eagle rhyton with black slip and brightly burnished are also known.[12]

The head of the second rhyton, also portraying a perched eagle, is missing (Fig. 5: Kt. k/k 34). 11.8 cm. in height and 7.5 cm. in width, it has a reddish-brown slip. The body is decorated with incised circles. The eagle has strong claws and a straight tail. Eagle rhyta of this type are peculiar to Kanish.

Hittite texts describing statues of Hittite deities mention some gods as holding gold, silver, ivory, iron and lead-covered eagles.[13] However, as H. G. Güterbock has pointed out, these texts do not say to which god the eagle was sacred.[14] Only the *BIBRU* in bird-form (drinking vessel) is mentioned.[15] The drinking vessels in eagle-form published here (*BIBRU* Á^{MUŠEN}) prove their existence.

IVORY FIGURINE
(*Fig. 6*)

In his "Ivory in Hittite Texts," H. G. Güterbock has greatly furthered our knowledge of Hittite ivory objects.[16] Aside from the finds from Assyrian Trade Colony Period Acemhöyük, Kanish, Alacahöyük and Alişar, we know very little about the ivory objects of this period.[17] In addition, in spite

12. Tahsin Özgüç, "An Assyrian Trading Outpost," Old World Archaeology: Foundations of Civilization, Scientific American, California, p. 202 (= Scientific American 208, 2, Feb. 1963, 96).

13. L. Rost, MIO 8, 1961, pp. 179, 181, 183–184 and 193.

14. Belleten VII/26, 1943, p. 313.

15. C. G. von Brandenstein, Bildbeschr., p. 23.

16. Anadolu (Anatolia) 15, 1971, pp. 1–7.

17. Nimet Özgüç, "Excavations at Acemhöyük," Anatolia 10, 1966, pp. 42ff.; Prudence Oliver Harper, The Connoisseur, 1969, pp. 156–162; and Nimet Özgüç, "An Ivory Box and a Stone Mould from Acemhöyük," Belleten XL/160, 1976, pp. 555–560; Tahsin Özgüç, Ausgrabungen in Kültepe 1948 (TTKY V/10), Ankara 1950, p. 208, pl. 67,435; Kültepe-Kanish (TTKY V/19), p. 107, pl. 34,2; Nimet Özgüç, Seals and Seal Impressions of Level Ib (TTKY V/25), p. 71, pl. 31,1; Erich Schmidt, The Alishar Hüyük Seasons of 1928 and 1929, Part I (OIP 19), Chicago 1932, p. 148, figs. 248–249, a430, b2102; H. H. von der Osten, OIP 29, fig. 249, c2656; and H. Z. Koşay and M. Akok, Ausgrabungen in Alacahöyük . . . 1940–1948 (TTKY V/6), Ankara 1966, pl. 31,i14 (1700 B.C.).

of the Hittite texts, we also know very little about objects from the Hittite Empire period.[18]

This ivory antelope was found in a refuse layer at Kanish (Fig. 6: Kt. i/k 19563). Its length is 3 cm. and its height 2.2 cm. It is sitting on its four folded legs and, in spite of its small size, bears details in the form of triangular eyes, curled horns, modeled ribs, and skillfully worked rump and forelegs. Two round holes, one at the neck and the other underneath, were meant to attach this piece to another object such as a gaming board.

The antelope was one of the most popularly depicted animals at Kanish. Among the rhyta, those in the form of an antelope are in the majority. Vivid renderings of antelopes in the native style on cylinder seal impressions, and especially in clay rhyta with carefully worked head and neck, are known from level II (Fig. 7: Kt. 82/k 98).

18. Kurt Bittel, Die Hethiter (Universum der Kunst), München 1976, figs. 187 and 248.

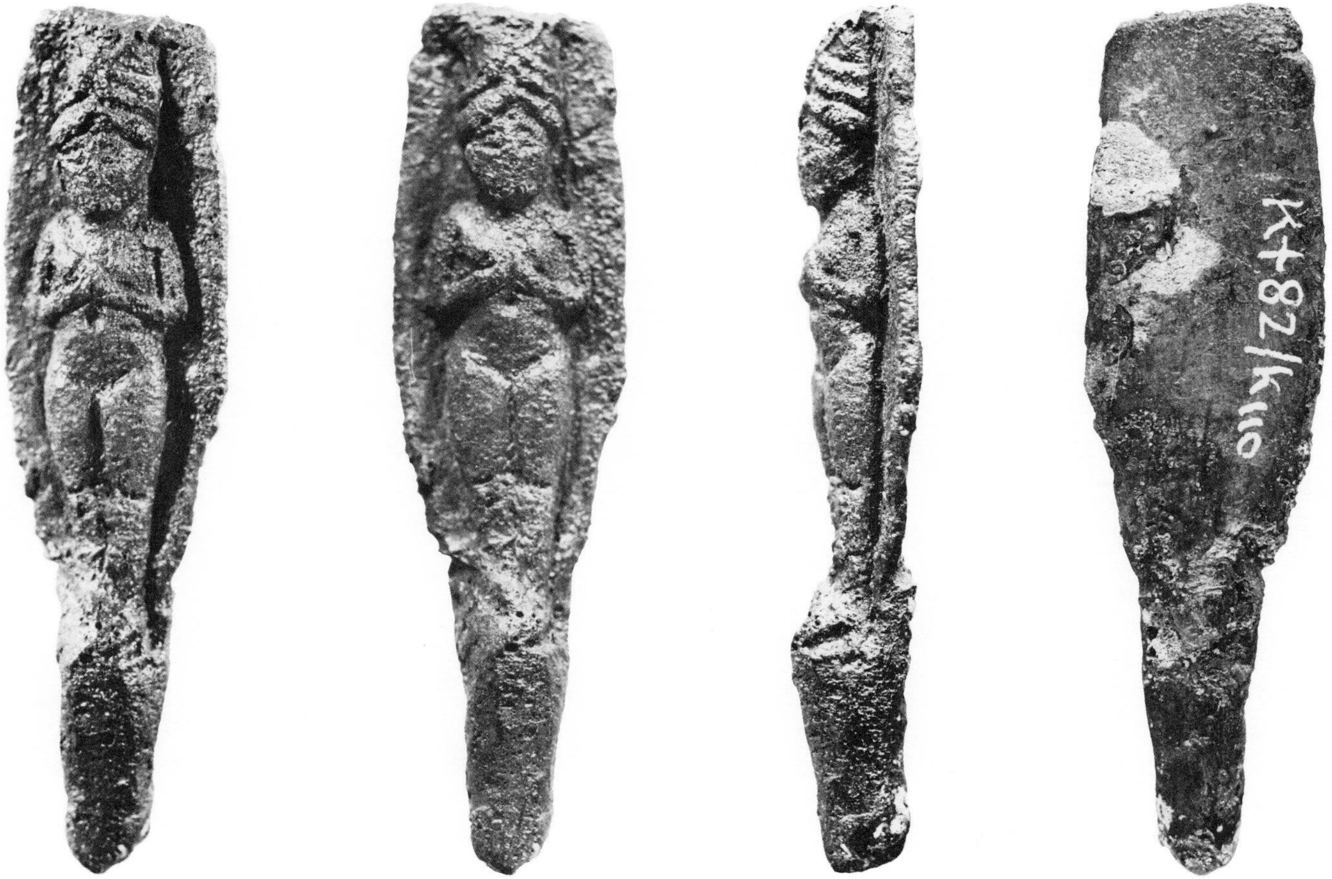

a *b* *c* *d*

Fig. 1.-Kt. 82/k 110

Fig. 2.-Kt. u/kga

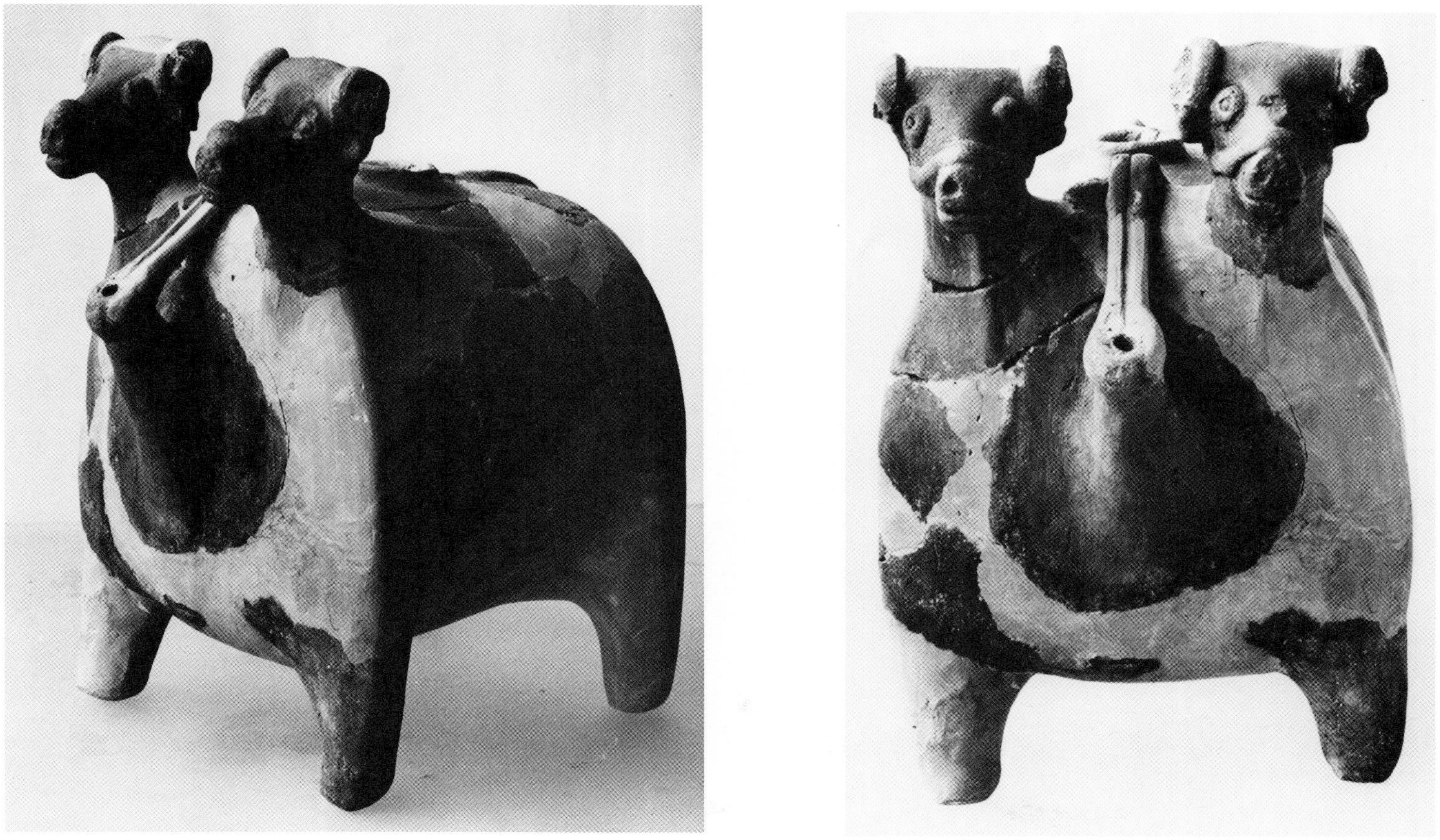

Fig. 3.-Kt. p/k 135; 94-12-64

Fig. 4.-Kt. e/t 200; 125-2-64

Fig. 5.-Kt. k/k 34

Fig. 6.-Kt. i/k 19563

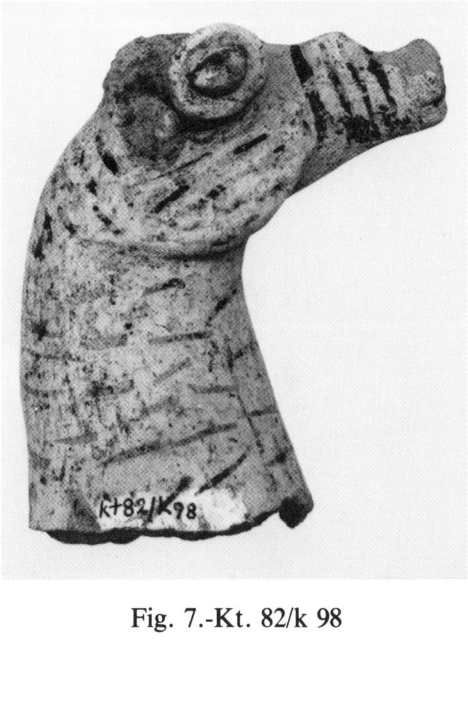

Fig. 7.-Kt. 82/k 98

SUPPLEMENT TO THE BIBLIOGRAPHY OF HANS GUSTAV GÜTERBOCK

1971

Materials for the Sumerian Lexicon 13, ed. M. Civil, with the collaboration of H. G. Güterbock, W. W. Hallo, H. A. Hoffner, and E. Reiner, Rome, Pontificium Institutum Biblicum.

1973

"Einige seltene oder schwierige Ideogramme in der Keilschrift von Boğazköy," *Festschrift Heinrich Otten,* Wiesbaden, Otto Harrassowitz, pp. 71–88.

"Ḫaššum/Ḫaššu(wa): Nach hethitischen Quellen," *Reallexikon der Assyriologie und Vorderasiatischen Archäologie* 4, p. 137.

1974

"Appendix: Hittite Parallels" to W. G. Lambert, "Dingir.šà.dib.ba Incantations," *Journal of Near Eastern Studies* 33, pp. 323–327.

"Boğazköy," in *Encyclopaedia Britannica* 14th ed., pp. 1181–83.

"The Hittite Palace," *Le palais et la royauté (archéologie et civilisation),* Compte rendu de la 19ième Rencontre Assyriologique Internationale, Paris 1971, Paris, Geuthner, pp. 305–314.

"Kleine Beiträge zum Verständnis der Ankara-Reliefs," *Baghdader Mitteilungen* 7 (= Festschrift A. Moortgat), pp. 97–99, pl. 13.

"Zwei hethitische Zeichnungen," *Mansel'e Armağan (Mélanges Mansel),* Türk Tarih Kurumu Yayınları VII/60, Ankara, Türk Tarih Kurumu Basımevi, pp. 421–24.

Review of U. Moortgat-Correns, *Die Bildwerke vom Djebelet el Bēḍā in ihrer räumlichen zeitlichen Umwelt,* in *American Journal of Archaeology* 78, pp. 298–99.

1975

"Hethiter, hethitisch: §1. Name, §2. Definition," *Reallexikon der Assyriologie und vorderasiatischen Archäologie* 4, pp. 372–375.

"Hieroglyphensiegel aus dem Tempelbezirk," in K. Bittel, H. G. Güterbock, G. Neumann, P. Neve, H. Otten, U. Seidl, *Boğazköy 5: Funde aus den*

Grabungen 1970 und 1971, Abhandlungen der Deutschen Orient-Gesellschaft 18, pp. 47–75.

"Ḫilammar," *Reallexikon der Assyriologie und vorderasiatischen Archäologie* 4, pp. 404–405.

"The Hittite Temple According to Written Sources," *Le Temple et le Culte*, Compte rendu de la 20ième Rencontre Assyriologique Internationale, Leiden, 1972, Publications de l'Institut Historique et Archéologique de Stamboul 37, pp. 125–132.

"Inschriften" and "Einschlägige Textstellen," in K. Bittel, J. Boessneck, B. Damm, H. G. Güterbock, H. Hauptmann, R. Naumann, W. Schirmer, *Das hethitische Felsheiligtum Yazılıkaya*, Boğazköy-Ḫattuša: Ergebnisse und Ausgrabungen 9, Berlin, Gebr. Mann, pp. 167–192.

"Yazılıkaya: Apropos a New Interpretation," *Journal of Near Eastern Studies* 34, pp. 273–277.

Review of J. Grothus, *Die Rechtsordnung der Hethiter*, in *Journal of Cuneiform Studies* 27, pp. 175–179.

1977

"Hittite Seals in the Walters Art Gallery," *Journal of the Walters Art Gallery* 36, pp. 7–16.

"Ištanu," *Reallexikon der Assyriologie und vorderasiatischen Archäologie* 5, pp. 209–10.

Obituary for "Gustavus Franklin Swift 1916–1976," *Archaeology* 30/1, p. 58.

1978

"Die Hieroglypheninschrift von Fraktin," *Assyriologia* 4 (Festschrift Lubor Matouš), Budapest, [appeared 1980], pp. 127–136.

"Hethitische Literatur," *Neues Handbuch der Literaturwissenschaft, I: Altorientalische Literaturen* (W. Röllig, ed.), Wiesbaden, Akademische Verlagsgesellschaft Athenaion, pp. 211–253.

Keilschrifttexte aus Boghazköi 26: Vokabulare, Mythen und Kultinventare (with C. W. Carter), Berlin, Gebr. Mann.

"Some Aspects of Hittite Prayers," *The Frontiers of Human Knowledge*, Skrifter rörande Uppsala Universitet, C:38, Acta Universitatis Upsaliensis, Uppsala, pp. 125–139.

Review of W. Schirmer, *Die Bebauung am unteren Büyükkale-Nordwesthang in Boğazköy* (*WVDOG* 81), in *Archiv für Orientforschung* 26 [appeared 1980], pp. 125–26.

1979

"Hieroglyphische Miszellen," *Studia Mediterranea* 1 (Festschrift P. Meriggi), Pavia, pp. 235–245.

"Some Stray Boğazköy Tablets," *Florilegium Anatolicum: Mélanges offerts à Emmanuel Laroche,* Paris, E. De Boccard, pp. 137–144.

1980

"An Addition to the Prayer of Muršili to the Sungoddess and its implications," *Anatolian Studies* 30 (Festschrift O. R. Gurney), pp. 41–50.

The Hittite Dictionary of the Oriental Institute of the University of Chicago 3/1 (ed., with H. A. Hoffner), Chicago, The Oriental Institute of the University of Chicago.

"Hittite hieroglyphic seal impressions," in M. Van Loon (ed.), *Korucutepe. Final Report on the Excavations of the Universities of Chicago, California (Los Angeles) and Amsterdam in the Keban Reservoir, Eastern Anatolia 1968–1970* vol. 3, Amsterdam, North-Holland Publishing Company, pp. 127–132, pl. 37–41.

"Randbemerkungen zu einigen hethitischen Gesetzen: 1. *annanuḫḫa-,* 2. *larputta,*" *Die Welt des Orients* 11 (Festschrift J. Klíma), pp. 89–92.

"Seals and Sealing in Hittite Lands," *From Athens to Gordion: The Papers of a Memorial Symposium for Rodney S. Young,* University Museum Papers 1, Philadelphia, pp. 51–63.

1982

"Einige sumerische und akkadische Schreibungen im Hethitischen: I. LUL und Verwandtes, II. *Mešedi,*" in *zikir šumim: Assyriological Studies Presented to F. R. Kraus* (G. Van Driel et al., eds.), Leiden, E. J. Brill, pp. 83–90.

Les Hiéroglyphes de Yazılıkaya: A propos d'un travail récent, Institut Français d'études anatoliennes: Éditions Recherche sur les civilisations: Synthèse 11, Paris.

"The Hieroglyphic Inscriptions on the Hittite Cylinder No. 25" (Appendix to E. Porada, "The Cylinder Seals found at Thebes in Boeotia"), *Archiv für Orientforschung* 28, pp. 71–72.

1983

"Hethitische Götterbilder und Kultobjekte," in *Beiträge zur Altertumskunde Kleinasiens: Festschrift für Kurt Bittel* (R. M. Boehmer and H. Hauptmann, eds.), Mainz-am-Rhein, Philipp von Zabern, pp. 203–217.

The Hittite Dictionary of the Oriental Institute of the University of Chicago 3/2 (ed., with H. A. Hoffner), Chicago, The Oriental Institute of the University of Chicago.

"Hittite Historiography: A Survey," in *History, Historiography, and Interpretation: Studies in Biblical and Cuneiform Literatures* (H. Tadmor and M. Weinfeld, eds.), Jerusalem, Magnes Press, pp. 21–35.

"The Hittites and the Aegean World: 1. The Aḫḫiyawa Problem Reconsidered," *American Journal of Archaeology* 87, pp. 133–138.

"A Hurro-Hittite Hymn to Ishtar," *Journal of the American Oriental Society* 103 (Festschrift S. N. Kramer), pp. 155–164.

"Kumarbi," *Reallexikon der Assyriologie und vorderasiatischen Archäologie* 6, pp. 324–330.

"Noch einmal die Formel *parnaššea šuwaizzi,*" *Orientalia* NS 52 (Festschrift A. Kammenhuber), pp. 73–80.

"The Second Inscription on Mount Sipylus" (with R. L. Alexander), *Anatolian Studies* 33 (Festschrift R. Barnett), pp. 29–32.

1984

"Hittites and Akhaeans: A New Look," *Proceedings of the American Philosophical Society* 128, pp. 114–122.

Forthcoming

Die hethitische Glyptik von Boğazköy II: Die Siegel und Siegelabdrücke der Unterstadt von Boğazköy (with R. M. Boehmer).

"Hittite Liver Models," in the Festschrift for E. Reiner.

"'Hittites' at Grinnell," in the Festschrift for M. Mellink.

"A Hittite silver vessel in the form of a fist," *Boston Museum of Fine Arts Bulletin*.

Materials for the Sumerian Lexicon 17: The Series Erim-huš = *anantu and* an-ta-gál = *šakû,* ed. A. Cavigneaux, H. G. Güterbock, and M. T. Roth with the assistance of G. Farber, Rome, Pontificium Institutum Biblicum.

"A Note on the Frieze on the Stag Rhyton in the Schimmel Collection," in the Festschrift for E. Akurgal.

"A religious text from Maşat," in Gedenkschrift U. B. Alkım.

"Troy in Hittite Texts? Wiluša, Aḫḫiyawa, and Hittite History," in a volume from the Symposium on the Trojan War held at Bryn Mawr College, Oct. 19, 1984.

Bibliography compiled by Richard H. Beal

INDEX

I. LEXEMES

A. Hittite
anda 86f.
antiyant- 17 with n.22
appa(n) 87
arḫa 87f.
ašatar 15 n.11
edi 88
ḫamenkant- 8 with n.24
ḫantezzi(ya)- DUMU.LUGAL 24 n.60
ḫapalki- 125ff.
ḫad/tauri 100, 102
ḫuprušḫi 113
irḫai- 160f.
iwaru 16 n.16
katta, kattan, kattanda 88
-ki, -ka 88f.
-ku 137 n.2
lē 86ff.
manqa 89
mugawar 121ff. with n.21
mukeššar 121 n.21
nakkuš 137ff.
nakkušša- 138 n.9
nakušši- 138ff.
nakkušatar 138 with n.9
natta 83ff.
nawi 86ff.
parā 88
parkuwatar 158 with n.23
purpura- 126
šakruwai- 157
šarā 88
GIŠ*šušiyazzakel* 132
tarant- 7f. with n.23
terip- 63
UZU*titita-* 71f.
ulili- 73f.
zinna- 160f.

B. Cuneiform Luwian
nakkušaḫit 138
pariyan 51
-ša 51
titit- 71f.
ululiyašši- 74

C. Hieroglyphic Luwian
(*350")*asharmis* 72
awayanawani-(URBS) 71
("SCUTUM")*harli-* 72
izista- 79f.
kukisati- 77
(*257)*piyatar*[72f.
(*245)*tanata-* 74f.
(LITUUS)*titita-* 71f.
("PANIS.SA_4")*tunikara-* 77
(TERRA+LA+LA)*walili-* 73f.
(*273)*warpi-* 76f.
(-)*kusati* 71
"PUGNUS"-*saha* 71
"*30"(-)*ir(a)nuwa* 73
*275-*ita* 71
L269 55
L399 55

D. Akkadian
aḫāzum 7 with n.18
biṣinnum 3 n.4
ḫ in Old Akkadian 2 n.4
mamman 145
nakkuššа/e 139
puḫrum 145

II. HITTITE GRAMMAR, ETC.

III. PROPER NAMES

IV. SUBJECT

V. CUNEIFORM TEXTS

VI. HIEROGLYPHIC TEXTS